THE
WOODWORKING
MANUAL

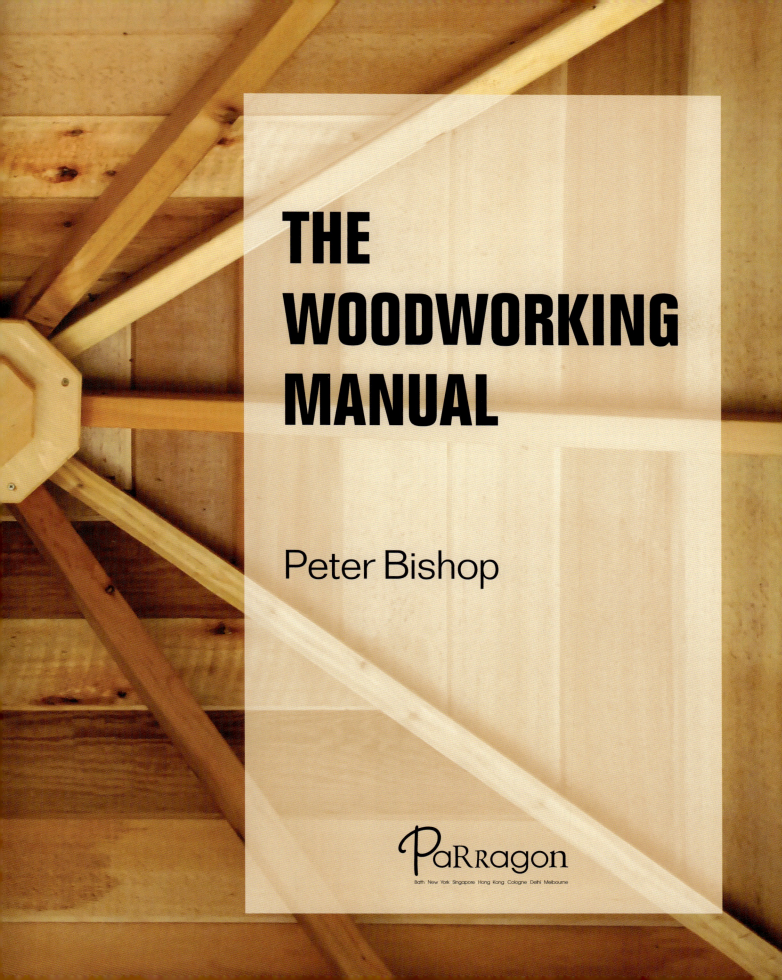

THE WOODWORKING MANUAL

Peter Bishop

PaRragon

Bath New York Singapore Hong Kong Cologne Delhi Melbourne

First published by Parragon in 2008
Parragon Books Ltd
Queen Street House
4 Queen Street
Bath, BA1 1HE

Conceived and produced by **Focus Publishing**, Sevenoaks, Kent
Project director: Guy Croton
Designers: Neil Adams; Heather McMillan
Illustrator: Heather McMillan
Editors: Guy Croton; Vicky Hales-Dutton; Caroline Watson
Indexer: Caroline Watson

See page 304 for photograph copyright details

ISBN 978-1-4075-1153-5

Printed in China

Contents

Introduction: the beauty of wood

Some of us believe that wood is one of the most beautiful natural resources available to mankind. It is tactile, textured, and richly endowed with other features that make you want to touch and feel it. For the user, it is most forgiving; errors can be corrected and repairs made with ease. Its versatility has led to its use in just about every application imaginable. Perhaps my enthusiasm for this material is a little extreme; however, let's hope that by the time you have read this book, you may also have a similar appreciation.

How wood grows

Wood largely grows by means of a process named photosynthesis. This takes place in the leaf structure of a tree, and is a complex chemical reaction between liquids drawn from the root network, carbon dioxide, and sunlight. The process creates sugars upon which the tree feeds and grows.

Above right Sunlight shining on leaves is a vital part of the process of photosynthesis and is central to the healthy growth of a tree.

The growth process

Water is transported up the tree, from the root system in the ground, via a process called osmosis, while food is transported downward from the leaves. The working cells, or cambium layer, immediately beneath the bark produce sapwood inside the tree and phloem, or inner bark, on the outside. As the tree grows, the bark expands, maintaining a protective sheath around the inner workings of the tree. Beneath this living, growing part of the outer structure is the sapwood and heartwood. The sapwood

Right The growth of a tree. The combined processes of osmosis —which transports water upward from the root system—and photosynthesis—which produces the nutrients on which a tree lives—are central to the successful growth of all species.

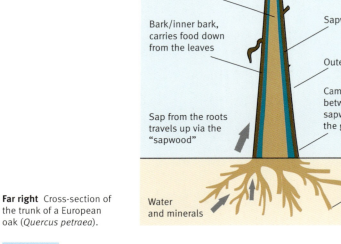

Carbon dioxide

Crown

Oxygen

Heartwood, providing strength

Trunk

Bark/inner bark, carries food down from the leaves

Sapwood

Outer bark

Cambium layer between bark and sapwood; this is the growing layer

Sap from the roots travels up via the "sapwood"

Roots

Water and minerals

Far right Cross-section of the trunk of a European oak (*Quercus petraea*).

Annual-growth ring
The layer of wood formed in one growing period, made up of large earlywood and small latewood cells.

Ray cells
Radiating sheets of cells that conduct nutrients horizontally; also called "medullary rays."

Heartwood
The mature wood that forms the spine of the tree.

Sapwood
The new wood, the cells of which conduct or store nutrients.

Pith
The central core of cells. This can be weak and may suffer from fungal and insect attack.

Bark
The outer protective layer of dead cells. The term "bark" can also include the living inner tissue.

Bast or phloem
The inner bark tissue that conducts synthesized food.

Cambium layer
The thin layer of living cell tissue that forms new wood and bark.

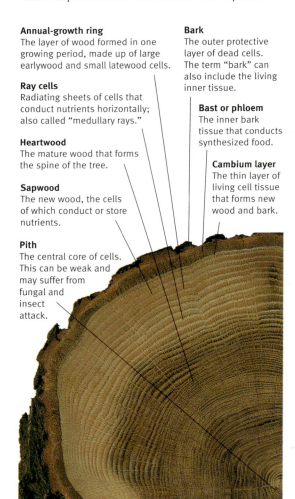

Softwood

Hardwood

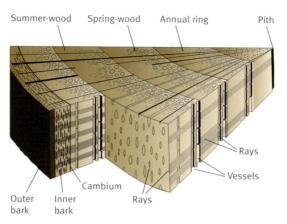

Summer-wood   Spring-wood   Annual ring   Pith

Rays

Vessels

Outer bark   Inner bark   Cambium   Rays

Annual ring   Pith

Spring-wood

Summer-wood

Heartwood

Rays

Sapwood

Cambium

Bark

Above left The cell structure—and hence the appearance—of softwood and hardwood are different.

Above The structural features of a hardwood.

transports liquids up to the leaf structures, ensuring that the growth process can continue, while the heartwood provides the mechanical structure that enables the tree to remain upright and grow to its full height.

Growth in softwoods

The conductive cells that provide strength and storage facilities within the outer section of the trunk vary slightly between hardwoods and softwoods. In the latter, long, thin-walled cells called tracheids control the flow of sap, while thick-walled tracheids, with smaller cavities, provide the mechanical strength. In spring, layers of the thin-walled tracheids are laid down, followed by thick-walled cells as the season progresses, creating the annual "ring" effect that can be seen when wood is cut into.

Growth in hardwoods

Hardwoods have a different cell structure. A pipe-like system, comprised of cells called vessels (usually visible only in hardwoods) transports fluids within the outer section of the growing tree. Vigorous growth takes place in spring and, when this slows, smaller, stronger cells form to provide the mechanical strength to the trunk, again creating the annual ring configuration. In some timbers, especially those from tropical countries, growth is continuous and the wood is called "diffuse-porous."

Both softwoods and hardwoods have storage cells that are named parenchyma. These small, boxlike cells are usually arranged horizontally within the wood and, in hardwoods, come in bands called rays. They provide the distinctive textual "figure" that is found in some woods such as oak and beech.

Below left The cellular structure of a typical hardwood, drawn at about x 33 enlargement. The pores and rays pit and run through the wood.

Below The main stem of a typical tree is known as a trunk or bole. This carries a crown of leaf-bearing branches.

Uses of wood

Human beings have used wood for thousands of years. The unique way in which it grows lends itself to the natural design of utensils and products. Hunter-gatherers used it to create tools and weapons and interesting configurations were turned into simple seats and head rests, without the use of sophisticated equipment.

Above right Ancient Egyptian mummy cases were made from wood.

Wood throughout the ages

The Ancient Egyptians valued their artifacts so much that these were buried with their owners for posterity. With few natural forests of their own, they were forced to import most of their requirements, including the highly prized cedar, cypress, and box. Local woods such as acacia and carob were used as the groundwork for veneer facings, which were made from the exotic imports. Ebony was combined with ivory to create intricate decorations. Overall, wood was used extensively in making mummy cases for burial. The type of wood used depended on the wealth of the family, but most cases were carved from softwood and then decorated. There is little doubt, also, that the Egyptians mastered the skills of furniture making. Many examples of how they used the mortise and tenon joint still survive to this day.

Below Many old buildings were based upon a wooden structure.

In medieval times, a simple plank and panel structure emerged in furniture making. Chests were hewn directly from logs and reinforced with iron, eventually becoming more intricate, with locking and pegged joints. Wall paneling developed, covering rough brick or stonework, while highly decorative patterns were produced in wood flooring. The natural shapes of the growing trees were used, to advantage, in timber-framed buildings. Some of the oldest examples are found in the European cruck frame buildings. A series of inverted Vs, made from curved lengths of timber, form the backbone of the buildings. As techniques improved, the timber-framed house became an art form, with many different shapes and panels contributing to the overall beauty of the buildings.

Out of necessity, some buildings were made entirely from wood. In Scandinavia, walls, floors, and ceilings were, and still are, constructed in wood, because of its widespread availability and its natural thermal properties. On other continents, where wood was abundantly available, different cultures developed a range of wooden structures on stilts. In Indonesia, houses shaped like boats represent how important the boat is to the survival of its culture. The use of stilts enabled occupiers to build over water and marsh, bringing them closer to sources of food and making better use of the available materials.

Wood for shipping

The origins of international shipping are based on wood. Without trees to build boats, trading and migration would not have occurred. Logs

with their cores burnt out and shaped into dug-outs are still used in Africa. Simple North American canoes were traditionally made by stretching birch bark over a wooden frame. In other cultures, boatbuilders used bamboo. Planks laid over a frame were joined by shaping and binding them in place. The Vikings developed clinker-built crafts, using scarfed joints and planks to produce the slender, graceful curves of their distinctive vessels. Many of the craft described above were also used as warships, with the Vikings, in particular, notorious for their seafaring aggression and colonial ambitions.

Harnessing natural resources

Wood has long been used in engineering to harness natural resources and exploit opportunities for development. Windmills and watermills began as simple structures and developed into sophisticated production units for grinding, cutting, and generating energy for other processes. Cogs and gears were first made from tight-grained woods such as apple, beech, holly, or hickory. As time moved on, these were replaced with iron gears and shafts. With the widespread introduction of steam power during the Industrial Revolution, these wood-based structures slowly became redundant.

Wood in general transportation

Wood is extremely versatile and has been key to the development of transportation. In the United Kingdom, for example, wooden lock gates in canals enabled links to be made at different levels. Huge frames and door structures—usually made from oak, and later, the more exotic woods like greenheart—resisted the weight of water and withstood the impact of canal boats. Since man first crossed a stream using a log, wood has been used for bridges. A good example are the ambitious log structures locked together up to eight tiers high which were built in North America during the expansion of the rail networks. Other engineers developed cantilever structures to bridge gaps across rivers and ravines.

Above Wood has been used in boats and ships of all descriptions for thousands of years.

Below From huge spans to more modest structures like this one, wood has always been a mainstay of bridge construction.

Harvesting wood

Wood harvesting techniques range from primitive methods involving the felling of a single tree right through to the extreme clear-fell or, at worst, slash-and-burn operations. In the latter, selective trees are felled for lumber and the rest of the forest is cut and burnt to provide short-term agricultural land.

Above right Freshly harvested timber awaiting collection.

Modern timber harvesting

In manmade, predominantly softwood forests, there is a clear and well defined cycle. Selected high-yield trees are planted. As these mature, they are thinned and the smaller logs utilized for pulp, chippings, or fencing materials. Once the main crop has matured it is clear-felled: highly efficient machines called harvesters will grab each tree, cut it through at the base, trim off all the branches automatically and cut the long logs into predetermined lengths. Piles of logs are then simply removed from the forest to the road side, using a forwarder, and collected for onward shipment to the sawmills by road. Then the cycle is repeated, about once every fifty years.

Below and opposite, left to right The stages of modern timber harvesting: mature trees are felled mechanically and stripped of their branches; they are then transported to a sawmill for conversion.

Logging in difficult conditions

Logging in the natural forests of North America continues. Here the trees are much larger and the terrain can be more difficult to traverse. In particularly hilly regions, the logging companies have developed special methods of extraction.

These will include the use of steel cabling systems. Mobile or fixed lines are strung up so that the logs can be lifted clear and dragged down a main line to a collection area. This may be the main extraction point, or the first in a series. In particularly tough terrain, if the lumber being extracted is considered worth it, helicopters are sometimes used.

In both North America and Scandinavia, sawmills were traditionally built downstream from the forests on the side of a river. Logs were cut, hauled, and dropped into the river to be taken downstream to the sawmill by natural means. On lakes the technique varied, with huge rafts of logs being gathered together and towed by tugs to the designated sawmill.

Huge equipment has been developed in order to handle larger tropical and temperate logs. Access roads are cut and laid to enable this equipment to access collection areas in the forest. Cranes and special lifting gear load the full-length logs onto special road transporters. Some of these transporters have adjustable

carriers so that they can cope with long lengths. The trips from the forest to the sawmill may be of many miles, and therefore the transporters need to carry their maximum weight whenever possible. At the sawmill, special lifting gear, or cranes, remove the logs. They are then sorted and visually graded and stored in a log yard, prior to being converted into lumber.

Low-impact harvesting

The techniques described above apply to highly commercial operations all around the world. So long as they are complemented by the appropriate reforestation and forestry practices, the cycle can be continuous. However, in the case of smaller operations in both third world countries and developed regions which seek to have a lesser environmental impact, more basic harvesting and extraction methods are employed. In some instances, this will involve the use of muscle power. If the logs extracted are small and of value they may be dragged from the forest by hand or with the help of oxen, mules, or horses. Providing each log has been selectively felled, the extraction damage is limited and soon naturally regenerates and repairs itself. In some countries like Myanmar, formerly Burma, elephants are still used to move logs around.

Conversion at source

The alternative to the low-impact extraction of logs is to harvest and convert the logs at source. After felling, a simple pit saw can be constructed to slice up the logs into manageable lumber which can then be extracted from the forest a piece or two at a time. Modern, cost-effective alternatives may replace the pit saw: there are a number of self-propelled sawing rigs available that can be taken in parts or on trailers into the forest.

Above Timber can be a difficult crop to harvest, due to the inaccessible terrain in which many trees grow.

Conversion

The objective of timber conversion is to get as much "yield" of usable timber, planks, boards, and scantlings from the round logs as possible. In high-production softwood mills, the yield can be as great as 80 percent, but it may be no more than 50 percent in a temperate hardwood mill. Tropical timber yields are somewhere in between.

Above right Logs and converted wood awaiting treatment and transportation at a lakeside sawmill.

Total conversion

Most softwood is produced with this yield factor in mind, with the possible exception of some top-quality North American species. With softwood, literally every part of the log is used: the bark is removed for fiber extraction or broken up for garden mulch; sawdust and unusable small pieces (which are chipped) are used for particle board manufacture; wood pulp is used for paper.

Hardwoods, especially temperate species from North America and Europe, are generally better for making furniture and cabinets and are consequently of more interest to the hobby woodworker. As a result, most of what is discussed here relates to them. Nonetheless, all conversion techniques are the same, whether for hardwoods or softwoods, and are universally applied.

Conversion techniques

There are a number of different sawing sequences and rigs used in the conversion of logs. Most conversion mills will have what is called a "green line" or "chain." This is a linked set of bandsaws processing the raw materials; it is called "green" because the wood has not yet been seasoned.

Below A log carriage type breaking-down unit can be used to produce back-sawn boards.

Headrig

The primary saw—called a "headrig," or "breaking down" saw—is used for the first and subsequent cuts in large logs. Conversion mills in tropical countries can handle logs up to nearly 6ft 6in (2m) in diameter. However, there is seldom the need for such large equipment in the conversion of temperate hardwoods and, as the log conversion process has moved back to source, it is unlikely that many large capacity headrigs remain in Europe. Conversely, they are still found in North America, due to the size of old growth softwood logs that are converted.

The headrig saw may make further cuts in the log sections, breaking them down into smaller sizes. The initial cuts are crucial and determine the eventual yield from the log. Most headrig sawyers are very experienced and can immediately see the best cuts to make in a log. Despite widespread mechanization in logging, it is difficult to replace the practiced eye of the sawyer when it comes to a bent hardwood log.

When cutting a log, many factors need to be taken into consideration, including its shape. Branch joints, damage, rot patches, and maybe the heart or pith of the log will all need to be cut

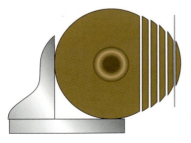
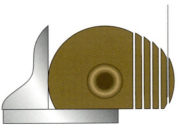
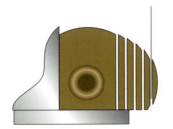
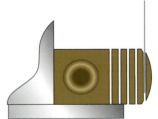

out or around. A good sawyer can make a vast difference to the quality and profitability of the sawmill operation.

Band resaw

A band "resaw" follows on from the headrig and is linked into the green line with, in most cases, fully automated conveyor systems. These second, smaller saws will break down further the slabs of wood to commercial sizes.

To avoid undue waste, the "kerf" of the saw blades (the width of cut) is reduced to a minimum. Less sawdust equals less waste. It all depends upon the thickness of the steel in the blade and its size. In large log conversion mills, these blades can be over 16in (400mm) wide, and may be over 40ft (12m) long. Where the production is out of small softwood logs for, say, thin fencing panels, a series of very thin bladed bandsaws will be set up to take the smallest cut possible, thereby increasing the yield from the log.

Cutting logs

The simplest way to cut a log is "through and through," producing lumber that has little quarter but a lot of plain-sawn material. This method is typically used on small to medium-sized logs. A step up from this, to try and increase the amount of figured, decorative lumber, is called "bastard quarter-sawn." The cuts follow, as closely as is practical, the tangential or cleavage line of the log. The aim is always to maximize the yield, regardless of what the end product will be.

The decision to cut logs in either the plain or quarter-sawn fashion is not always directly related to the yield, especially for hardwoods. Plain-sawn is usually more than adequate for most jobs but, because of the way in which it is cut, the wood is more likely to move, distort, or shrink in thickness during the drying process. Some Australian species of eucalyptus are more prone to defects if plain-sawn. So, to avoid high levels of downgrade, it is common practice to cut these on the quarter if possible. You might also want to cut on the quarter to ensure quality and stability, or if including decorative features. However, true quarter-sawing is very wasteful, and that makes it expensive. Generally, quarter-sawing has been modified to the bastard quarter cut.

Through and through

Simple boxed heart

True quarter cut

Bastard quarter cut (1)

Bastard quarter cut (2)

There can also be very good reasons for plain-sawing as opposed to quarter-cutting. Douglas Fir, for example, shows a great deal more character if plain-sawn. Some other species are less likely to split when nailed. Plain-sawn logs produce wider boards. They dry more quickly and are easier to cut. In summary, there are many different factors involved in the conversion of logs into lumber.

Above A variety of common log sawing patterns.

Below Stacked logs after initial cutting.

Grading

One of the major dilemmas when working with wood concerns grading—which grade to use for the job in hand, what that grade means with regard to quality and what it might be used for. The following information refers to visually graded wood, sometimes called appearance or commercial grades.

Above right The growing conditions that applied throughout its life will affect the grading of timber when it comes to be harvested.

Below
Comparing softwood grade classifications.

Grading standards

Visually graded material should not be confused with mechanically stress-graded material, which is used for constructional purposes.

Let us not forget that timber is a natural product. Each tree, plank, and piece of wood is individual, which is what makes it so attractive. Although "grades" of timber should be used as a guide to general quality, in the final selection, the end use will determine exactly what is required in terms of grade.

As our timber resources diminish, we should always consider using a substitute material that utilizes our wood resources more efficiently or has an economical benefit to the country of origin. That might mean selecting the best timber for the "faces" of a project and using poorer quality or cheaper substitutes for the sub-framing and hidden work. In recent years, several organizations have promoted lower grades of timber. For example, American and European oak, with a greater preponderance of knots, is being marketed as "character" oak. Some hardwoods, from the Pacific Rim, are sold in Europe as "pin hole no defect" (PHND), which results from an attack by the larvae of wood boring beetles. Most recently, there has been greater use of manmade boards like MDF, which have a number of advantages over solid wood.

Softwood grading

Generally, softwood grading is based on a "defects" system, whereby grading rules define

Source	Grades			
	Highest			Lowest
UK/Europe	I clear	I, II	III	IIII
Scandinavia, Poland, and Eastern Canada		I, II, III, IV (unsorted)	V	VI
Russia and the former Soviet Block countries		I, II, III (unsorted)	IV	V
Canada and Pacific coast of North America	No 1 clear No 2 clear No 3 clear	Select merchantable, No 1 merchantable	No 2 merchantable	No 3 common

the maximum allowable size of the defect for each grade in relation to the size of the timber. Therefore, one large defect in a wide board may be as acceptable as a smaller one in a narrow board to qualify for a particular grade. Defects taken into account when grading wood include knots, splits, twists, cup bows, ring width, wane, sap-stains, and rot.

Grade comparisons

The table on the opposite page shows a simple way of comparing classifications of grades from different sources. The general rule of thumb is that "clears" should be virtually defect-free and suitable for those special jobs, "unsorted" should contain a fair amount of good material and be suitable for most joinery projects, with the rest getting progressively poorer in quality with the increasing numbers.

Grade marks

It is worth noting that many primary lumber production mills end-mark every piece of timber with a shipping mark, defining their grading interpretation. These often take the form of stars, crowns, and capital letters stamped onto the ends of each board. Such marks are a mine of information, showing the country of origin, the production mill, the shipper, grade, and species.

Hardwood grading

There are a confusing number of hardwood grading systems, including some that are similar to those applied to softwoods. The most popular form is based on the "cutting system." The object is to assess the amount of usable/defect-free timber in relation to the whole board. Assessment is usually made through a notional rectangle of 12 square inches (three centimeters square). Definition of the grades follows the establishment of minimum areas of cutting acceptable as a fraction of the whole piece.

It is assumed that a perfect piece of lumber would be defect-free for twelve-twelfths of its surface, with each twelfth being one of the notional rectangles mentioned previously. As the grade of each plank is assessed, it may be twelve/twelfths, eleven/twelfths, ten/twelfths and so on.

Source	Grades			
	Highest			Lowest
UK/Europe	1	2	3	4
Square edged	10/12	8/12	9/12	8/12
Unedged	11/12	10/12	9/12	8/12
America/Africa/	Firsts	Seconds	Selects	No 1 common
Australia	11/12	10/12	9/12	8/12
South-East Asia	Prime	Selects	Standard	
	10/12	9/12	8/12	

Grade comparisons

The table above outlines the most likely grades and clear cutting units to qualify with the most common sources found.

It is a good idea to get some advice if you are unsure about which hardwood timber to use.

Grade marks

Like the crown and star marks found on some softwoods, you might also find end marks on hardwoods. These usually consist of two or three different colors in patches on the ends, maybe with some contrasting spots over-painted. Producers also stencil names and grades across the side of each stack of banded lumber. Alternatively, you may find a simple "prime" or "FAS" stamp on the face of each board.

Above
Comparing hardwood grade classifications.

Left Various grading marks may be stamped onto the ends, edges, and faces of timber as it progresses from the sawmill to the timber merchant.

Storage and drying

Wood needs to be looked after carefully. If it is left in a pile with little or no air circulating, it will become moist, an ideal breeding ground for both fungi and wood-eating insects. Whether you are dealing with a small amount of lumber or an entire timber yard, the following basic principles apply.

Above right Drying wood correctly is an art. Too moist, and it will bend; too dry, and it will crack and degrade.

Stacking timber

When wood is first cut from the log it can contain more than its own weight in moisture, which must be removed without damaging the structure too much. Ideally, you should stick and stack the planks so that they can be "air dried" initially, and then "kiln dried" if necessary, to remove further moisture. When being air dried, the planks are set out, layer by layer, with thin strips of equal size and distribution laid upon each consecutive layer to enable air to circulate.

Stacks should be situated on clear ground free of weeds, undergrowth, and direct moisture. Pairs of concrete or wooden blocks, up to 1ft

Right Stacks of wood being air dried. It is important that these are kept in a clean, dry environment, well away from plants and other sources of moisture.

(300mm) in height and about 3ft 3in (1m) wide are ideal. These should be placed about 3ft 3in (1m) apart from one another. Stout timber bearers should be laid across them, followed by the first layer of planks. Thin strips are then placed directly over these bearers and another set of planks laid down. And so the process continues, until the stack is formed.

The strips, or stickers, as they are sometimes known, are of a uniform thickness, most commonly ¾in (18mm). Some timbers, especially in thicker planks, will suffer if they dry out too quickly. Their outer surfaces may shrink faster than the core, creating surface checks and splits. To avoid this, lumber over, say, 2in (50mm) thick should be placed on strips of ½in (12mm). Thinner stock can go on the standard or even thicker strips up to 1in (25mm) thick.

As the stack is built up, the strips must be kept in line with the original bearers, to keep the weight evenly transferred down through the stack and so as to avoid unnecessary distortion of the wood. It is often helpful to weigh down the last layer with more solid blocks to prevent planks at the top from warping out of shape. If left outside, these stacks should be covered and a slight backward tilt of the whole stack will help to avoid moisture pooling on surfaces. As the wood dries, also ensure that nearby weeds or plants are completely removed so they cannot interfere with the stack. After the appropriate drying period the wood will either be ready for use or for the next stage of drying. There is an old adage: "an inch a year," suggesting that it will take one year to air-dry timber one inch thick, three years for three inches thick, and so on.

Artificial drying techniques

The lowest average moisture content achieved through air drying is mostly between 18–20 percent, making wood dried in this manner unsuitable for use in modern houses. Further, artificial, drying techniques are called for. For example, de-humidifying chambers (made up from simple box chambers and in old shipping containers) draw out the moisture under controlled conditions, while sealed vacuum cylinders use heat and pressure to remove moisture. Correct use of this technique produces the lowest number of defects. Large-scale drying takes place in progressive kilns in which wood is loaded one end, dried, and removed ready for use, at the other. Other common kilns use heat and humidity to draw out moisture.

Within the modern, well-insulated, heated home and office, the ideal moisture content is around eight to ten percent. Anything higher than this could result in further shrinkage; anything lower might lead to movement as moisture is gained. The process of drying and measuring the residual moisture is based on averages. Samples are taken from each charge and the average dictates when it has dried to the required levels. By its very nature, wood has variable structures, and so it is likely that one or more planks will be wetter, and others will be drier, than average. When making top-quality furniture, it is important that the wood's moisture content matches that where it will eventually be located. It is therefore a good idea to store the nominal components in a similar environment for a week or two before work starts.

Working with recently dried wood

As a result of the drying process, wood will change size and shape. A fair proportion of this will be attributed to shrinkage and some to movement, as stresses are set up in the wood during the process. Whenever possible when designing, jointing, and making wood products, these factors should be taken carefully into account. Before work starts the woodworker should be confident that any further movement in the finished structure will be minimal. When making tops for structures, try alternating the grain orientation to avoid too much movement in

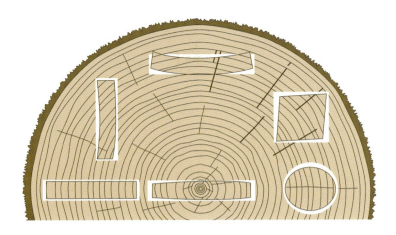

either direction. Where stability is required, opt for quarter-sawn material.

Design has evolved to make allowances for movement in wood, which is why drawer bottoms should not be permanently fixed with glue. The grooves into which the drawer slots should allow for further movement in both directions. Larger tops should be attached with "buttons" rather than solid screw fixings, to allow the top to expand and shrink naturally as the seasons change without causing splits. With care and thought, many items can be successfully made to accommodate the natural vagaries of this extremely versatile resource.

Above The amount and direction of shrinkage and distortion in a piece of wood will vary depending upon which part of the tree trunk it has been cut from.

Below Wood about to enter a hot air and vent kiln drier.

Veneers

The basic principle of veneers is to make better use of some of the fine-figured woods by cutting them thinly and attaching them to a stable "ground." The ground is usually made up from a much cheaper material, thus making the final piece more cost-effective than a solid section of expensive wood.

Above right Veneers have been used in furniture for centuries. This bureau dates from the 17th century reign of Louis XIV of France.

Veneering—a potted history

The art of veneering has been refined over many centuries. The Ancient Egyptians were the first to use decorative timbers applied to plain cores, technically known as "grounds" or "groundwork." Apart from being cheaper than using top-quality wood for the entire piece, the other benefits of veneering are that a more stable component is likely to result from the procedure and the maker has much more license to produce free-flowing shapes. In addition, by positioning the veneers in different forms, they can produce true works of art.

Before mechanization occurred in the 19th century, wooden veneers were cut by hand. Slicing up the sections as thinly as possible would have been hard and tedious work. Fortunately, water and steam power were soon developed and saws were made to cut more accurately. It was still a wasteful process, though, with nearly as much sawdust as actual veneer produced.

Modern methods of making veneers

As technology has developed over the centuries, slicing the wood mechanically to make veneers has become the norm. Logs or baulks of wood are placed in ponds of cold or warm water so that they become more pliable and easier to cut. Sometimes the object piece is fixed in a machine and the blade mechanism is driven across, at a pre-determined space, to produce a very thin veneer. At other times, the object piece is fixed into a holding mechanism that drops onto the cutting edge. As each cut is made, it is notched forward by the required thickness and the process is repeated. Using either of these methods, the depths of cut can be remarkably precise. In both these cases there will always be a residual piece left over where the machine "dogs" have held it in place. These are called backboards and are highly prized for making top-quality, solid wood cabinetry.

Right Slicing a veneer with a blade.

Far right Cutting a veneer with a saw.

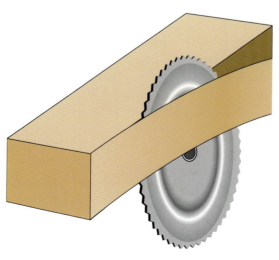

Making veneers by rotary cutting

Both the above methods are used to produce the best veneers with top-quality figuring. The alternative, and most efficient, way to produce veneers is by rotary cutting. After centering, each end of a log is mounted in a mechanism that is driven. This is then presented to the cutting edge and the cutting process begins. The log is moved forward at an even, progressive rate, so that as it rotates a veneer is peeled off, just like a roll of paper.

This is a more economical way of producing veneers, because the final thickness can be less than half of that produced by the slicing method. Peeled veneers tend not to be too decorative, although an exception to this is bird's eye maple, which is efficiently produced in this way. The rotary cut technique is used extensively to produce plywood. Cheaper, poorer-quality timbers are used for the cores and these can be faced up with a veneer or a simple defect-free covering.

Types of veneer

Veneers are cut from the most decorative face of the wood, mostly along the quarter-sawn section. The result will depend upon the structure of the wood. Interlocking grain, such as that found in sapele, will produce a striped, or ribbon figure. When the grain alignment includes undulations, this produces a number of interesting variations including wavy, curly, and fiddleback figures. Maple and birch both produce blister- and quilted-like figures and one of the best known is

Above A selection of different wood veneers.

bird's-eye maple figure. European oak cut in the same way will expose the medullary rays, creating the easily recognizable flower figure.

Burrs

Defects also create interesting effects. Burrs, or burls, are large, bulbous growths that can occur on any tree. One theory is that damage through fire, frost, or mechanical injury will set off a reaction that creates the growth. The grain fibers in a burr are totally out of line and irregular. When sliced into veneers, the resulting spectacular grain effect is highly prized.

Left Rotary cutting a veneer.

Other effects

Natural growth features can also create interesting veneers. The fork in a tree or a large branch sprouting from the trunk can produce a crotch or curl figure. Mahogany is prized for this and a lot of antique furniture displays the curl-like figure. The same growth configuration produces feather, moonshine, and swirl crotch figures, depending upon the individual structure and orientation of the tree's grain.

Being inventive can produce good results. The cone cutting technique, for example, produces some outstanding figures, which are best displayed when incorporated into a round table top.

Above Cone cutting veneers.

Sheet materials

Improvements in manufacturing techniques have resulted in a plethora of new manmade wood products on the market. This development is driven by the need to utilize wood in more efficient ways, to create products that meet specific needs and to generate profit for the manufacturing companies involved.

Above right A close-up of a piece of Orientated Strand Board (OSB).

Types of sheet materials and composite boards

Sheet materials and composite boards are broadly split into three main classifications: particle boards; fiber boards; and laminated boards. The following lists the main features of each and a little basic information about their uses.

Particle boards

As well as wood, particle boards comprise other cellulose-based materials. The boards are created by a process that mechanically produces particles of various sizes. These are combined

Below Some common classifications for sheet materials.

INT	Interior use	Obviously for interior use only. It is likely that both the binder and the wood itself are not that durable.
MR	Moisture and moderately weather resistant	The boards with this classification will stand moderate exposure to cold water and damp conditions, but not hot, wet applications.
BR	Boil resistant	Although the binders in these panels may have been tested for boil resistance, they are likely to fail under prolonged exposure.
WBP	Weather and boil proof	The binders used for these panels are most suitable for external use under most conditions. The timbers used in WBP panels will probably be less durable than the binders. The manufacturer's recommendations for their protection must be followed.

with a resin binder, extruded out into flat sheets and subjected to a high temperature pressing process that forms the board.

Chipboard

Most chipboard is constructed from sawmill residues, wood waste, and forest thinnings and is an ideal way to maximize the use of wood. Although it can be produced for external use, chipboard is best used internally or in protected or less harsh external locations. Any moisture increase usually results in a swelling of the panel that eventually leads to a breakdown of the structure.

Orientated Strand Board (OSB)

OSB is made up in a similar manner to chipboard but consists of thin wood wafers that are laid in a specific way. The board is constructed in three wafer layers, similar to plywood. It is held together with a resin binder that generally allows for external use. The manipulation of the wafers—their "orientation"—led to its name. OSB is stronger than chipboard, especially in the longitudinal plane.

Wafer board

This board is also created from wood wafers. Like OSB, wafer board is stronger than chipboard and is used where appearance is not critical.

Odds and ends

Other particle boards can be made up from various residues produced as a result of other processes. These can sometimes be more economical to use than those listed here.

Fiber boards

The manufacturing process that produces fiber board starts by separating the fibers of the wood raw material. These are refined at high temperature and can be mixed with water and/or resin binders, extruded and pressed in a similar method to that of particle board production.

Hardboard

Hardboard is a fairly cheap, multipurpose panel product that has a range of uses from floor lining to furniture drawer bottoms. Standard hardboard, smooth on one face only, is not suitable for external use.

Medium board

Medium board is produced in the same way as hardboard. The main difference is the density —medium board is about half as dense as hardboard. It is not suitable for external use.

Soft board

At about a quarter to a third of the density of hardboard, soft board is mainly used for insulation only.

Medium Density Fiber board (MDF)

MDF has become tremendously popular in recent years. It is manufactured from fibers that have been dried, had resins added and are pressed to produce the board, which has two smooth faces. MDF can be worked like wood and is an ideal product from which to make baseboards and other second fix internal moldings.

Laminated boards

The most common and easily recognized laminated board is plywood. Logs are peeled to produce veneers that are bonded together in alternating grain directions to produce the ply board. Blockboard and laminboard are variations on the theme, using larger sections of solid wood in the core.

Plywood

The minimum number of veneers used in plywood is three and moves upward, two at a time, to a multilayered board. The product range

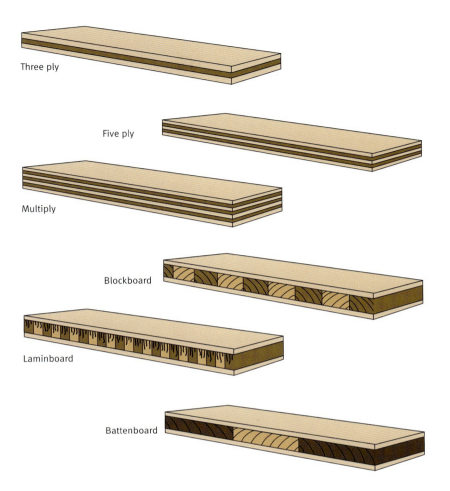

Three ply

Five ply

Multiply

Blockboard

Laminboard

Battenboard

Above Various types of commonly used manmade boards.

is huge and includes some that are metal- or plastic-faced for specific applications.

Blockboard

The inner core of this panel product is comprised of solid strips of wood, which can be hardwood or softwood, depending on the grade and end use of the material.

Laminboard

Although it is made up in a similar way to blockboard, laminboard is superior in quality. The core strips of solid wood are much thinner and are edge-glued as the board is constructed. A strong panel product that is used in furniture production with veneer faces.

Battenboard

An uncommon panel product, battenboard is created using wider solid strips of wood.

Wood and the environment

We must not lose sight of the fact that trees are the only natural, regenerating resource available to us. If managed carefully, they will continue to grow and flourish long after other resources, such as petrochemical and metal products, become exhausted. If used up without replenishment, the consequences will be dire.

Above right Established woodlands and forests need care and maintenance in order to survive the vagaries of modern life.

Environmental concerns

We also have to face up to the impact of global warming. One of the key issues affecting the climate of the world is the release of carbon dioxide (CO_2) into the environment. Because trees take up, and lock in, carbon dioxide in healthy wood, the more trees and forests we have, the more the environment will benefit. Despite this widely accepted fact, however, planting and growing trees is not the sole answer to the problem.

If a forest is left to develop naturally, it will eventually reach equilibrium, with new growth occurring only as old trees die or are destroyed by pest attack or fire. Natural regeneration will take place, but only up to the levels of the

biomass balance. The term "biomass" refers to various kinds of organic materials that are used as sustainable fuels, of which wood is the principal one. New growth will continue to capture carbon dioxide, but decayed, dead, or burnt trees will emit it in equal amounts, directly counteracting efforts made to stabilize the environment through the extensive replanting of woods and forests.

So, what is the answer? Providing forests can be managed and sound wood, in the form of lumber, can be extracted, there will always be benefits. Lumber, with its carbon content locked in during its useful life, becomes a commodity with a commercial value. Then, once lumber production trees are removed, new growth can be introduced and encouraged to extend the natural cycle and, if this is maintained, in the long term the benefits will outweigh any disadvantages.

However, trees alone will not save the world! There need to be significant reductions in the world's industrial carbon emissions, as well —on a progressive basis, starting right now. Many countries of the world now recognize this course of action as a necessity, but not all. Some question whether global warming actually exists as a phenomenon at all. Suffice to say that global warming and its future ramifications for the planet is a huge and emotive subject that will long be debated. In the meantime we, as workers of wood, should take a positive stance and encourage the establishment of new tree growth projects and increasing levels in the use of wood in whatever ways we can. Of course, the responsible usage of wood should go hand in hand with this approach.

Right Planting new trees is one way to sustain the environment and combat the worldwide effects of mass deforestation and climate change.

Opposite Acid rain, global warming, and other environmental phenomena affect trees significantly in many parts of the world.

Directory of wood

There are many hardwoods and softwoods to choose from, offering an incredible array of qualities and characteristics which have a bearing on their suitability for a multitude of applications. In this selective directory of woods, you will find nearly 100 of the finest and most versatile. Perhaps the most important criterion for the selection of woods in the following pages is their availability: many woods are now under threat, so only plentiful and popular species have made it into this directory.

Introduction

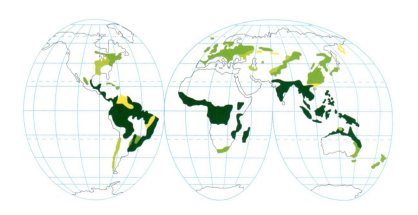

So, which wood is for you? Hopefully the wealth of information provided in this directory will give you more than enough choice. Once you have selected the wood you require, if you are in any doubt as to which tools and adhesives to use with it, refer to the other sections of the book, which are full of helpful advice.

Above right Wood is a beautiful worldwide resource which we must use responsibly and renew with care.

Selection criteria

The choice of woods described in this section has been determined by a number of factors. In the selection I have aimed to include:

- A representative cross-section of both hardwoods and softwoods that are available on the open market, such as ash, mahogany, oak, teak, pine, and spruce
- A number of woods that are easily recognized but not always readily available, such as apple, boxwood, ebony, pear, walnut, and yew
- A range of decorative woods, such as cocobolo, goncalo alves, rosewood, snakewood, and zebrano
- A number of more utilitarian woods that are commercially available but less recognizable, such as abura, bintangor, dahoma, jarrah, nyatoh, Californian redwood.

My original, longer list was whittled down by a careful review of the endangered species listing, which is maintained by CITES, Convention on International Trade in Endangered Species.

This listing grades woods from a total trade ban through to local or international approved but regulated trading.

Hardwoods

The term "hardwood" can be confusing at times if one considers that within this classification we have woods ranging from the relatively soft basswood through to the ultra-tough Lignum Vitae. In reality, the classification relates to some fundamental differences in cellular structure and botanical grouping rather than any physical characteristics or properties. Hardwoods make up a botanical group known as angiosperms. This group has broad leaves with encased seed pods. They grow both in temperate and tropical regions. Those from the former tend to drop their leaves in winter while the latter do not. However, this is not a hard and fast rule. Different species will grow in different climates and this will affect the rate and type of growth structure within the wood itself. Temperate woods generally have a clear,

Below The worldwide distribution of hardwoods.

Key

Broadleaved evergreen forest

Broadleaved deciduous and coniferous mixed forest

Broadleaved deciduous forest

Broadleaved evergreen and deciduous hardwood forest

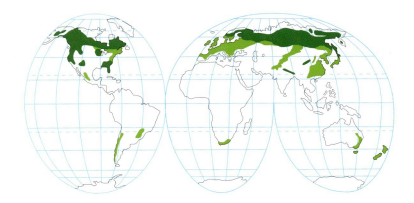

annual growing cycle that can be seen in the grain pattern. Tropical woods tend to grow continuously with little demarcation for the seasons.

There are a huge number of hardwoods growing worldwide. Some of these are available in commercial quantities and others are rare, only coming onto the market occasionally. Some will be used for utility and structural purposes while others will be prized for a property such as grain pattern, stability, or weight. The choice and variety of hardwoods is much greater than in the softwood grouping, and you will always be able to find one that is suited to your needs.

Softwoods

Like hardwoods, this term does not always directly relate to the property of the woods in this grouping. For example, the extremes in our selection go from the hardest, pitch pine and yew, down through to the softest which, in this case, is Western red cedar. Once more, it is a classification of a botanical grouping, gymnosperms, which predominantly have

needle-shaped leaves, are cone-bearing, and evergreen. However, once more, this is not a hard and fast rule. Larch, for example, drops its needles annually. Commercial softwoods predominantly grow in the northern hemisphere, where their growth patterns reflect the varying seasons. Where some of these species have been introduced into a different climate, as a managed plantation crop, the impact can sometimes be dramatic. Growth rates can accelerate and wood properties can alter.

The number of softwood species available worldwide is much fewer than hardwoods. Those available in bulk and broadly sold as redwood or whitewood will be used for a wide range of purposes from pallets to paneling. Others may have some limited decorative use and/or some particular property for which they are valued. As interested parties, we will have come across more softwood in use than hardwood.

Working properties

In the narrative descriptions of the following woods, reference is often made to the working properties and gross features of the wood in question. In addition, there is a quick reference guide to the associated working properties of each wood. Each of these comprises the following headings, whose rationales and criteria for selection are outlined below.

Above The worldwide distribution of softwoods.

Below and below left Summary boxes like these are provided for each wood in the directory. The more checks or diamonds, the greater the availability or price of the wood.

Working properties

Weight (per ft³)	35lb (16kg)
Durability	Very durable
Bendability	Moderate
Hardness	Hard
Sawing and usability	Take care
Splitting	Average
Gluing	Good

Uses					Availability	Price
VENEER	PLYWOOD	FURNITURE	JOINERY	CONSTRUCTION	✓✓✓	◆◆◆
✓	✓	✓	✓	✓		

Weight

If the text describes the weight as about "average when dry," this refers to wood that has a moisture content of around 12 to 15 percent and, at that point, weighs about 40 pounds per cubic foot (18 kilograms per cubic foot). That is about 1,412 pounds per cubic meter (635 kilograms per cubic meter). Therefore, a lightweight wood will be anything from the low to middle twenties, in pounds, per cubic foot and the really heavy ones will be anything up to and over, say, 70-odd pounds per cubic foot.

The weight of wood is mainly affected by two factors; the density of the wood structure and the moisture content therein. What may influence the first is the way in which, when the wood grows, the cellular structure is formed, as well as the growth cycles of the tree, climatic conditions, and so on. The second will simply be how much moisture is in the wood at the time it is measured.

Often, when wood has been converted into lumber from the log, it is sticked and stacked for air drying. The idea here is to remove as much moisture as possible before it might then go on to be artificially dried. Under these circumstances the wood is in the process of "air drying." As a rule of thumb, air drying will only enable the stacked wood to reach a moisture content of around 18 percent. In order to reach our average weight comparison at 12–15 percent moisture content, some further artificial drying needs to take place.

Durability

In the description of each wood that follows I often refer to how the heartwood of a particular timber may be considered to be nondurable, durable, and very durable. In this case durability means how the wood will perform in conditions that might encourage it to be attacked by fungi that will eventually destroy the structure and integrity of the wood itself.

There are lots of factors that might affect durability; the cellular structure and its resistance to moisture or water ingress, the density of the wood, where it comes from, chemical and mineral inclusions, growth rates, and so on. Therefore, when a particular description states that the wood is, say, heavy, it does not follow that it will be durable. Care needs to be taken to ensure the correct wood is chosen for the end use purpose or, if the wood is not considered durable enough, a suitable preservative treatment is applied.

Bendability

Some woods will naturally bend and flex in use and others need to be bent artificially into particular shapes. All wood is elastic to some extent. That means that if it is simply pulled out of line it should return to its original shape once released. The bendability of wood is normally tested under laboratory conditions. Samples of a predetermined size are held firm while pressure is applied to see how far it will deflect before sheering takes place.

Hardness

Hardness is simply rated by seeing how far a constant-sized nail penetrates into a standard wood sample about ½in (13mm) from the end. The penetration in relationship to the split, if or when it occurs, is what is measured and reported upon. In the text, reference is often made as to whether any predrilling is required prior to screwing and nailing fixings. Hardness will also affect the choice of wood for specific end uses.

Sawing and usability

Sawing, planing, chiseling, and turning qualities are all important to those who use wood regularly. The factors that will affect how each wood works will be variable. They include grain configuration, hardness, moisture content, how the wood has been dried, and any elements in the wood such as oils or minerals, knots, and so on.

Generally speaking, when both hand and machine planing, the cutting angle should be about 30 degrees. At this angle, most woods will produce a satisfactory finish, providing there are no other elements such as interlocking grain involved. Softer, low density woods may benefit from some reduction in cutting angle to help avoid producing a woolly surface.

It is always a good idea, and sometimes critical, that tools are looked after and sharp edges maintained. A blunt planing iron will definitely produce a poor quality finished surface. The same applies for turning and carving chisels and gouges.

Splitting

Most woods will split if forced to, some more easily than others. In general, hardwoods will tend to split more readily than softwoods, although this is not always the case. In this classification, advice is given as to whether the timber needs predrilling prior to fixing (see also "Hardness" above.)

Gluing

When comment is made on the gluing properties of a particular wood, it is referring to a solid wood section rather than veneers. Factors like open grain, resin, chemical, and mineral content will all have some impact on the gluing

process. The moisture content of the wood to be jointed may alter the expected performance of the adhesive. In addition, how much pressure is exerted during the process and on through until the glue has cured will possibly determine the ultimate quality of a joint. In most cases, we assume that the surfaces to be jointed are clean, dry, and a close fit, if appropriate. Glue should always be used in accordance with the manufacturer's specification.

The type of glue used may also have some influence on completing a successful jointing process. Some, like Elmer's Glue (polyvinyl acetates) do not set rigidly and should not be used where the joint may come under pressure. For rigid joints, a resin glue is probably best.

Above Ensure that the wood you select can be sawed and otherwise worked with sufficient ease for your purpose.

Below Keep in mind that wood with a very open grain will be difficult to glue and fit.

ACER PSEUDOPLATNUS

Sycamore

This wood is commonly named **Sycamore** and is also known as **Scotch Plane**, **Sycamore Plane**, **Plane**, **Great Maple**, **Weathered Sycamore**, or **Harewood**.

The Sycamore tree is found throughout Europe. Occasionally, there is some confusion over its common name when other trees are given the same local name. For example, in Scotland European Plane is also called sycamore. *Acer pseudoplatnus* should not be confused with North American sycamore, *Platanus occidentalis*; it is more closely related to maple. The trees are not tall, reaching heights of around 100ft (30m). Clear bole lengths will depend on local growing conditions but can be up to 65ft (20m) long in managed forests. When freshly cut, the heartwood is a pale off-white cream color with little or no delineation between this and the sapwood. Darker streaking is often found and the wood is usually sorted off the saw for the lighter more uniform color. It has a mild, finely textured grain.

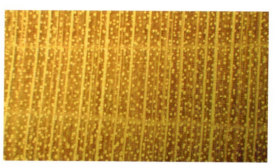

Top Grain when radially cut. **Middle** Grain when tangentially cut. **Bottom** Cross-section.

Source Throughout Europe

Working properties

Weight (per ft³)	37lb (17kg)
Durability	Perishable
Bendability	Good
Hardness	Soft
Sawing and shaping	Take care
Splitting	Good
Gluing	Good

Properties of the wood

A lightweight, soft wood which is not considered to be durable. All sycamore wood is susceptible to what is called "shadow staining" if stacked wet on stickers; a darker mark where the sticker has lain. To avoid this the wood is often end stacked for long periods before the final drying process takes place. Working sycamore can be difficult if it has heavily interlocked grain. Saws tend to bind and burn and planing can produce a woolly surface. It should nail and screw with ease and has good adhesion. Staining properties are good, but care needs to be taken near end grain. A fine surface finish can be achieved.

Uses of the wood

Sycamore turns well and is therefore used for a wide range of craft related items. As a neutral type of timber the white wood is often used for kitchen cutting boards, and so on. Lumber that displays a fiddleback figure is often literally used for musical instrument backs. It can be sliced for veneers. Sycamore is used for inlay work where it can be easily colored.

Uses					Availability	Price
VENEER	PLYWOOD	FURNITURE	JOINERY	CONSTRUCTION		
✓	✓				✓	◆◆

Top Grain when radially cut. **Middle** Grain when tangentially cut. **Bottom** Cross-section.

ACER SACCHARUM and NIGRUM
Maple

The common name of this wood is **Maple** and it is also known as **Rock**, **Hard**, **Sugar**, **Black**, **White**, or **Black Sugar Maple**.

These are the two species of maple that are grouped together and generally sold as Rock or Hard Maple. The trees grow throughout the central and northern parts of North America and favor the colder climates of this region. These species of maple are farmed to produce maple sugar and syrup. The trees are not tall, averaging around 82ft (25m), but can, on occasion, exceed 120ft (35m). Clear boles can be produced up to 30–50ft (10–15m), but these are probably the exception. The heartwood is a creamy to light brown when freshly cut and the sapwood is not always clearly defined. Where paler heartwood is adjacent to the lighter sapwood, this is often marketed as White Maple. The grain is fairly tight and can be straight or curly with some pith flecks included. Occasionally fine figures are present. These can be recognized as fiddleback, curly, and birds-eye.

Properties of the wood

These species of maple are fairly hard and heavy. However, the heartwood is not considered to be durable. The wood dries slowly with a high level of shrinkage and there is a possibility that further movement will subsequently occur. Care needs to be taken when sawing and planing to avoid burning and chatter. This wood is reasonably receptive to nails, but predrilling before fixing with them or with screws is recommended. Maple has good adhesive properties and can be successfully stained, if required.

Its grain structure lends itself to producing a fine surface finish.

Uses of the wood

With the differentiation between heart and sapwood sometimes difficult, it is best to use this wood internally. When the decorative figures are apparent, maple is often used as a veneer. Over the centuries it has been employed in fine cabinet work, furniture, and joinery. With a fairly high resistance to wear, it also makes an ideal flooring material for both domestic and sporting venues.

Source North America

Working properties

Weight (per ft³)	46lb (21kg)
Durability	Perishable
Bendability	Good
Hardness	Hard
Sawing and shaping	Take care
Splitting	Average
Gluing	Good

Uses					Availability	Price
VENEER	PLYWOOD	FURNITURE	JOINERY	CONSTRUCTION	✓✓	◆◆
✓		✓	✓			

AFZELIA SPP.

Afzelia

This wood is generally called **Afzelia** and is also known as **Apa**, **Alinga**, **Aryian**, **Bilinga**, **Bolengu**, **Chanfuta**, **Doussie**, **Kontah**, **Lingue**, **Malacca Teak**, **Mkora**, **Mbembakofi**, **Mussacossa**, **Papao**, or **Uvala**.

The Afzelia trees can be found right through the central band of Africa. These are not huge trees in comparison with some others found in Africa. Heights generally vary between 65–82ft (20–25m). A clear, straight bole can be harvested of around 50ft (15m) without branches. Afzelia is coarse-grained and a mucky yellow to reddishbrown in color when first cut from the log. On exposure, the heartwood deepens to a more uniform dark red to brown with a clear distinction between this and the sapwood, which is yellowish in color. A feature often found is the inclusion of a white or yellow calcium deposit in the cell cavities. Absorbed during the growing process, this material can help to distinguish the timber from other species.

Top Grain when radially cut. **Middle** Grain when tangentially cut. **Bottom** Cross-section.

Source West, Central, and East Africa

Working properties

Weight (per ft³)	46lb (21kg)
Durability	Durable
Bendability	Poor
Hardness	Hard
Sawing and shaping	Satisfactory
Splitting	Average
Gluing	Take care

Properties of the wood

The wood is fairly hard and considered reasonably heavy when dried. With some spiral grain found, it does require care while seasoning. However, once the appropriate moisture content levels have been achieved, it is exceptionally stable. Classified as a very durable wood, Afzelia does not need preservative treatment in most instances. If applied, due to the occasional calcium deposits, preservatives do not penetrate well. Afzelia is a tough wood to work. Hand and machine planing need some care and the latter is best achieved with specialist tools. Predrilling for nailing and screwing is a good idea.

Uses of the wood

Afzelia has been traditionally used for heavy construction work. Uses typically include bridges, quay, and dock works and other potential areas of high wear. With care it has potential to be used in joinery and a good surface finish can be worked up. This latter feature has led to its occasional use as a kitchen worktop surface and for flooring.

Uses					Availability	Price
VENEER	PLYWOOD	FURNITURE	JOINERY	CONSTRUCTION		
✓		✓	✓		✓✓	◆◆

Top Grain when radially cut. **Middle** Grain when tangentially cut. **Bottom** Cross-section.

ALNUS SPP.

Alder

The common English name is **Alder** and it is also known as **Black**, **White**, **Gray**, **Red**, **Western**, and **Oregon Alder**.

Alder is not a large tree and is often considered a weed due to its ability to regenerate after being cut back. Found throughout Europe and central north America, depending upon location the overall height of the tree will reach, at most, around 82ft (25m). In Europe it is often found growing in wet and boggy soil conditions, in which it thrives. Larger trees are found in North America, where it can grow in a variety of conditions. Boles are generally not large, with short logs being produced. Depending upon the species, the wood varies from a light creamy color through to a pale pink when first cut. These colors will often noticeably darken after drying and then pale again. Careful selection at this stage can produce material that is nearly white in color. There is generally little or no differentiation between heart and sapwood. Some figuring can be present if lumber is cut on the quarter, but this is not consistent.

Properties of the wood

Alder is fairly light in weight once dried and is not considered a durable wood. Surprisingly, when completely immersed in water, it will last for years. In fact these properties have led to it being used for piles in wet and boggy situations. The most famous of these can be found under the city of Venice! Unfortunately, if used in external locations, this wood can be susceptible to insect attack. Although it will readily accept preservatives, it is best used internally. With fairly straight, mild grain, alder is easy to work and finish but where wild grain is present some care needs to be taken to avoid it plucking up from the surface.

Uses of the wood

Apart from its use as a specialist pile in wet conditions, this wood has another claim to fame. Many Stradivarius violins are made from alder. General use will include such things as plywood cores, small finished components such as brushes, smaller moldings, and other less prominent furniture use.

Source Mainly Europe and North America

Working properties

Weight (per ft³)	33lb (15kg)
Durability	Perishable
Bendability	Poor
Hardness	Medium
Sawing and shaping	Satisfactory
Splitting	Good
Gluing	Good

Uses					Availability	Price
VENEER	PLYWOOD	FURNITURE	JOINERY	CONSTRUCTION	✓✓	◆◆
✓		✓	✓			

ASTRONIUM FRAXINIFOLIUM

Goncalo Alves

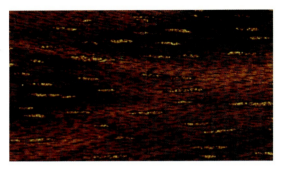

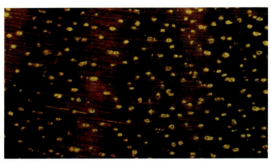

This hardwood is generally named **Goncalo Alves** and is also known as **Yoke**, **Locustwood**, **Kingwood**, **Tigerwood**, **Zebrawood**, **Courbaril**, or **Roble Gateado**.

The Goncalo Alves tree is fairly rare but found throughout Central and tropical South America. Most of the commercially available lumber comes from Brazil. The tree can stand at up to 130–150ft (40–45m) high. Branching occurs at about half this height, giving a fairly short clear bole length. When freshly cut, the heartwood ranges from a light brown to a much darker brown, in stripes—hence the "Tigerwood" common name. Depending upon the plane with which the lumber is cut, there may be uniform stripes or irregular ones. The effect of this color variation in the wood is dramatic and extremely attractive. The grain is interlocked and irregular, contributing to the overall effect. The sapwood is clearly lighter in color and easily distinguishable.

Top Grain when radially cut. **Middle** Grain when tangentially cut. **Bottom** Cross-section.

Source Central and South America

Working properties

Weight (per ft³)	59lb (27kg)
Durability	Very durable
Bendability	Poor
Hardness	Hard
Sawing and shaping	Difficult
Splitting	Poor
Gluing	Take care

Properties of the wood

This is a hard, dense, and heavy wood that is classified as durable and strong. These particular qualities are not often tested, due to the types of end use to which it is put. As with similar timbers, some predrying on thin stickers will help to avoid too much surface checking and distortion. As this is a hard wood, tools will need to be kept sharp to avoid burning while sawing and chattering while planing and molding. If nailed, screwed, or glued, care needs to be taken. The density does not help the latter and predrilling is recommended for the former. An excellent surface finish can be achieved.

Uses of the wood

At source, Goncalo Alves is sometimes used for structural purposes but, in the main, the lumber from this tree is prized for its decorative appearance. This has led to its use in furniture, where the marked color variations of the grain are displayed. Because the wood turns reasonably well, it is often used in craft applications for bowls, dishes, and similar items.

Uses					Availability	Price
VENEER	PLYWOOD	FURNITURE	JOINERY	CONSTRUCTION		
✓		✓			✓	◆◆◆

Top Grain when radially cut. **Middle** Grain when tangentially cut. **Bottom** Cross-section.

AUCOUMEA KLAINEANA

Gaboon

Gaboon is also known as **Okoume**, **Gaboon Mahogany**, **Gaboon Wood**, **Angouma**, **Mofoumou**, **N'goumi**, **Ongoumi**, or **Zouga**.

This wood is predominantly found in West Africa but most specifically in Gabon, from which the most common name is derived. The Gaboon tree is taller than average but not huge, at around 115–150ft (35–45m). Taller trees can be found but are rare. The bole can be buttressed to a height of just under 10ft (3m). This tends to result in clear boles of around 65ft (20m). When the logs are first cut the heartwood is a light, salmon pink color that quickly darkens on exposure. The sapwood is clearly distinct, being a lighter, paler pink. If cut on the quarter, gaboon sometimes shows similar grain patterns to mahogany. Coupled with the darkening of the heartwood, it can easily be confused with mahogany at times. Cross shakes are a feature often found in gaboon and these will affect its appearance and strength properties.

Properties of the wood

Gaboon is a lightweight wood that is classified as nondurable. The inclusion of silica during the growing process makes it particularly resistant to treatment with preservatives; therefore, it is recommended for internal use only. The silica can have an adverse affect on the sawing and planing of this wood. Care needs to be taken to ensure all tools are sharp and, to avoid plucking out the surface when planing or molding, a reduced cutting angle might be beneficial. The light, woolly nature of gaboon makes it fairly easy to nail and screw. Adhesion properties are also good. If the wood is to be stained, it has a high absorption rate. With care, a reasonable final finished surface can be achieved.

Uses of the wood

At source gaboon is peeled for veneers and cut for cores in blockboard. Its tendency to include shakes precludes it from any structural uses. Its similarity to mahogany does lead it toward use as a substitute in furniture, paneling, and molding.

Source West Africa

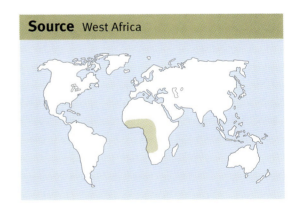

Working properties

Weight (per ft³)	26lb (12kg)
Durability	Perishable
Bendability	Poor
Hardness	Soft
Sawing and shaping	Take care
Splitting	Average
Gluing	Good

Uses					Availability	Price
VENEER	PLYWOOD	FURNITURE	JOINERY	CONSTRUCTION	✓✓	◆◆
✓	✓	✓	✓			

BETULA SPP.

European Birch

The common English name is **European Birch** and it is also known as **Finnish**, **Swedish**, **English**, and so on, depending upon origin. Other names are **Silver**, **White**, and **Masur Birch**.

Birch trees are not substantial and do not grow to a great height. At a maximum of around 65ft (20m), they have a slim bole that produces clear wood logs up to 33ft (10m) in good growing conditions and locations. Another tree that is often seen as a weed, birch is found throughout Europe and is easily recognized with its silvery, flaking bark. It grows quickly in poor condition soils. It can be scattered throughout a mixed woodland and will take over cleared areas of land fairly rapidly. Cutting from the log, there is no discernible difference in color between the sap and heartwood. This ranges from a white through to a light brown and is plain in appearance. It has no definite figure or grain pattern, but does have some slight silvering and darkening that is easily recognized.

Top Grain when radially cut. **Middle** Grain when tangentially cut. **Bottom** Cross-section.

Source Throughout Europe

Working properties

Weight (per ft³)	40lb (18kg)
Durability	Perishable
Bendability	Moderate
Hardness	Medium
Sawing and shaping	Satisfactory
Splitting	Poor
Gluing	Good

Properties of the wood

The lumber from birch is of medium weight when dried. It is usually fairly straight-grained and, when grown slowly in colder climes, it produces a much sought-after, tight-grained wood. Initial drying can produce some distortion but it does dry quickly. Birch should be converted and dried as soon as possible to avoid fungal attacks which might produce staining. It is not classified as a durable timber and therefore should not be used externally. Sawing and planing are reasonable, but the grain can tend to pluck or break out and this is particularly prevalent around knots. A good wood to stain to match others, it can be finished to produce a good, smooth surface.

Uses of the wood

Larger logs are peeled to produce birch plywood, which is used in a variety of forms from drawer bottoms, to cupboard backs, etc. Its ability to be stained well has led to use as the subsidiary wood in cabinet work. It is often painted and turned; the tight grain lends itself to this well.

Uses					Availability	Price
VENEER	PLYWOOD	FURNITURE	JOINERY	CONSTRUCTION		
✓	✓				✓✓	◆◆

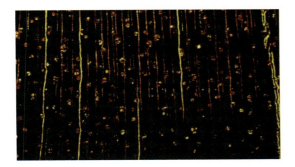

BROSIMUM AUBLETII

Snakewood

This wood is generally known as **Snakewood** and is also called **Letterwood**, **Conouru**, **Cardinal Wood**, **Letterhoot**, **Tortoiseshell Wood**, or **Leopard Wood**.

The Snakewood tree is not found in huge quantities, so its wood only comes onto the market occasionally and in small lots. The market name snakewood is also applied to other rather obscure and rare woods that sometimes become available. This tree grows in the north-eastern parts of South America, obtaining heights of no more than 65–82ft (20–25m). Boles can be straight and free of branches for upward of 26ft (8m) or so. Because it is highly prized for its heartwood, the sapwood, which is a clearly defined off-white color, is often hewn off and the wood is sold by weight. When first cut the heartwood has a deep red base that is mottled with patches of darker brown. This gives the characteristic figuring that attracts some of the imaginative names above. The grain is often straight with some interlocking. It has a fine, even texture.

Top Grain when radially cut. **Middle** Grain when tangentially cut. **Bottom** Cross-section.

Properties of the wood

Snakewood is hard, heavy, and dense when dry. Its heartwood is considered to be very durable. Drying the boles and billets that are produced can be troublesome. If it is to be cut and artificially dried, some predrying on thin stickers is advisable. A high level of surface checking and end splitting may result without due care during the process. However, once the wood has reached a satisfactory moisture content, it remains fairly stable. As you would expect, working snakewood can also be difficult.

Sharp saws and planer blades are essential. Predrilling is advised for fixings. This wood's adhesive properties are satisfactory with care. A fine finished surface can be produced.

Uses of the wood

Snakewood is often sliced for veneer production and can be used as an inlay. It is valued for its unique figuring and used for musical instrument parts, craft, and hobby items. It turns well and is often made into decorative, fancy turned pieces.

Source South America

Working properties

Weight (per ft³)	81lb (37kg)
Durability	Very durable
Bendability	Poor
Hardness	Hard
Sawing and shaping	Difficult
Splitting	Poor
Gluing	Take care

Uses					Availability	Price
VENEER	PLYWOOD	FURNITURE	JOINERY	CONSTRUCTION	✓	◆◆◆
✓		✓				

BUXUS SEMPERVIRENS

European Boxwood

Widely known as **European Boxwood**, this wood is also sometimes known as **Box**, **Iranian**, **Persian**, **Turkey**, or **Turkish Box**, depending upon origin.

This is the true boxwood tree. It is small in stature, only growing to around 33ft (10m), and is often found to be much shorter than that. Clear logs are also short and may only be around 5ft (1.5m) long. Boxwood grows throughout Europe and in similar climates on through to Iran. It should not be confused with the plethora of other timbers marketed under the boxwood name. Although they may have similar properties to the true Boxwood, they are not related. When the wood is cut from the log it produces a tight-grained lumber. There is no perceptible differentiation between the sap and heartwood, which varies from a light straw color to a pale yellow. The grain configuration can vary depending upon the growing conditions. In many cases it simply grows as a bush.

Top Grain when radially cut. **Middle** Grain when tangentially cut. **Bottom** Cross-section.

Source Europe and the Middle East

Working properties

Weight (per ft³)	55lb (25kg)
Durability	Durable
Bendability	Good
Hardness	Hard
Sawing and shaping	Take care
Splitting	Poor
Gluing	Good

Properties of the wood

Boxwood is dense and fairly heavy in comparison to other woods. Coupled with this, the location of the trees and the conditions of their growth tend to make it a difficult timber to dry. It will surface and end split easily and, if kept in the round, will split right through from the outside to the core if dried too rapidly. There are a number of chemical potions that have been used to try and alleviate checking, but how successful these are is not clear. As a hard, dense wood, it is sometimes difficult to cut. Boxwood should be held firmly when planing, to avoid it chattering and producing an uneven surface. In the unlikely event of it needing to be nailed or screwed, predrilling is thoroughly recommended.

Uses of the wood

The tight, close grain of boxwood makes it perfect for use in high quality turning and carving work. It is used in cabinet work for inlays and components for musical instruments. Old fashioned wooden rules were made from box because of its quality of finish and its stability once dry.

Uses					Availability	Price
VENEER	PLYWOOD	FURNITURE	JOINERY	CONSTRUCTION		
✓		✓			✓	◆◆

Top Grain when radially cut. **Middle** Grain when tangentially cut. **Bottom** Cross-section.

CALOPHYLLUM SPP.

Bintangor

The common English name of this wood is **Bintangor** and it is also known as **Bunut**, **Mentangol**, or **Penagayyer**.

Bintangor, as one of the Calophyllum genus of trees, is found throughout South-East Asia, ranging in location from coastal areas and swamp through to mountain forests. This wood is mainly sourced from Malaysia. It is a medium height tree, normally reaching around 100ft (30m). Clear, straight boles are normally produced at around 50–65ft (15–20m). When first cut from the log the heartwood is a pinkish red through to reddish brown, which darkens on exposure. The sapwood is distinct from the heartwood and varies from a lighter yellow brown through to a slight orange hue. The grain of this wood is coarse and interlocked, which can produce a striped figure effect on the quarter cut. The surface of through and through boards may have a darker zigzag configuration. When planed, bintangor has a smooth, lustrous finish, but the timber is not that attractive overall.

Properties of the wood

Slightly less than medium weight, bintangor is not heavy once dried. As with a number of these tropical timbers, care needs to be taken when drying. Too rapid moisture removal will result in a high level of warping, twisting, and splitting. Prior to artificial drying, a period of slower, air drying is recommended. Once the wood has been dried there is little further movement. Sawing and planing can be difficult, on occasions, especially if there is a high degree of interlocking grain or the wood has been case-hardened during the drying process. Bintangor is only moderately durable and should be preservative-treated for external use; penetration is reasonable. It will split, especially near end grain; therefore, predrilling is a good idea. The open grain takes stains well, but be careful toward the ends. Produces a good finished surface, but may need filling.

Uses of the wood

Indigenous uses of bintangor include boatbuilding, masts, and spars. When exported, it is often molded and planed for use in joinery and light construction work.

Source South-East Asia

Working properties

Weight (per ft³)	40lb (18kg)
Durability	Perishable
Bendability	Poor
Hardness	Medium
Sawing and shaping	Satisfactory
Splitting	Poor
Gluing	Good

Uses					Availability	Price
VENEER	**PLYWOOD**	**FURNITURE**	**JOINERY**	**CONSTRUCTION**	✓✓	◆◆
✓	✓		✓			

CARAPA GUIANENSIS

Andiroba

Top Grain when radially cut. **Middle** Grain when tangentially cut. **Bottom** Cross-section.

Andiroba is also known as **Crabwood**, **Cedro Macho**, **Krappa**, **Figueroa**, **Tangare**, **Bastard Mahogany**, **Demerara Mahogany**, or **Carapa**.

This is a fairly large tree, reaching heights of around 100–130ft (30–40m). Clear, cylindrical boles of anything up to 50ft (15m) or more, can be harvested. Andiroba is found throughout north and central parts of South America. Although it has a number of other names, the most common of these is crabwood. This wood is closely related to the mahoganies, hence its associated names. The heartwood can vary from a light pink through to a fairly dark red when first cut. This tends to darken to a more uniform and consistent color over time. The sapwood is clearly defined and a paler brown in color. Andiroba resembles mahogany, but has no natural luster. The sapwood is distinctly lighter than the heartwood. Occasionally, depending upon the cut from the log, a fiddleback figure can be seen.

Source South America

Working properties

Weight (per ft³)	40lb (18kg)
Durability	Moderately durable
Bendability	Poor
Hardness	Medium
Sawing and shaping	Satisfactory
Splitting	Poor
Gluing	Good

Properties of the wood

Andiroba has a fairly coarse grain with some tendency toward interlocking. Of medium weight, it has reasonable strength properties. Drying can be problematical and takes time. Some splitting will occur early on and the process needs to be monitored to avoid distortion. Shrinkage is a factor but is not significant. Andiroba is considered to be moderately durable but can be susceptible to insect attack when freshly cut. The wood works reasonably well with care. Some surface plucking can take place when planing, due to the occurrence of interlocking grain. To avoid splitting, predrilling is a good idea when nailing and screwing. Takes adhesives and stains well and can produce a good surface finish, with work.

Uses of the wood

As a rather plain wood, andiroba does not have a high profile in furniture manufacturing outside the countries of origin. When exported it is more often used in construction and general joinery and has been associated with boatbuilding and mast work.

Uses					Availability	Price
VENEER	PLYWOOD	FURNITURE	JOINERY	CONSTRUCTION		
✓	✓		✓		✓✓	◆◆

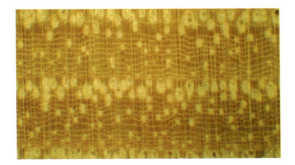

Top Grain when radially cut. **Middle** Grain when tangentially cut. **Bottom** Cross-section.

CARAYA SPP.

American Hickory

American Hickory is also known as **Water**, **Bitternut**, **Pecan**, **Nutmeg**, **Mockernut**, **Pignut Shagbark**, **Shellbark**, **Red**, and **White Hickory**.

Hickory trees are found throughout Canada and the United States. The tree is grown for a variety of reasons, including nut production. Under well-managed growing conditions, the trees can reach a height of up to 115ft (35m). However, these are the exceptions, with most only reaching 65ft (20m) or so. Once more, under well-managed growing conditions, clear boles can be found up to half the height of the tree. This tends to restrict the length of lumber produced. When freshly cut there is some color differentiation between heart and sapwood. The sapwood can be wide and a creamy, off-white color. This is often selected out and sold as white hickory. The heartwood tends to be a lightish, reddish brown. Hickory grain is generally straight but does become interlocked on occasions and can be coarse in texture.

Properties of the wood

Wood from the hickory tree is tough and slightly above average in weight when dry. High levels of shrinkage will occur when drying and this might lead to greater amounts of degrade from the process. The thicker sizes can benefit from some predrying, on thin stickers, to help avoid surface checking. The wood is classified as nondurable and the sapwood, in particular, should be treated with preservatives for external use. During sawing there can be a tendency to bind and burn on the blade; a wider kerf is beneficial. Lumber with interlocked grain can pluck out when planed. Gluing is reported to be average but difficult at times. Predrilling is recommended when nailing or screwing. If it is required, a fine finish can be achieved with effort.

Uses of the wood

With its reputation for toughness, hickory has found a niche end use as a tool handle. Hammers and other similar tools benefit from its high levels of shock resistance. At source it is often turned into flooring, and some cabinet and furniture work.

Source North America

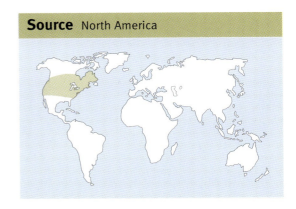

Working properties

Weight (per ft³)	46lb (21kg)
Durability	Perishable
Bendability	Good
Hardness	Hard
Sawing and shaping	Take care
Splitting	Average
Gluing	Good

Uses					Availability	Price
VENEER	PLYWOOD	FURNITURE	JOINERY	CONSTRUCTION	✓✓	◆◆
✓	✓	✓	✓			

CASTANEA SATIVA

Chestnut

Normally called **Chestnut**, this wood is also known as **Sweet**, **Spanish**, or **European Chestnut**.

A fairly large tree, for Europe and North Africa, chestnut reaches around 100ft (30m). Clear bole lengths can be up to 20ft (6m), before any branching occurs. The trunk can sometimes clearly display a twisting effect in growth that produces a difficult, spiral grain. Most trees grow in mixed woodland, unless they have been cultivated for harvesting their nuts. This chestnut should not be confused with horse chestnut, *Aesculus hippocastanum*, which is a much lesser tree with little or no commercial value. When cut freshly from the log the heartwood is colored a light straw yellow through to pale brown. On occasions the heartwood can be much darker. Sapwood is clearly visible and slightly lighter. A quick glance might confuse chestnut with oak, but it does not have the decorative and distinct medullary rays of that wood.

Top Grain when radially cut. **Middle** Grain when tangentially cut. **Bottom** Cross-section.

Source Throughout Europe

Working properties

Weight (per ft³)	33lb (15kg)
Durability	Durable
Bendability	Poor
Hardness	Medium
Sawing and shaping	Satisfactory
Splitting	Poor
Gluing	Good

Properties of the wood

Chestnut is a lightweight wood when dried. Both the sap and heartwood are susceptible to wood boring insect attack and should be treated with an appropriate preservative if they are likely to be exposed to that threat. Interestingly, the heartwood is classed as durable and has been traditionally used in Europe for fencing posts. Care needs to be taken with the selection of fittings, due to the inclusion of acidic chemicals in chestnut that can cause discoloration. Nonferrous metals are best if there is any possibility of exposure to moisture. Spiral grain aside, chestnut will saw and plane relatively easily, producing a good, smooth surface. Good to nail and screw into, it also takes adhesives well.

Uses of the wood

Although not available in huge commercial quantities, chestnut has a history of use. Because of its similarities to oak, it is often used alongside that timber for cabinet and furniture work. Traditional coffins were made from chestnut, due to the widths available.

Uses					Availability	Price
VENEER	PLYWOOD	FURNITURE	JOINERY	CONSTRUCTION		
✓		✓	✓		✓	◆◆

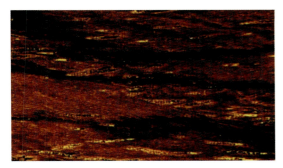

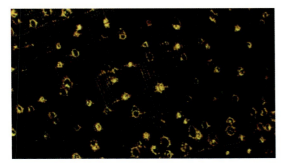

Top Grain when radially cut. **Middle** Grain when tangentially cut. **Bottom** Cross-section.

DALBERGIA RETUSA

Cocobolo

Cocobolo is the most common name of this hardwood, but it is also known as **Granadillo**, **Nambar**, or **Palo Sandro**.

Cocobolo can be found throughout Central America, but the small, commercial production of the lumber mainly takes place in Nicaragua and Costa Rica. This is not a large tree compared to some, reaching a maximum height of around 65–82ft (20–25m). The boles are not long and are buttressed at the bottom, producing relatively short lengths of lumber. Similar in nature to rosewood, this timber is prized for its extremely decorative heartwood. When freshly cut from the log it displays a range of streaky colors from orange through to a much deeper reddish brown. Although slightly fading on exposure, this color contrast is maintained. In contrast, the sapwood is a dirty cream or gray color and is clearly visible. The grain is usually straight, open, and quite coarse in texture. This wood gives off an attractive scent until it is sealed.

Properties of the wood

This is a well above average weight wood that is dense and feels cold to the touch. The heartwood is attractive as described and there is a clear delineation between this and the gray sapwood. Due to its density, drying can be lengthy and problematical. However, once this has been achieved, the wood tends to be very stable. Unlikely to be used in exposed applications, cocobolo is very durable. Its hardness causes problems with blunting when sawing and planing. Some care needs to be taken, especially when sawing, to avoid dust contact with the skin. On occasions the effect will be to cause an orange staining of the skin or a mild form of dermatitis. If the cutters are sharp a very smooth surface finish can be obtained.

Uses of the wood

Due to its decorative features, and relative scarcity, cocobolo is used for many craft applications. It turns and carves well and is often used as a decorative accessory for jewelry products. In cabinet work it can produce some interesting effects when inlaid.

Source Central America

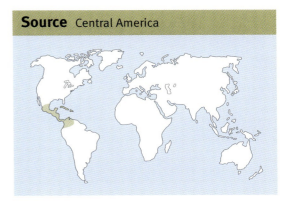

Working properties

Weight (per ft³)	70lb (32kg)
Durability	Very durable
Bendability	Poor
Hardness	Hard
Sawing and shaping	Take care
Splitting	Poor
Gluing	Poor

Uses					Availability	Price
VENEER	PLYWOOD	FURNITURE	JOINERY	CONSTRUCTION		
✓		✓			✓	◆◆◆

DALBERGIA STEVENSONII and *D. LATIFOLIA* Rosewood

The common English name is **Rosewood** and it is also known as **Nagaed**, **Honduras**, **Indian**, **East Indian Rosewood**, **Blackwood**, **Bombay Blackwood**, **Shisham**, **Sonokelin**, **Angsana Keling**, or **Java Palissandre**.

These two rosewood trees are reviewed here together due to their similar properties and uses. D. *stevensonii* is sourced from Honduras and D. *latifolia* from India. Honduras rosewood is found in northern parts of South America up through to Central America. Indian rosewood is found on the Indian sub-continent, right through to Indonesia and surrounding islands. Trees from Central America are likely to be slightly taller than the Indian rosewood, but local growing conditions introduce some variation in the heights that the trees are able to achieve. On average they will reach heights of around 80–100ft (25–30m). Under favorable growing conditions clear boles can reach lengths of around 60–80ft (20m).

Top Grain when radially cut. **Middle** Grain when tangentially cut. **Bottom** Cross-section.

Properties of the wood

Rosewood is a hard, heavy, and dense wood when dry and the heartwood is considered to be very durable. It is a dark purplish brown with characteristic darker flecks and streaks and gives off a roselike odor when freshly cut. The sapwood is clearly defined as a creamy, off-white color. Rosewood's grain is medium-fine in texture, interlocked and open. Drying is not difficult and results in fairly low levels of degrade if care is taken. Some surface checking and end splitting might occur. Working rosewood needs sharp tools. Edges are taken off fairly quickly and planer blades will chatter. Predrilling for fixings is essential and care needs to be taken when gluing to ensure coverage and penetration. A good finished surface can be achieved with fillers and effort.

Uses of the wood

Rosewood is a decorative wood that has been highly sought after for fine furniture and cabinet work. It is also used for musical instrument parts, cutlery handles, and smaller turned items.

Source Central America; India; South-East Asia

Working properties

Weight (per ft³)	59lb (27kg)
Durability	Very durable
Bendability	Poor
Hardness	Hard
Sawing and shaping	Difficult
Splitting	Poor
Gluing	Take care

Uses					Availability	Price
VENEER	PLYWOOD	FURNITURE ✓	JOINERY	CONSTRUCTION	✓	◆◆◆

Top Grain when radially cut. **Middle** Grain when tangentially cut. **Bottom** Cross-section.

DIOSPYROS EBENUM and SPP.

Ebony

Widely known as **Ebony**, this hardwood is also known as **Nigerian**, **Cameroon**, **Indian**, **Macassar**, **Ebony**, and so on, depending upon origin. Additionally known as **Adaman Marblewood** or **Zebrawood**.

The trees from which the commercial, black ebony wood is harvested come in a variety of sizes from different continents. Ebony trees from the Indian sub-continent through to Madagascar are short, with a maximum height of around 23ft (7m). They are often shorter, growing like large bushes. Bole size is small and narrow. African Ebony trees are not large but can stand up to 65ft (20m). The sapwood is clearly delineated from the heartwood, being lighter in color. Interestingly, we might assume that all the heartwood of ebony is black, the color for which this wood is known. However, some of the sub-species that make up the grouping can be striped, variegated, and gray.

Properties of the wood

Although most people assume that the color of ebony is always black, often the only way in which to tell the true color of the wood is to split the log. This is another reason why only small sections of truly black ebony are commercially available. Most ebony is heavy, even when dry. This density makes the drying process difficult. Fine, long hairline surface cracks can appear in larger pieces. It is often best to reduce the size of the blank before drying. Some trees are girdled while they are still standing. This is a process in which the bark is completely cut through around the bole and the tree dies and starts to dry as it stands. Machining ebony is also difficult and sharp tools are essential. With effort, a really good surface finish can be achieved.

Uses of the wood

Ebony is generally used as decorative components. Small handles, turned items, chessmen, and musical instrument parts are common. As a contrasting wood it is often used as an inlay in furniture and such like.

Source Africa, East India, and Indonesia

Working properties

Weight (per ft³)	57lb (26kg)
Durability	Very durable
Bendability	Poor
Hardness	Hard
Sawing and shaping	Difficult
Splitting	Poor
Gluing	Take care

Uses					Availability	Price
VENEER	PLYWOOD	FURNITURE ✓	JOINERY	CONSTRUCTION	✓	◆◆◆

DIPTEROCARPUS SPP.

Keruing

Keruing is also known as **Yang**, **Apitong**, **Gurjun**, **Bajac**, **Hieng**, **Eng**, **In**, **Keruing Belinbing**, **Minyak Keruing**, **Dau**, or **Engurgun**.

Commercial keruing lumber comes from a large range of Dipterocarpus trees growing through the Indian sub-continent and into South-East Asia. All the up to 70 or so species from which the wood is sourced have similar features. Due to this number, trees vary in height, but can be anything from 100–200ft (30–60m) tall. Depending upon the species, some buttressing is apparent but most boles are straight and clear. Lumber is produced up to and over 23ft (7m) or so. When freshly cut, the wood is a plain, coarse-grained pinkish brown through to a darker brown. The sapwood is distinct and is usually gray in color. A sticky resin easily and freely exudes from all surfaces. This hardens on exposure and, after drying, can sometimes cease to be a problem.

Top Grain when radially cut. **Middle** Grain when tangentially cut. **Bottom** Cross-section.

Source India, Myanmar, and South-East Asia

Working properties

Weight (per ft³)	46lb (21kg)
Durability	Moderately durable
Bendability	Poor
Hardness	Hard
Sawing and shaping	Difficult
Splitting	Poor
Gluing	Take care

Properties of the wood

Keruing is slightly above average weight, is fairly dense, and the heartwood is considered to be moderately durable. If artificially dried it can produce high levels of down-grade material. Cupping, distortion, and splitting are common features. If high temperatures are employed, the resin, when present, will tend to leach out and pool on adjacent surfaces. Saws and planes quickly gum up if attention is not paid to them when working this wood. The inclusion of silica in some species will rapidly blunt tools, leading to the potential for binding and burning. This is not a wood that lends itself to creating a fine, finished surface. If the resin is present it will work its way out through paints and sealers.

Uses of the wood

Where appearance is not important keruing can be a useful, reasonably strong, structural timber. Truck beds, railroad rolling stock, and some external joinery applications are ideal uses. Some stuff-over furniture frames are also made from this wood.

Uses					Availability	Price
VENEER	PLYWOOD	FURNITURE	JOINERY	CONSTRUCTION		
	✓			✓	✓✓	◆◆

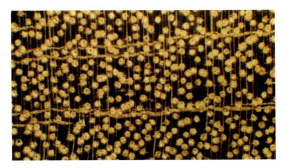

Top Grain when radially cut. **Middle** Grain when tangentially cut. **Bottom** Cross-section.

DRYOBALANOPS SPP.

Kapur

Kapur is also known as **Borneo Camphorwood**, **Kapor**, **Kapur Sintok**, **Kapur Paji**, **Kapoer**, **Tulai**, **Malampait**, **Santjulit**, **Brunei Teak**, or **Enteng**.

This is another tall tree from South-East Asia. It can reach heights of 200ft (60m). It generally has a straight bole, above buttressing, that can produce long lengths of lumber. When freshly cut from the log, kapur has a camphor-like smell, hence the name Borneo Camphorwood, which diminishes over time. Each time the wood is subsequently cut this odor will recur. If it is stacked in wet conditions, a dark, brown-green stain leaches out of the wood. Once dry, this problem disappears. The heartwood can be an insipid yellow brown through to a deeper, reddish brown. The sapwood is distinct and a paler version of this. There are no significant features to the grain; it is usually coarse and fairly straight with some interlocking. Often fine resin ducts are apparent, but this does not exude onto the surface.

Properties of the wood

Kapur is a slightly above medium weight hardwood. However, this does depend on the source and local growing conditions. Its heartwood is considered to be very durable and resistant to treatment with preservatives. It dries fairly slowly with a tendency to cup across the width of the board. Surface checking is apparent and can increase if it is dried too rapidly. Sawing kapur can be a little troublesome at times. Blunting can occur, which might lead to some burning in the cut. During planing and molding it is important to keep all cutters sharp to help avoid producing a woolly surface. Kapur splits easily and therefore predrilling is recommended when nailing and screwing.

Uses of the wood

As a rather plain utilitarian wood, kapur tends to be used for applications that take full benefit from its positive properties. An excellent construction and structural timber, it can also be used for some external joinery components, heavy-duty flooring, and similar wear-resistant locations.

Source South-East Asia

Working properties

Weight (per ft³)	46lb (21kg)
Durability	Very durable
Bendability	Moderate
Hardness	Hard
Sawing and shaping	Take care
Splitting	Poor
Gluing	Take care

Uses					Availability	Price
VENEER	PLYWOOD	FURNITURE	JOINERY	CONSTRUCTION		
	✔		✔	✔	✔✔	◆◆

DURIO ZIBETHINUS and SPP.
Durian

The common English name of this hardwood is **Durian** and it is also known as **Daun**.

The name Durian is derived from the fruit of this tree, which grows in Malaysia. The fruit, about 6in (15cm) in diameter, is of conical shape with a spiny case. It is much sought after for its taste but not for its smell! However, the fruit is of a value that is sometimes worth more than the lumber produced from the tree. Durian is the trade name for a collection of closely related species. The trees grow throughout the South-East Asian region and obtain an average height of around 100ft (30m). Boles are fairly straight and cylindrical with small buttresses. When freshly cut from the log, the heartwood ranges in color from an orange through to a deeper red brown. The sapwood can be clearly distinguished by its lighter shade. The grain is not distinct, being fairly open, coarse, and even. Some interlocking grain is apparent, with dark deposits in the vessels being common.

Top Grain when radially cut. **Middle** Grain when tangentially cut. **Bottom** Cross-section.

Source South-East Asia

Working properties

Weight (per ft³)	37lb (17kg)
Durability	Perishable
Bendability	Poor
Hardness	Medium
Sawing and shaping	Take care
Splitting	Good
Gluing	Good

Properties of the wood
Dry weight can vary due to the mix of species included under the durian name. On average it is slightly lighter than a medium weight wood and, as a general classification, is considered not to be durable. Treatment with preservatives is recommended for external use. During the drying process cupping can often occur. Once at a satisfactory moisture content, it is reasonably stable. The mix of densities tends to make sawing and planing interesting; some boards will cut and finish with ease while others are more difficult.

Durian has no natural tendencies to split; therefore, unless working near end grain, there is no particular need to predrill. The naturally open grain lends itself to adhesion and will need to be filled to obtain a good surface finish.

Uses of the wood
Local use of the lumber includes packing cases, tea chests, and other nonstructural items. It can be peeled to form plywood cores. If planed and molded, it can be used for internal fixings, but should not be used for joinery without treatment.

Uses					Availability	Price
VENEER	PLYWOOD	FURNITURE	JOINERY	CONSTRUCTION		
✓	✓		✓		✓✓	◆◆

Top Grain when radially cut. **Middle** Grain when tangentially cut. **Bottom** Cross-section.

DYERA COSTULATA and D. LOWII

Jelutong

This hardwood is widely known as **Jelutong** and is also sometimes referred to as **Jelutong Paya**, **Jelutong Bukit**, **Djelutung**, **Tinpeddaeng**, **Andjarutung**, or **Letung**.

Jelutong is a large tree found throughout the South-East Asian region. Sometimes growing up to heights of 200ft (60m), a straight, clear bole of 100ft (30m) is not uncommon. When freshly cut from the log the wood is almost white in color. This does slightly darken on exposure with little or no differentiation between heartwood and sapwood. The trees are sometimes tapped for latex, which can be problematical when producing lumber. Often, staining from fungal attack occurs adjacent to these workings. In addition, latex that has turned solid is often found and can easily be pulled out. This affects both the visual and strength properties of the wood. Jelutong is a plain timber and there are no discernible grain features. It is usually straight, with a fine and even slightly lustrous texture.

Properties of the wood

A lightweight wood that is not considered durable. Once cut into, lumber drying should follow fairly rapidly to avoid surface staining from fungal attack. At source it is often dipped or sprayed with a fungicide to help alleviate this problem. Fortunately, most stock dries fairly easily, with little distortion or shrinkage. Thicker stock can take time to relinquish core moisture and therefore some predrying is advisable. Jelutong is not a strong or hard wood and can be dented easily. Both sawing and planing is relatively easy, it takes nails and screws well, and has good adhesion properties. If required, a satisfactory surface finish can be worked up.

Uses of the wood

The inclusion of the latex ducts and passages often makes jelutong a difficult wood to find in large sections free and clear of defects. Locally it is employed as a core in plywood and door manufacture. Its best attributes are the combination of stability and ease of shaping. This maintains its use as an engineering pattern-making material.

Source South-East Asia

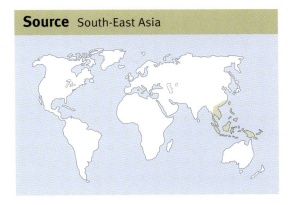

Working properties

Weight (per ft³)	29lb (13kg)
Durability	Perishable
Bendability	Poor
Hardness	Soft
Sawing and shaping	Satisfactory
Splitting	Good
Gluing	Good

Uses					Availability	Price
VENEER	PLYWOOD	FURNITURE	JOINERY	CONSTRUCTION	✓✓	◆◆
	✓		✓			

ENTANDRAPHRAGMA CYLINDRICUM

Sapele

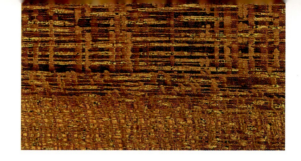

Sapele is also known as **Aboudokro**, **Sapele** or **Scented Mahogany**, **Sapele Wood**, **Penkwa**, **Lifaki**, **Botsife**, **Liboyo**, **Sapelli**, or **Acajou Sapelli**.

This is a red, African hardwood that is found in the west through to the heart of the continent. It is a tall tree, reaching heights of around 180ft (55m) or so. Broad buttresses are a feature, which enable clear boles of around 82–100ft (25–30m) to be found. Sapele has a number of different local colloquial names, one of which is scented mahogany. This, it is believed, comes from the rich, spicy, cedar-like scent that the wood distinctively gives off when freshly cut. In fact this scent is one of the only gross features that will differentiate it from its close cousin, Utile. Sapele can be confused with African mahogany on occasions; it comes from the same family, Meliacea. However it is a bit heavier and there are some slight color variations, with sapele tending to be a little more orange.

Top Grain when radially cut. **Middle** Grain when tangentially cut. **Bottom** Cross-section.

Source Africa, predominantly West Africa

Working properties

Weight (per ft³)	40lb (18kg)
Durability	Moderate
Bendability	Poor
Hardness	Hard
Sawing and shaping	Take care
Splitting	Poor
Gluing	Good

Properties of the wood

The wood itself, which is of a medium weight when dry, is quite tough and difficult to saw, especially if it has the interlocking grain feature that produces the stripe. The varying grain can also help toward some distortion when the timber is dried. Planing can also be a bit tiresome but, with care, a good surface can be produced. It is only moderately durable and therefore should not be used in continuously damp or wet conditions. Due to its cellular structure, it does not take preservatives particularly well.

When fixing, even with nails, pilot holes should be drilled to avoid splitting the wood or bending nails. The wood can be stained and brought up to a good surface finish.

Uses of the wood

Probably best known for striped veneer flush door facings, sapele can be used for many other purposes. Often employed as a substitute for mahogany in furniture manufacture, it is also used extensively in joinery manufacture. Window and door frames are favorite uses.

Uses					Availability	Price
VENEER	PLYWOOD	FURNITURE	JOINERY	CONSTRUCTION		
✓	✓	✓	✓		✓✓	◆◆

ENTANDROPHRAGMA UTILE

Utile

The common English name is **Utile** and it is also known as **Sipo**, **Mufumbi**, **Cedar**, **Assie**, **Mvovo**, **Tshimaie**, or **Kalungi**.

The Utile tree grows throughout West Africa and into parts of Central Africa; it is related to the mahogany family. The trees are tall, growing up to heights of 150ft (45m) plus. Boles can be clear and straight for about half this height. It is similar in growth shape to sapele, but generally has a larger trunk. When freshly cut from the log the heartwood is usually a uniform reddish brown that darkens slightly on exposure. The sapwood is clearly distinct and a paler color. The open grain is partially interlocked and uneven. This creates a similar striped pattern to sapele, with which it is easily confused. Telling these two woods apart using the gross features, weight, color, texture, and so on, is difficult. Experienced woodyard people will tell you that it is only the spicy scent of sapele that gives it away. Utile does not have a particularly strong odor, and this is the main difference between the two woods.

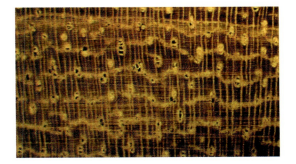

Top Grain when radially cut. **Middle** Grain when tangentially cut. **Bottom** Cross-section.

Properties of the wood

Utile is an average weight wood when dry and the heartwood is considered to be durable. Drying the wood can be a bit problematical at times, depending upon the levels of interlocked grain found. Some twisting and distortion can occur and if splits or shakes are apparent these may enlarge. Once the wood is dried to the desired moisture content, it remains reasonably stable. The working properties of utile are normally good and it turns well. Predrilling for fixings is recommended close to the end grain and its adhesive properties are satisfactory. The wood stains easily and a good surface finish can be achieved after filling.

Uses of the wood

Utile is a fairly mild, generally useful red African hardwood. At source, it is employed for a full range of applications. When exported, it is often used as a substitute for mahogany and can produce fine furniture and cabinet work. It is easily molded into solid wood profiles, cut into veneers, and turned.

Source Predominantly West Africa

Working properties

Weight (per ft³)	42lb (19kg)
Durability	Durable
Bendability	Poor
Hardness	Hard
Sawing and shaping	Satisfactory
Splitting	Average
Gluing	Good

Uses					Availability	Price
VENEER	**PLYWOOD**	**FURNITURE**	**JOINERY**	**CONSTRUCTION**	✓✓	◆◆
✓	✓	✓	✓			

53

ERISMA UNCINATUM

Cambara

The hardwood **Cambara** is also known as **Quarubarana**, **Jaboty**, **Jaboti**, **Vergalho-de-Jabuti**, **Quarubatinga**, **Cedrinho**, **Singri-Kwari**, **Manonti Kouali**, **Felli Kouali**, **Quaruba Vermelha**, **Mureillo**, and **Brazilian Cherry**.

Cambara is not a huge tree, but it produces clear boles of up to 80ft (25m) or more. Cambara, Quarubarana, and Jaboty are the most common names associated with the export of lumber from this tree, which is found growing in forests throughout central and northern South America. It is one of those slightly less known species that is not always available in large commercial quantities, but it makes a good alternative to some of the Far Eastern and African hardwoods. Lumber, when freshly cut from the log, has a pinkish cream through to light brown heartwood that darkens on exposure. The sapwood is clearly delineated and is lighter in color. The grain is fairly straight, with some inclination to waver, is plain, and has no distinct features.

Top Grain when radially cut. **Middle** Grain when tangentially cut. **Bottom** Cross-section.

Source   South America

Working properties

Weight (per ft³)	44lb (20kg)
Durability	Moderate
Bendability	Moderate
Hardness	Medium
Sawing and shaping	Satisfactory
Splitting	Average
Gluing	Good

Properties of the wood

Once dried, cambara is, on average, a medium weight wood. However, depending upon local growing conditions, this can vary and will affect the amount of wastage during drying. Care needs to be taken when drying thicker lumber, due to its tendency to surface check. The wood is not classified as durable and can be susceptible to wood boring insect attack. Preservative treatment is relatively effective, due to the permeability of the wood. The working properties of cambara are reasonable. It saws and planes easily enough with sharp tools.

Predrilling is recommended when screwing or nailing, especially near end grain. It can be glued, stained, and finished with ease.

Uses of the wood

Cambara is rather a plain wood but has the potential to be used for a number of applications. Local uses include furniture, moldings, packaging, and craft items. The logs are peeled for the production of plywood. When imported, it is often used as a replacement for the meranti type woods and lends itself to molding into joinery sections.

Uses					Availability	Price
VENEER	PLYWOOD	FURNITURE	JOINERY	CONSTRUCTION		
	✓		✓		✓✓	◆◆

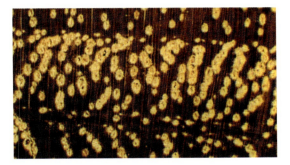

Top Grain when radially cut. **Middle** Grain when tangentially cut. **Bottom** Cross-section.

EUCALYPTUS DIVERSICOLOR

Karri

The common name of this Australian hardwood is **Karri**.

Apart from jarrah (see page 56), karri is probably the other best known hardwood tree that is grown in Western Australia and converted to lumber for export. As one of Australia's largest, it is a taller, bigger tree than jarrah, reaching up to heights of around 200ft (60m) or more in good growing conditions. Clear, straight boles can be harvested of well over 100ft (30m) in length. When freshly cut from the log, the wood is a reddish brown color with a slightly paler, narrow sapwood; all darkens down on exposure. The grain is coarse but fairly evenly textured. With some interlocking present, a striped figure can be apparent, depending upon the cut from the log. This wood is difficult to tell apart from jarrah. A simple test to distinguish between them is to burn a sliver of the heartwood of each. If the residual ash is white, the burnt wood is karri, if the ash is black, it is jarrah.

Properties of the wood

This is a heavy and hard wood of which the heartwood is considered to be durable. If preservative treatments are applied, it is very resistant to these. Drying the wood can be problematical. Thinner stock tends to distort and all thicknesses show signs of surface checking. A slow, predrying period on thin stickers is recommended to help reduce the volume of downgrade. Its hardness and density make for difficult working conditions. Saws will burn and planes will chatter; sharp tools are essential. To avoid bending or breaking, predrilling for fixings is important. On the occasions that this wood is used internally, a good surface finish can be achieved.

Uses of the wood

Although heavier than jarrah, karri is not as durable, and therefore should not be used in applications where it is subject to continuously damp or wet conditions. As a strong wood, it is ideally suited to use in the construction of structural components and such like. At source, it is used for bridge building, joists, rafters, and beams.

Source Western Australia

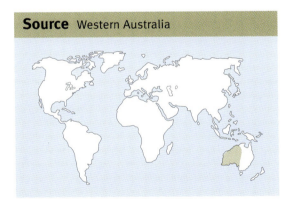

Uses					Availability	Price
VENEER	PLYWOOD	FURNITURE	JOINERY	CONSTRUCTION	✓✓	◆◆
	✓		✓	✓		

Working properties

Weight (per ft³)	57lb (26kg)
Durability	Moderate
Bendability	Moderate
Hardness	Hard
Sawing and shaping	Difficult
Splitting	Average
Gluing	Good

EUCALYPTUS MARGINATA

Jarrah

The common English name is **Jarrah** and it is also known as **Curly Jarrah**.

Jarrah is one of the most important Western Australian eucalyptus trees. It predominantly grows in the south-western part of the state. Trees reach an average height of around 130ft (40m). Clear boles of about half that length are common before branching. The heartwood is a rich reddish brown, similar to mahogany when freshly cut. This turns darker on exposure. The sapwood is clearly defined, a paler color, and tends to be fairly narrow in older trees. In most cases, the grain of this wood is rather insignificant, coarse, even, and with some darker flecking appearing. On occasions jarrah will have a wavy, curly grain, hence the addition to its common name. Gum can also be present in pockets or vein-like deposits. Jarrah and karri, another Australian eucalyptus hardwood (see page 55), are visually difficult to tell apart.

Top Grain when radially cut. **Middle** Grain when tangentially cut. **Bottom** Cross-section.

Source Western Australia

Working properties

Weight (per ft³)	50lb (23kg)
Durability	Very durable
Bendability	Moderate
Hardness	Hard
Sawing and shaping	Take care
Splitting	Poor
Gluing	Good

Properties of the wood

A fairly heavy timber, the heartwood of jarrah is considered to be very durable. During drying a fairly high degree of distortion can take place, especially with the curly grained stock. Thicker material should be predried on thin stickers to avoid too much surface checking. Working jarrah can be difficult. The interlocking grain may cause pinching and burning of saws. Planing and molding cutters need to be sharp and probably have a reduced cutting angle to produce a reasonable finish. Adhesion properties are good, while predrilling is recommended for nailing and screwing. Although it is unlikely to be utilized in high quality, finished work, a good surface can be achieved with effort.

Uses of the wood

At source jarrah has been used for a wide range of products. In the main these are focused toward structural and constructional uses, such as railroad ties, bridges, heavy-duty flooring, decking, fencing, etc. Other uses include sea defenses and dock work, where its durability and strength is utilized.

Uses					Availability	Price
VENEER	PLYWOOD	FURNITURE	JOINERY	CONSTRUCTION		
	✓		✓	✓	✓✓	◆◆

Top Grain when radially cut. **Middle** Grain when tangentially cut. **Bottom** Cross-section.

FAGUS SYLVATICA

European Beech

European Beech is also known as **English**, **Danish**, **French**, **Romanian**, **German Beech**, and so on, depending upon its place of origin. Also known as **White** or **Steamed Beech**.

The Beech tree, also sometimes called the Queen of the Woods, is found throughout Europe. It grows in mixed woodland, stands, and open locations. The tree can reach heights of over 115ft (35m), but is generally shorter. Depending upon the growing conditions, clear boles are often in the region of 40ft (12m), and can be large and buttressed at the base. The wood is a creamy white when cut, with some variations through light brown to dark streaking. The lighter, whiter lumber, without any darker coloration, is usually selected out when converted. To help produce a more consistent color, planks are often put through a steaming process that turns the wood a more uniform pink to brown. There is little or no distinction between heart and sapwood, with one blending into the other.

Properties of the wood

Beech is a medium weight wood when dry that is often used as a comparison for others when their weights need to be established. During the drying process there can be some distortion, especially if the tree has grown in exposed conditions. It will check and split without care and shrinkage is significant. Because of the varying growth conditions, beech can be a bit problematical when sawing and planing. It can burn easily if pinched on the saw and will often chatter while planing. However, a good finish is achievable with the right tools. Predrilling for nailing and screwing is recommended. The wood is considered perishable and susceptible to insect attack; this is definitely not one to be used outside. Beech stains and finishes well.

Uses of the wood

A useful wood that has many applications from bentwood furniture and cabinetwork through to tool handles, flooring, plywood, and such like. Its close grain makes beech an excellent wood for turning.

Source Throughout Europe

Working properties

Weight (per ft³)	44lb (20kg)
Durability	Perishable
Bendability	Good
Hardness	Medium
Sawing and shaping	Satisfactory
Splitting	Average
Gluing	Good

Uses					Availability	Price
VENEER	PLYWOOD	FURNITURE	JOINERY	CONSTRUCTION	✓✓✓	◆◆◆
✓	✓	✓	✓	✓		

FRAXINUS AMERICANA, F. NIGRA and F. PENNSYLVANICA

American Ash

American Ash is also known as **White**, **Red**, **Green**, **Black**, or **Brown Ash** with local variations calling it **Tough**, **Medium**, or **Soft Textured Ash**.

Ash grows throughout central North America. The trees can reach heights of around 100–115ft (30–35m) plus. Although reaching these heights, in relative terms the boles tend to be fairly short before branching. Lumber is not usually produced much longer than 15–20ft (5–6m) as a maximum. Depending upon which sub-species the wood is cut from, there is often quite a lot of color variation. White ash is particularly desirable and is often selected and sorted out when the logs are converted. Although called white, it is generally an off-white, pale cream color. Darker colors are also prevalent, with the wood sometimes a consistent light brown color with darker streaks. With the exception of the lighter colors, the sapwood is clearly distinct. This wood has an open, straight grain.

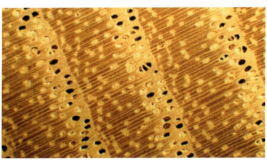

Top Grain when radially cut. **Middle** Grain when tangentially cut. **Bottom** Cross-section.

Source North America

Working properties

Weight (per ft³)	40lb (18kg)
Durability	Perishable
Bendability	Good
Hardness	Medium
Sawing and shaping	Satisfactory
Splitting	Poor
Gluing	Good

Properties of the wood

During grading the denser, harder boards are separated from the lighter, whiter ones. The former have good strength properties and are about an average weight when dried. The latter are selected for their appearance rather than their strength or durability, hence the application of names as above. Depending upon the grain structure, shrinkage and distortion whilst drying are minimal. It can be worked reasonably well without too much blunting during sawing and planing. Pre-drilling is advised when fixing with nails or screws because the wood easily splits. American ash is not considered durable and should be preservative-treated when used externally.

Uses of the wood

The heavier, tougher ash is used for striking tool handles and in similar applications where its resistance to shock is well recognized. Although not considered durable, it was often used in the production of spokes for wooden wheels. The softer, white ash is used for furniture, internal joinery, and trims.

Uses					Availability	Price
VENEER	PLYWOOD	FURNITURE	JOINERY	CONSTRUCTION	✓✓	◆◆
✓	✓	✓	✓			

Top Grain when radially cut. **Middle** Grain when tangentially cut. **Bottom** Cross-section.

FRAXINUS EXCELSIOR

European Ash

The common English name is **European Ash** and it is also known as **English**, **Belgium**, **German**, depending upon its country of origin, as well as **Olive Ash**.

This is a slightly smaller tree than its American cousin. Found throughout Europe, it probably only reaches a maximum height of around 100ft (30m). Of a similar but small stature, the lumber produced is short to medium in length. Occasional long boards are available, but these are rare. With a small bole diameter, board widths are also limited. When cut through and through there is usually quite a high level of waste from both the heart and wane. The freshly sawn wood is slightly pink in color with darker streaks. This tends to go off after the wood has dried. The sapwood is not distinctive enough to stand out from the heartwood unless this is particularly dark. Flat-sawn surfaces show well-defined grain patterns due to the strong growth rings. The grain is normally fairly straight but coarse.

Properties of the wood

An open-grained wood, ash can have some attractive features, including streaks of color. Occasionally fiddle-back or other decorative figures can be found and these are extremely attractive. All the comments applying to American ash (see opposite page) can also be applied to this wood. Distortion during drying can be a problem and care needs to be taken when stacking. End splits will occur if the process is undertaken too quickly. European ash cuts and joints well with a good level of adhesion. This wood can be finished well, but its open grain does not allow a perfectly smooth finish without filling. It will take a preservative reasonably well.

Uses of the wood

European ash is prized for its toughness and has been extensively used for for centuries as tool handles, spokes and oars, and such like. It has the ability to be easily bent, so it has traditionally been used in the production of country-style furniture in many different countries of Europe.

Source Throughout Europe

Working properties

Weight (per ft³)	42lb (19kg)
Durability	Perishable
Bendability	Good
Hardness	Medium
Sawing and shaping	Satisfactory
Splitting	Average
Gluing	Good

Uses					Availability	Price
VENEER	PLYWOOD	FURNITURE	JOINERY	CONSTRUCTION	✓✓	◆◆
✓	✓	✓	✓			

GOSSWEILERODENDRON BALSAMIFERUM Agba

The common English name is **Agba** and it is also known as **Achi**, **Moboron**, **Noboron**, **Tola**, **Tola Branca**, or **White Tola** and **Pink Mahogany**.

Agba trees can be very tall, with top canopies found at up to 200ft (60m). The boles of the trees are fairly straight and, before branching, they will produce clear lengths of up to 65–82ft (20–25m). Predominantly found in West Africa, mainly in and around Nigeria, agba lumber is a pale creamy white when it is first cut from the log. This darkens on exposure and there is little or no difference between the heart and sapwoods. The grain is similar to and has been compared with mahogany on occasions, hence one of the common names above. The lumber of this species can be fairly resinous and this is occasionally found in large pockets. During the drying period, this resin exudes from the pockets, leaving small, surface deposits or large globules behind.

Top Grain when radially cut. **Middle** Grain when tangentially cut. **Bottom** Cross-section.

Source Predominantly West Africa

Working properties

Weight (per ft³)	30lb (14kg)
Durability	Durable
Bendability	Good
Hardness	Medium
Sawing and shaping	Satisfactory
Splitting	Good
Gluing	Good

Properties of the wood

Not a heavy or particularly strong wood, agba does have a tendency toward "brittle heart"; these are shakes across the grain of the wood. Therefore, care needs to be taken when selecting this wood for individual components. Agba is a stable wood during and after drying. Once the resin has exuded during this process, it hardly ever appears again. If agba is treated with preservatives there is some resistance, due to the presence of the resins. This hardwood is easily worked with only some care needing to be taken to avoid resin building up on the tools. Easy to nail, screw, glue, and finish, agba is an attractive wood with many potential uses.

Uses of the wood

Classified as durable, agba has traditionally been used for both internal and external applications. Joinery and construction work, such as sills and treads, through to furniture carcass work and non show-wood features are commonly undertaken with this wood. When stained it can be used as a cheaper substitute for mahogany.

Uses					Availability	Price
VENEER	PLYWOOD	FURNITURE	JOINERY	CONSTRUCTION		
		✓	✓		✓✓	◆◆

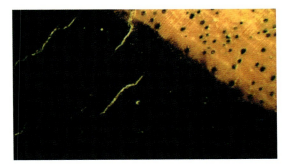

Top Grain when radially cut. **Middle** Grain when tangentially cut. **Bottom** Cross-section.

GUAIACUM SPP.

Lignum Vitae

Lignum Vitae is also known as **Bastard Lignum Vitae**, **Guaiacum Wood**, **Bois de Gaiac**, **Porkholz**, **Pokhout**, or **Lignum Sanctum**.

Lignum Vitae is one of the hardest timbers that is commercially available. It grows in and around Central America and the northern parts of South America. The trees of the three main species from which Lignum Vitae is sourced are not tall. At most they are likely to reach a height of around 33ft (10m) or so. Boles are also not large and tend to be harvested in the round in short lengths. These can have the sapwood hewn off and are sold as bolts or billets up to 10ft (3m) long. The main species, G. officinale, is a dark, greenish brown through to a deep brown near black color. Sapwood is narrow, distinct, and sharply defined as a yellowish color. The grain is interlocked and finely textured. This hardwood feels cool, slightly oily to the touch, and has a pleasant odor.

Properties of the wood

Lignum Vitae is hard, heavy, and dense—it can sink in water. The heartwood is considered to be very durable. Drying can be lengthy and, without care, will result in surface checking and splitting. The presence of interlocking grain makes it difficult to saw and plane. The finely textured grain does lend itself to turning. All tools need regular sharpening to maintain an edge. With an inclusion of naturally self-lubricating resins, the adhesive properties of this wood are not good. Predrill when fixing to avoid splits. The heavy nature of the wood enables a very fine surface finish to be achieved.

Uses of the wood

The name Lignum Vitae translates as "Wood of Life." Historically it has been prized for the medicinal properties associated with the resins found in this wood. These have also had a bearing on the uses to which it has been put. The self-lubrication properties led to its use as bushes and bearings in ships' propellers, rollers, turned items, and expensive sports goods such as bowls. It is good for turning.

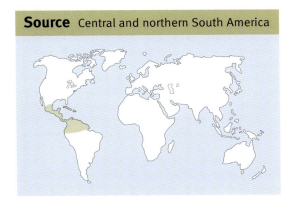

Source Central and northern South America

Working properties

Weight (per ft³)	81lb (37kg)
Durability	Very durable
Bendability	Poor
Hardness	Hard
Sawing and shaping	Difficult
Splitting	Average
Gluing	Poor

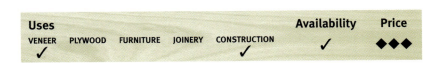

Uses					Availability	Price
VENEER	PLYWOOD	FURNITURE	JOINERY	CONSTRUCTION		
✓				✓	✓	◆◆◆

HERITIERA LITTARALIS and H. SIMPLICIFOLIA Mengkulang

This South-East Asian hardwood is called **Mengkulang** and is also known as **Palapi**, **Dungan**, **Chumprak**, **Kembang**, **Chumprag**, or **Lumbayan**.

A number of additional species to those identified above can be marketed together under the Mengkulang name. The tree, which grows throughout South-East Asia, is a little over average height, standing up to 130ft (40m) plus. Clear boles of over 66ft (20m) are produced after the large buttresses. When freshly cut, an unpleasant odor can be detected from this wood, but this soon goes off. The heartwood is a pinkish brown through to a darker brown, sometimes with a yellow tinge. The sapwood is paler and not always clearly delineated. Darker streaking can be visible on some surfaces when cut on the quarter. Mengkulang is a fairly coarsely grained wood with an open interlocked structure. It can also feel greasy or oily to the touch.

Top Grain when radially cut. **Middle** Grain when tangentially cut. **Bottom** Cross-section.

Source South-East Asia

Working properties

Weight (per ft³)	44lb (20kg)
Durability	Perishable
Bendability	Moderate
Hardness	Medium
Sawing and shaping	Difficult
Splitting	Poor
Gluing	Take care

Properties of the wood

Mengkulang is slightly above average weight when dried; however, the heartwood is not considered to be durable. The drying process is relatively swift, with little distortion occurring. Some surface checking can be apparent, depending upon the density of the differing species. The working properties of mengkulang are not particularly good. Edges soon go off on tools and resharpening is required to maintain a reasonable finish. Once more, a reduction in cutting angle will help to avoid break-out on the surface when planing. It requires predrilling when nailing and screwing and has poor adhesive properties. With effort, if required, a good surface finish can be achieved with some filling.

Uses of the wood

This is a general utility timber that can be used for structural and construction purposes. At source it is often found in furniture components and is used for internal trims. It has often been used as a vehicle flooring material. Not particularly useful for cabinet work.

Uses					Availability	Price
VENEER	PLYWOOD	FURNITURE	JOINERY	CONSTRUCTION		
	✓	✓	✓		✓✓	◆◆

Top Grain when radially cut. **Middle** Grain when tangentially cut. **Bottom** Cross-section.

HERITIERA UTILIS

Niangon

Niangon is also known as **Ogoue**, **Nyankom**, **Cola Mahogany**, **Wismore**, or **Wishmore**.

The Niangon tree is found throughout West Africa, growing in lower swamp land zones through to high zone tropical rain forests. The tree is not large, with anything over 100ft (30m) or so being an exception. Straight boles of roughly 66ft (20m) can be harvested. When growing in swamps, the trunks of these trees can twist and distort out of line. Niangon heartwood varies from a pale pink through to a reddish brown when first cut from the log. This all darkens down to a more uniform color after exposure. Although not clearly defined, the sapwood is a paler color. With an open, interlocked grain texture, niangon has a wavy grain that can produce a striped effect on quarter-cut boards. There often appear to be some resins present and it also has a greasy feel. When resin is present, it can make this wood very difficult to work effectively.

Properties of the wood

Niangon is an average weight wood when dry. It dries fairly rapidly and easily, with little shrinkage and distortion. There is a tendency to twist slightly, particularly in wood grown in swampy sources. If resin is present, the drying process can tend to encourage this to leach out onto the sawn surfaces. The heartwood is considered to be durable and if attempts are made to treat it with preservatives these are resisted. Working niangon can be difficult. If resins are present there is potential for cutting tools to gum up. Regular cleaning and sharpening will help to alleviate this problem and provide a better finish with some of the highly interlocked grain material. The wood does not have the best adhesive properties. Care needs to be taken with fixings and predrilling is recommended. If the grain is filled, a satisfactory surface finish can be achieved.

Uses of the wood

Niangon is used at source for furniture manufacture, joinery, and lightweight structural applications. It can be used as a substitute for other more expensive woods.

Source West Africa

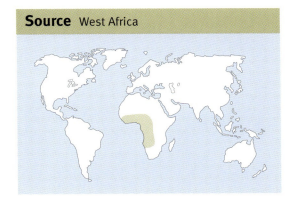

Working properties

Weight (per ft³)	40lb (18kg)
Durability	Durable
Bendability	Poor
Hardness	Medium
Sawing and shaping	Take care
Splitting	Poor
Gluing	Take care

Uses					Availability	Price
VENEER	PLYWOOD	FURNITURE	JOINERY	CONSTRUCTION	✓✓	◆◆
	✓	✓	✓			

INTSIA SPP.

Merbau

Merbau is also known as **Mirabow**, **Borneo Teak**, **Merbau Darat**, **Kajubesi**, **Ipi**, or **Kwila**.

This is a well above average height tree, growing throughout the South-East Asian and south-west Pacific region. Standing up to 130ft (40m) or so, it can produce clear boles of around 66ft (20m) after buttressing. When freshly cut from the log, merbau can have a striking yellowy orange heartwood. This quickly dulls down to a more uniform dark, reddish brown. The sapwood is a clearly and sharply defined pale yellow or cream color. Characteristically, the grain of this wood contains sulphur-like deposits. When yellow, these are sometimes extracted for dye and can often lead to a mistaken identification of the wood as Afzelia (see page 34). In damp conditions these deposits tend to leach out and stain any adjoining surfaces. Merbau's grain is open with some interlocking apparent, which can be wavy, on quarter-cut surfaces.

Top Grain when radially cut. **Middle** Grain when tangentially cut. **Bottom** Cross-section.

Source South-East Asia

Working properties

Weight (per ft³)	50lb (23kg)
Durability	Durable
Bendability	Poor
Hardness	Hard
Sawing and shaping	Difficult
Splitting	Poor
Gluing	Good

Properties of the wood

At an above average weight when dry, merbau is a fairly hard and dense wood. The heartwood is considered to be very durable under most conditions. However, it reacts poorly when in sustained damp, moist, and poorly ventilated conditions. With a difficult-to-penetrate cell structure, it is also resistant to treatment with preservatives. This wood dries fairly quickly, with little shrinkage or distortion. It is difficult to work when dry. Saws tend to bind and planer blades chatter. A reduced cutting angle for the latter is helpful. Predrilling for fixings is more than recommended, due to a tendency to split. Merbau has good adhesive properties. It needs work if a fine surface finish is required.

Uses of the wood

Merbau is used at source for heavy constructional and structural work where moisture is not a problem. Its reasonable levels of stability and low shrinkage factors lend themselves to use in general joinery and similar applications. Merbau has a natural resistance to wear and is often used for flooring.

Uses					Availability	Price
VENEER	PLYWOOD	FURNITURE	JOINERY	CONSTRUCTION		
	✓	✓	✓	✓	✓✓	◆◆

Top Grain when radially cut. **Middle** Grain when tangentially cut. **Bottom** Cross-section.

JUGLANS NIGRA

Black Walnut

Black Walnut is also known as **American Black** or **American Walnut**, and sometimes **Gumwood**.

Black walnut is found throughout the central parts of North America. The tree is much taller than its European cousin. In good growing conditions, it can reach heights of up to 150ft (45m) or thereabouts. Clear boles free of branches tend to be relatively short, at around 50ft (15m) or more. When freshly cut from the log, the heartwood varies from a light brown through to a chocolate, sometimes dark purple, brown with attractive streaking. There is a noticeable musky odor to the wood that diminishes but does not disappear. The sapwood is clearly distinct and a pale, off-white color. Over time the heartwood darkens. Occasionally, the wood is steamed to try and produce a more uniform spread of color and darken the sapwood. The coarse grain is fairly straight but can have a tendency toward being wavy or curly.

Properties of the wood

Of average weight, black walnut has very durable heartwood. However, the sapwood is subject to attack by wood boring beetles and should be avoided if at all possible. Drying black walnut can be troublesome, especially with the thicker sizes. There is a tendency for honeycombing to appear if care is not taken. Some predrying of these thicker stocks is probably advisable. Once the wood has been dried to a satisfactory moisture content it remains relatively stable. Working properties are good. It can be nailed and screwed relatively easily and has good adhesive properties. It will stain well and a really fine surface finish can be achieved with some effort.

Uses of the wood

Black walnut is a very attractive wood that is sought after for its decorative properties. It is mainly used in the production of fine furniture and cabinet work. It has applications for internal joinery, paneling, and moldings. It is often sliced for veneers and when burrs are found, these are sliced and prized for their decorative use.

Source North America

Working properties

Weight (per ft³)	40lb (18kg)
Durability	Very durable
Bendability	Moderate
Hardness	Hard
Sawing and shaping	Satisfactory
Splitting	Average
Gluing	Good

Uses					Availability	Price
VENEER	PLYWOOD	FURNITURE	JOINERY	CONSTRUCTION	✓	◆◆
✓		✓				

JUGLANS REGIA

Walnut

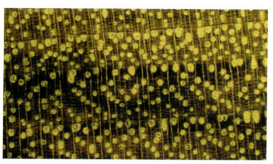

The common English name is **Walnut** and it is also known as **Circassian**, **European Walnut**, and it can be prefixed with the country of origin, for example, **French**, and so on.

This walnut tree is found throughout Europe and on eastwards. It is thought that it probably originated in Turkey. It was most likely introduced elsewhere as a source of food and oils from its nuts, in addition to the production of lumber. The trees themselves only reach heights of around 82ft (25m) in good growing conditions. Branching can be fairly low down, therefore clear boles are not often found over 20ft (6m) or thereabouts. The heartwood is variable in color, from a grayish brown through to a darker brown with distinctive streaking. None of these colorations are uniform and can be affected by the local conditions in the country of origin. The sapwood is clearly defined as a pale off-white color. Grain can be variable, depending upon where the tree has grown. It is usually fairly coarse and can be straight or wavy.

Top Grain when radially cut. **Middle** Grain when tangentially cut. **Bottom** Cross-section.

Source Throughout Europe

Working properties

Weight (per ft³)	37lb (17kg)
Durability	Moderately durable
Bendability	Moderate
Hardness	Hard
Sawing and shaping	Take care
Splitting	Average
Gluing	Good

Properties of the wood

A slightly less than average weight when dry, the heartwood of this walnut is only considered to be moderately durable. It dries relatively well but slowly, with some tendency toward honeycombing. Once dried to the required moisture content, it remains fairly stable. This wood is not quite as easy to work as its American cousin, due to the more varied growing conditions that pertain across the tree's area of provenance and the grain configurations in the wood, which are more numerous. Sharp tools are essential to avoid saws binding and surfaces plucking out. It can be fixed relatively easily and has good adhesive properties. Staining is satisfactory and with care a fine finished surface can be produced.

Uses of the wood

Another sought-after wood for its use in fine furniture and cabinet work. Sliced quarter-cut lumber and burrs are particularly attractive. Walnut is traditionally used for making expensive gun stocks, due to its resistance to shock and ease of carving.

Uses					Availability	Price
VENEER	PLYWOOD	FURNITURE	JOINERY	CONSTRUCTION		
✓		✓			✓	◆◆

Top Grain when radially cut. **Middle** Grain when tangentially cut. **Bottom** Cross-section.

KHAYA SPP.

African Mahogany

This hardwood is generally called **African Mahogany** and is also known as **Ogwano**, **Ngollon**, **Khaya**, **Khaya Wood**, **Krala**, **Acajou Blanc**, or **Acajou d' Afrique**.

This is a West African hardwood which mainly grows in tropical forests. There are up to five different species that are collectively sold as African Mahogany and, when enough volume is available, some are selected to be sold separately as Heavy Mahogany. This latter group, probably only two species, tends to grow in drier zones. On occasions the exported lumber is named after the country of origin or port of shipment. The trees stand above average at about 100–130ft (30–40m) tall. With buttressing, clear boles of around 66ft (20m) or more can be found. After being freshly cut the heartwood turns a medium to dark, reddish brown, depending upon species and growing conditions. The sapwood is clearly distinct, often a pale pink or straw color. The grain is fine and interlocked, producing a striped effect on quarter-cut boards.

Properties of the wood

A lightweight timber, the heartwood of this mahogany is considered to be durable. Drying is fairly straightforward, with cupping only on wider boards being the main problem. If the grain is a bit wild, planing and molding African mahogany can result in some plucking out or woolly sections of surface. As a lighter wood, with fairly high levels of interlocking grain, nailing and screwing are relatively easily achieved. Adhesive properties are good and it takes stains reasonably well. With care, and vigorous polishing, a more than satisfactory surface finish can be achieved.

Uses of the wood

African mahogany has always been and continues to be used as an alternative to the true mahoganies from Central and South America. Now it is rightfully used on its own merits for furniture, interior joinery and fittings, stairs, windows, and cabinet work. It has also been employed in boatbuilding for both decking and sidings, for flooring, and veneers.

Source West Africa

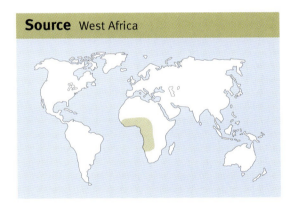

Working properties

Weight (per ft³)	33lb (15kg)
Durability	Moderately durable
Bendability	Poor
Hardness	Medium
Sawing and shaping	Take care
Splitting	Average
Gluing	Good

Uses					Availability	Price
VENEER	PLYWOOD	FURNITURE	JOINERY	CONSTRUCTION	✓✓	◆◆
✓	✓	✓	✓			

LIRIODENDRON TULIPIFERA

Tulipwood

Tulipwood has many other commonly used names, including **American Tulipwood**, **Tuliptree**, **Canary Wood**, **Canary Whitewood**, **American Whitewood**, **Basswood**, **Yellow**, or **Tulip Poplar**.

This tulipwood is another fairly big tree from North America. It grows throughout the eastern states, perhaps more profusely through the south-east. The tulipwood tree can reach heights of up to 164ft (50m), but is more probably only likely to be around 100ft (30m) or so. The boles can be thick and straight up to branching, producing a range of lumber up to 20–23ft (6–7m). When freshly cut from the log, a slight musky odor is detectable. The heartwood varies in color from a pale off-white brown through to an olive green. Often there are patches of these differing color ranges adjacent to each other. The sapwood is slightly lighter and it is often difficult to see a clear difference between this and the heartwood. The grain is fine, even, and usually straight.

Top Grain when radially cut. **Middle** Grain when tangentially cut. **Bottom** Cross-section.

Source Eastern North America

Working properties

Weight (per ft³)	30lb (14kg)
Durability	Perishable
Bendability	Poor
Hardness	Soft
Sawing and shaping	Satisfactory
Splitting	Good
Gluing	Good

Properties of the wood

A lightweight wood that is not considered to be durable and, if used for external purposes, which should be treated with preservatives. Drying this wood is normally trouble-free; however, there can be some marked levels of shrinkage. The working properties of tulipwood are good. It both saws and planes relatively easily. Nailing and screwing are easily carried out and it has good adhesive properties. It stains well and can be brought up to a satisfactory finished surface, as long as it has been correctly sealed.

Uses of the wood

Tulipwood is used at source for a whole range of purposes, from light construction work through joinery to furniture and cabinet work. Some thought needs to go into where it is placed, due to the slightly softer nature of the wood. Exterior use must be accompanied by staining. Its fine grain lends itself to being used as a carving wood. The heavier examples are the best for furniture, but most would be for stuff-over, drawer sides, and similar applications. Poorer quality wood is used for pallets and packing cases.

Uses					Availability	Price
VENEER	PLYWOOD	FURNITURE	JOINERY	CONSTRUCTION		
✓	✓	✓	✓	✓	✓✓	◆◆

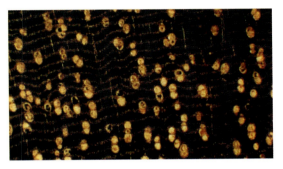

Top Grain when radially cut. **Middle** Grain when tangentially cut. **Bottom** Cross-section.

LOPHIRA ALATA

Ekki

This African hardwood is called **Ekki** and is also known as **Azobe**, **Kaku**, **Bongossi**, **Akoura**, **Eba**, **Red Ironwood**, **Ironpost**, or **Hendui**.

Trees yielding commercial quantities of lumber are found from West Africa through Central Africa to the east. Ekki is a large tree, reaching up to 150–164ft (45–50m). With little buttressing at the base, the bole is straight and long. Clear timber lengths are readily available. When freshly cut, Ekki's heartwood is a dark reddish brown that darkens on exposure. The sapwood is clearly visible and lighter in color, making it easy to distinguish from the heartwood. The grain is often interlocked, coarse, and open, with what appears to be a lighter mineral deposit included. Ekki has a natural resistance to acids and this leads to its use in cider and other fruit presses. So long as the surface finish is not important, ekki has superb qualities that can be put to good use in a wide variety of ways.

Properties of the wood

Ekki is a plain-looking wood. It is hard and one of the heaviest commercial timbers available. The heartwood is classified as very durable making it, probably, the most durable timber available out of Africa. All these factors lead to a difficult drying process that often ends up with surface and end checks and splitting. To help avoid this, a lengthy period of predrying on thin stickers is recommended. Sawing and planing ekki can also be troublesome. Where possible, it is best to use tungsten carbide-tipped tools that will retain their cutting edge for longer. Boring can be difficult but is essential for near end work. In addition the inclusion of minerals in the pores does not help with adhesion.

Uses of the wood

Ekki is ideally suited for use where there is likely to be a high degree of wear, and resistance to decay or insect attack is important. It has been traditionally used in dock and wharf construction, where it can last for many years. Railroad ties, bridges, and other construction works are also typical uses.

Source Africa

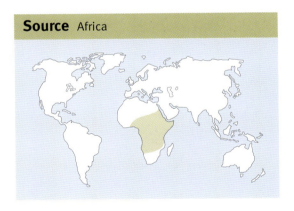

Working properties

Weight (per ft³)	66lb (30kg)
Durability	Very durable
Bendability	Poor
Hardness	Hard
Sawing and shaping	Difficult
Splitting	Poor
Gluing	Take care

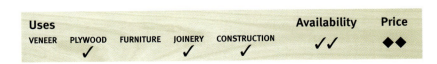

Uses					Availability	Price
VENEER	PLYWOOD	FURNITURE	JOINERY	CONSTRUCTION	✓✓	◆◆
	✓		✓	✓		

LOVOA TRICHILIOIDES

African Walnut

The common English name is **African Walnut** and it is also known as **Alonawood, Apopo, Bibolo, Bombolu, Congowood, Tigerwood, Sida, Noyer du Gabon, Noyer d' Afrique, Lovoawood, Eyan, Dilolo Fiote, Dibetou**, and can be prefixed with the country of source.

This is a relatively short tree found throughout West Africa and into parts of Central Africa. It stands up to about 130ft (40m) tall and, in profile, looks similar to the true walnut trees. Clear bole lengths are usually around half the height at, say, 60ft (18m) or so. The heartwood is golden brown in color with occasional darker streaks. This coloration may have led to its loose association as walnut. These darker streaks are actually gum canals and can often be clearly seen on end grain. The sapwood is delineated and is slightly paler. The grain is fairly fine and interlocked, which produces a striped effect when cut on the quarter. Although often marketed as walnut, it is in fact a member of the mahogany family.

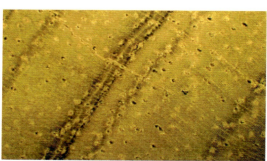

Top Grain when radially cut. **Middle** Grain when tangentially cut. **Bottom** Cross-section.

Source Predominantly West Africa

Working properties

Weight (per ft³)	35lb (16kg)
Durability	Moderately durable
Bendability	Moderate
Hardness	Medium
Sawing and shaping	Take care
Splitting	Average
Gluing	Good

Properties of the wood

This is a lightweight wood when dry and the heartwood is only considered to be moderately durable. Drying is fairly rapid with little distortion if care is taken. Some splits and surface checking may occur with thicker stocks. The interlocked grain sometimes makes working with this wood difficult. Sharp tools are essential to avoid binding on saws and plucking out of planed surfaces. A reduction of the cutting angle when planing may help to alleviate this problem. The wood takes fixings well—although predrilling near the end grain is advised when using nails and screws—and has good adhesive properties. It will stain with ease and a fine surface finish can be achieved with work and fillers.

Uses of the wood

The weight of African walnut precludes it from anything too structural. It is most often used for furniture and cabinet work and peeled or sliced for veneers. It can be used for internal joinery works and moldings, shopfitting, and paneling.

Uses					Availability	Price
VENEER	PLYWOOD	FURNITURE	JOINERY	CONSTRUCTION		
✓	✓	✓	✓		✓✓	◆◆

Top Grain when radially cut. **Middle** Grain when tangentially cut. **Bottom** Cross-section.

MALUS SYLVESTRIS and M. DOMESTICA
Applewood

The wood of the apple tree is unsurprisingly known as **Applewood** but is also referred to generically as **Fruitwood**, when it is combined with other timbers such as pear.

Found throughout Europe and North America, the apple tree is not grown on a commercial basis for its wood. Trees will vary in size, possibly reaching a maximum height of around 16–33ft (5–10m). Boles are short and often distorted, with the lumber yield being minimal. When freshly cut from the log, the lumber is light brown with a pink or reddish hue and can vary quite a bit. There is little distinction between the heartwood and the sapwood. The grain of apple is generally close, with a fine, uniform texture. During growth some trees tend to spiral, which can at times produce a difficult grain. Slower grown wood, from the north, tends to have the tighter grain. Valued for this tighter grain and, when it is not too interlocking or spiraled, this wood is used for craft turning and carving.

Properties of the wood

For a fairly heavy wood, apple, from the little data available, is not particularly durable. It can be susceptible to insect attack even when dry and should not be used in exposed or external situations. Drying can be fraught at times. Slow air circulation needs to be maintained in both air and kiln drying situations to prevent the wood from drying too quickly. If it does, the incidence of distortion and splitting will increase dramatically. If the grain is irregular, spiral, or interlocking, then sawing and planing become problematical. Tools will often overheat if trapped while cutting. However, it can be worked up to a fine surface finish. Apple's adhesion properties are fairly good, and it also stains and finishes well.

Uses of the wood

Although not available in huge commercial quantities, apple has traditionally been used, on a local basis, for country-made furniture and joinery. Often combined with other timbers such as pear and used under the generic fruitwood name, it can be found in chairs, tool handles, doors, and small items of treen.

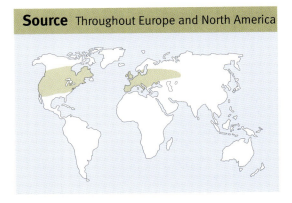

Source Throughout Europe and North America

Working properties

Weight (per ft³)	44lb (20kg)
Durability	Perishable
Bendability	Moderate
Hardness	Hard
Sawing and shaping	Take care
Splitting	Good
Gluing	Good

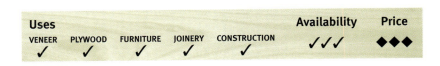

Uses					Availability	Price
VENEER	PLYWOOD	FURNITURE	JOINERY	CONSTRUCTION	✓✓✓	◆◆◆
✓	✓	✓	✓	✓		

MANSONIA ALTISSIMA

Mansonia

The common name of this hardwood is **Mansonia** and it is also known as **Aprono**, **Bete**, or **Ofun**.

The Mansonia tree grows in the tropical rain forests of West Africa. Of average height, it stands around 100ft (30m) tall. The boles are not excessively long and tend to be not very large in diameter, with narrow buttresses. When freshly cut, the heartwood can be a rich reddish brown, but this frequently fades into a dull uniform dark brown. Initially, there may be some purple streaking or tinges in the heartwood as well, but these soon fade upon exposure. The sapwood is clearly defined, is wide, and whitish in color. The fine grain is fairly evenly textured. Occasionally this wood has been offered on the commercial market as African black walnut. It should not be confused with *Lovoa trichilioides*, the other African wood that has been attributed with this name. It is possible that the grain characteristics once led to this former, inappropriate name.

Top Grain when radially cut. **Middle** Grain when tangentially cut. **Bottom** Cross-section.

Source West Africa

Working properties

Weight (per ft³)	37lb (17kg)
Durability	Very durable
Bendability	Good
Hardness	Medium
Sawing and shaping	Satisfactory
Splitting	Good
Gluing	Good

Properties of the wood

Mansonia is a slightly less than average weight wood when dry. Distortion during drying is not a major problem, but splits and shakes around knots may extend. The heartwood of mansonia is considered to be very durable and resistant to preservative treatment. The fine dust created when working the wood has been known to cause dermatitis and other irritations to eyes, nose, and throat. Of those woods which can cause these problems, mansonia is considered to be one of the worst. The actual working of the wood is not difficult, with good sawn and planed surfaces produced. It should not need predrilling for fixing and has good adhesive properties. With its fine grain structure, a good finished surface can be achieved.

Uses of the wood

At source, mansonia is peeled for plywood manufacture and used in joinery and furniture manufacture. It can be employed to make a whole range of furniture and cabinet works, perhaps where the figured grain is not so important.

Uses					Availability	Price
VENEER	PLYWOOD	FURNITURE	JOINERY	CONSTRUCTION		
✓	✓	✓	✓		✓✓	◆◆

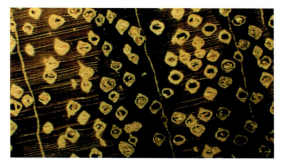

MICROBERLINIA BISULCATA and M. BRAZZAVILLENSIS Zebrano

Zebrano is also known as **Zingana** and sometimes **Zebrawood**. Although accepted, the use of both the names Zebrawood and Zebrano can be confusing. In several cases, other African and South American timbers are known by these names.

The two species of trees that are brought together to produce the small quantities of this zebrano are found mainly in West Africa. They are fairly tall trees, reaching heights of just over 150ft (45m). Boles can be straight and clear for 66ft (20m) or more. The heartwood alternates in narrow bands from a pale golden brown to a darker reddish brown. This striping is particularly striking with quarter-cut material and lends itself to the common name. The sapwood, which is often adzed off, is apparent and a paler color. The coarse grain is interlocked and wavy. With a hard feel to it, the lumber can have some resins present.

Top Grain when radially cut. **Middle** Grain when tangentially cut. **Bottom** Cross-section.

Properties of the wood

Zebrano is slightly above average weight when dry and the heartwood is thought to be durable. Drying the wood can be a problem, especially with thicker materials. Twisting can be reduced if lumber is cut on the quarter from the log. Some predrying of thicker stocks is essential to avoid too much surface checking. Working zebrano can be difficult at times, due to the interlocking grain. Some saw binding can occur and the surface can be plucked out when planing. Predrilling for fixings is probably advisable. This hardwood has good adhesion properties. Although it is unlikely that you would wish to stain this wood, with care a fine finish can be produced.

Uses of the wood

This wood is not available in large, commercial quantities. It is prized for its decorative appeal and most often sliced or peeled for veneers. When available, it is a popular timber for use in craft-related items, such as turning and intricate inlay work.

Source West Africa

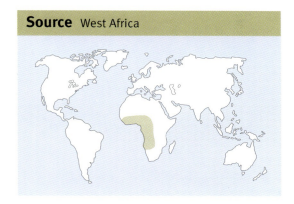

Working properties

Weight (per ft³)	42lb (19kg)
Durability	Durable
Bendability	Poor
Hardness	Hard
Sawing and shaping	Take care
Splitting	Average
Gluing	Good

Uses					Availability	Price
VENEER	PLYWOOD	FURNITURE	JOINERY	CONSTRUCTION		
✓		✓			✓	◆◆◆

MILICIA EXCELSA and M. REGIA

Iroko

The widely grown African hardwood **Iroko** is also known as **Odum, Odoum, Kamba, Kambala, Tule, Intule, Moreira, Mereira, Mvule, Bang, Abang, Bangui, Mulundu, Lusanga, Roko**, and **Rokko**.

Iroko can be found throughout West, Central, and East Africa, hence the large number of common names of which the above listing is not definitive. It is a large, deciduous tree, standing up to 164ft (50m) tall on occasions. With little or no buttressing clear, straight boles of up to 66ft (20m) can be produced. With a distinct whitey cream sapwood, the heartwood can be a bright yellow when first cut. This darkens fairly quickly to a light brown and, after full exposure will darken further to a dark, golden brown. Also, when freshly cut the wood has a distinct, not unpleasant, musky odor. The grain is fairly open and has a tendency to be interlocked. The wood has a slightly oily feel to it when dry. On occasions large calcium deposits can be found in pockets or sheets.

Top Grain when radially cut. **Middle** Grain when tangentially cut. **Bottom** Cross-section.

Source Africa

Working properties

Weight (per ft³)	40lb (18kg)
Durability	Very durable
Bendability	Moderate
Hardness	Medium
Sawing and shaping	Difficult
Splitting	Poor
Gluing	Good

Properties of the wood

Although of medium weight the heartwood is considered to be very durable. However, it should not be used in conditions that are continuously moist or wet. With an interesting cellular structure, it is resistant to attempts to treat it with preservatives. Drying iroko can be problematical. Although it dries fairly rapidly, there can be high instances of distortion, depending upon the grain structure. Sawing and planing can also be difficult if the wood has not been conditioned. Pinching and burning can occur and the calcium-like deposits, when present, quickly blunt saws. Adhesion is good, despite the slightly oily texture. With a tendency to split, predrilling is advisable when screwing and nailing. A good surface finish can be achieved.

Uses of the wood

Iroko is a popular timber for joinery—both internal and external—and home and backyard furniture, the latter because it is often used as a substitute for teak. It is reasonably hard-wearing for floors and has some use in structural and marine works.

Uses					Availability	Price
VENEER	PLYWOOD	FURNITURE	JOINERY	CONSTRUCTION		
✓	✓	✓	✓		✓✓	◆◆

Top Grain when radially cut. **Middle** Grain when tangentially cut. **Bottom** Cross-section.

MILLETTIA LAURENTII
Wenge

The common English name of this hardwood is **Wenge** and it is also known as **Dikela** or **Palissandre du Congo**.

The Wenge tree is found from West and Central to East Africa, with most of the commercial production coming out of Central Africa. This is not a very big tree, only reaching heights of around 66ft (20m) or so. Clear boles are short and may only be at best around 20ft (6m). When freshly cut from the log, the wood gives off a slightly musky smell that disappears over time. The heartwood is a deep chocolate brown alternating with a near black, which produces a marked narrow striping effect. The sapwood is clearly distinct from the heartwood and is yellowish brown to cream in color. The grain of this wood is coarse, open, and interlocked. It feels cold to the touch and is slightly oily. Wenge is sometimes confused with M. *stuhlmannii*, which grows in the same areas, has similar properties and is known as Panga Panga.

Properties of the wood

Although quite variable, wenge is probably above average weight when the wood is dry. The heartwood is considered to be durable, but both that and the sapwood are susceptible to attack by wood boring beetles. If this has occurred it is often difficult to spot due to the very dark coloration of the heartwood. Drying can be problematical and is slow. End splits will lengthen and surface checking will occur, especially on thicker stocks. With these, some predrying in thin stickers would be advantageous. Wenge is not easy to work. Tools are blunted fairly quickly and the grain configuration can lead to saws binding and planer blades chattering. Predrilling for all fixings is essential. Its adhesive properties are good, helped on by the open grain. Unlikely to be stained, a satisfactory surface finish can be achieved with effort.

Uses of the wood

This is an interesting wood that has some attractive decorative properties. It is used to produce furniture and dark-faced veneered panels. It wears well and makes a striking flooring material.

Source West and Central Africa

Working properties

Weight (per ft³)	40lb (18kg)
Durability	Durable
Bendability	Poor
Hardness	Hard
Sawing and shaping	Take care
Splitting	Poor
Gluing	Take care

Uses					Availability	Price
VENEER	PLYWOOD	FURNITURE	JOINERY	CONSTRUCTION	✓✓	◆◆
✓		✓	✓	✓		

MITRAGYNA SPP.

Abura

The African hardwood known as **Abura** is sometimes also called **Elilom**, **Elelom**, **Bahia**, **Maza**, **Mujiwa**, **Mushiwa**, **Subaha**, **Voukou**, or **Vuku**.

Abura is predominantly found in the rain forests of West Africa; however, it can also be found in parts of central Africa. The tree can grow to around 100ft (30m) tall, and has a long, straight bole. Its leaves are extremely toxic, and smoking them when they have been dried can be more dangerous than smoking opium, with similar effects! This is a plain wood which, when freshly cut, can give off a fairly unpleasant odor; this disappears once the wood has been dried. Both the heartwood and the sapwood are colored a yellowish brown and there is no clear definition between them. The core can be slightly grayish in color. Abura's grain is generally straight, but there is a tendency toward interlocking or spiral grain. The occurrence of a wavy grain can at times produce a birch-like figure.

Top Grain when radially cut. **Middle** Grain when tangentially cut. **Bottom** Cross-section.

Source Predominantly West Africa

Working properties

Weight (per ft³)	35lb (16kg)
Durability	Perishable
Bendability	Poor
Hardness	Medium
Sawing and shaping	Satisfactory
Splitting	Average
Gluing	Good

Properties of the wood

Once dried, this is a fairly lightweight wood which leads to its classification as perishable. It is reasonably stable during the drying process, with little or no distortion, depending upon the grain formation. End splitting does occur due to a fairly high degree of shrinkage from green. Not a particularly strong wood, it needs preservative treatment, which it easily absorbs, if used externally. Abura takes adhesives well and joints can be stronger due to the lightness of the wood. Staining works well, but end grain needs some care due to higher levels of absorption. The tendency to split is alleviated by predrilling when screwing or nailing.

Uses of the wood

Abura is not a durable wood and therefore has traditionally been used internally. Abura's plainness and ability to take stain has led to its use in furniture manufacture, where it can be matched in for the less obvious components. It is naturally resistant to the effects of acids and has sometimes been used in applications where this has been beneficial.

Uses					Availability	Price
VENEER	PLYWOOD	FURNITURE	JOINERY	CONSTRUCTION		
✓	✓	✓	✓		✓✓	◆◆

Top Grain when radially cut. **Middle** Grain when tangentially cut. **Bottom** Cross-section.

NAUCLEA DIDERRICHII

Opepe

The common English name of this African hardwood is **Opepe** and it is also known as **Obiache**, **Ubulu**, **Badi**, **Belinga**, **Ekusawa**, **Kusia**, **Kusiaba**, **Kusiabo**, **Akondoc**, **Kantate**, **Bonkese**, **Maza**, **Bonkangu**, **Ngulu**, **Gulu**, or **Alama**.

This is a large tree producing strong, durable, and versatile wood that grows from West through Central to East Africa. Most commercial quantities available come from West Africa. Overall heights of this tree can reach around 164ft (50m) tall. With little buttressing, clear boles are often found at around 82ft (25m). Opepe's heartwood is a distinct light yellowy orange when first cut, darkening over time. The sapwood is clearly distinct and a paler version of the heartwood. The grain of this wood can be interlocked, which produces an attractive stripe effect. It is also straight and of a slightly coarse grain nature, due to its large pore structure. Opepe has reasonable working qualities with little occurrence of blunting to tool edges.

Properties of the wood

Opepe is of above average weight when dry. It is hard and dense and the heartwood is considered to be very durable. As it is often used in large sizes, drying can be difficult. A high level of surface checking and splitting can occur, especially with through-and-through cut material. Predrying on thin stickers is recommended. Once dry, there is little further movement. Opepe's working properties are surprisingly good for such a hard wood. Some reduction in cutting angles might be beneficial when planing the interlocked grain timber. It will need predrilling when fixing to avoid splitting or screws shearing. It has good adhesive properties, due to its open grain structure. With work and fillers, a satisfactory surface finish can be achieved.

Uses of the wood

This wood is traditionally used in heavy construction and structural work. Generally in large sizes, it is ideal for dock and wharf work. It makes a very hard-wearing decking and flooring material. It also has some use in external joinery applications.

Source West and Central Africa

Working properties

Weight (per ft³)	46lb (21kg)
Durability	Very durable
Bendability	Poor
Hardness	Hard
Sawing and shaping	Satisfactory
Splitting	Poor
Gluing	Good

Uses					Availability	Price
VENEER	PLYWOOD	FURNITURE	JOINERY	CONSTRUCTION	✓✓	◆◆
	✓		✓	✓		

NESOGORDONIA PAPAVERIFERA

Danta

Danta is also known as **Kotibe**, **Apru**, **Otutu**, **Epro**, **Olborbora**, **Ovoue**, or **Tsanya**.

Danta is not one of the largest African trees, only growing to around 100ft (30m). It is found throughout West Africa, tending to be more commercially available to the south. Boles are clear, with small buttresses, reaching lengths of around 50ft (15m). When freshly cut from the log the heartwood can be a bright, deep crimson red that darkens on exposure. The sapwood is a clearly defined pale brown color. There is nothing particularly striking about the grain, which feels slightly oily or greasy. However, it does sometimes produce a stripe on the radial face that is similar to sapele (see page 52), but generally a lot narrower. In some instances there can be evidence of small pin-like knots or darker, damaged tissue. With some interlocking apparent, quarter-sawn material does occasionally produce a narrow, stripped figure.

Top Grain when radially cut. **Middle** Grain when tangentially cut. **Bottom** Cross-section.

Source Predominantly West Africa

Working properties

Weight (per ft³)	46lb (21kg)
Durability	Durable
Bendability	Moderate
Hardness	Hard
Sawing and shaping	Satisfactory
Splitting	Average
Gluing	Take care

Properties of the wood

Danta is dense, hard, and above average weight when dry. Its density slows down the drying process, but wastage and shrinkage are limited. Occasional case hardening does occur and, if included, there can be some splitting around knots. For such a dense wood, danta is only classified as durable. Sharp tools are required for sawing and planing. Predrilling when screwing or nailing is recommended. Due to the presence of natural oils, care needs to be taken when using adhesives. This inclusion can also have a detrimental effect on the quality of finish obtained. Cleaning the surfaces before sealing will help and a fine polished luster can be achieved.

Uses of the wood

A hard-wearing wood, danta is traditionally used for construction and structural purposes. Its resistance to wear makes it ideal as a flooring material. Danta's natural color has led to its use in joinery for both internal and external uses. At source it has been used as a boatbuilding material, especially useful for planking.

Uses					Availability	Price
VENEER	PLYWOOD	FURNITURE	JOINERY	CONSTRUCTION		
✓	✓	✓	✓	✓	✓✓	◆◆

Top Grain when radially cut. **Middle** Grain when tangentially cut. **Bottom** Cross-section.

OCOTEA RODIAEI

Greenheart

The common English name of this wood is **Greenheart** and it is also known as **Demerara**, **Black**, **Brown**, **Yellow** and **White Greenheart**, **Groenhart**, or **Sipiroe**.

An evergreen tree, greenheart is found throughout north and central South America. The main source of this wood is Guyana, with further smaller amounts commercially available from Surinam. It is a very hard, heavy, and durable wood. The Greenheart tree stands at a little above average height, reaching up to around 130ft (40m) tall. With some buttressing, clear boles are produced at about half this length. The freshly cut heartwood is a dull, light olive green with some darker streaking on occasions. The sapwood is not always clearly defined. All the wood darkens on exposure. Greenheart's grain, although rather plain, is mainly straight and finely textured, although interlocking does occur. Occasional gum pockets can be found and sometimes there are deposits in the pores.

Properties of the wood

Greenheart's natural durability negates the need for preservative treatment, which is resisted due to the pore structure. Drying can be troublesome and can produce high levels of degrade with thicker sizes. Surface checking is also apparent. If the wood is to be artificially dried, then predrying on thin stickers is recommended. The hardness and density of the wood can cause problems when working. If there is a high level of interlocking grain, this will be exacerbated further. Sharp tools are essential. The inclusion of some gum makes the adhesion properties of greenheart poor. All fixings should be predrilled or bored out to avoid splitting.

Uses of the wood

Greenheart is a wood that lends itself to structural uses. The heartwood has a natural resistance to marine borer attack and has therefore been used extensively in dock, wharf, and other water-related environments. Decking, pier works, and lock gates are commonly made from greenheart. Heavy constructional and structural uses are other areas of use.

Source South America

Working properties

Weight (per ft³)	73lb (33kg)
Durability	Very durable
Bendability	Moderate
Hardness	Hard
Sawing and shaping	Difficult
Splitting	Poor
Gluing	Take care

Uses					Availability	Price
VENEER	PLYWOOD	FURNITURE	JOINERY	CONSTRUCTION ✓	✓✓	◆◆

PALAQUIUM SPP. and PAYENA SPP.

Nyatoh

The common name of this South-East Asian hardwood is **Nyatoh** and it is also known as **Njatuh**, **Padang**, **Balam**, and **Chay**.

Nyatoh trees grow throughout the South-East Asian region. They are not tall in comparison to other tropical timbers, reaching average heights of around 100ft (30m) or so. Boles can be straight and fluted. Due to the fact that there are a number of species grouped together to form commercial lots of nyatoh, there are some variations in the properties of the wood. When freshly cut from the log, the heartwood can vary in color from a deep pinkish brown through to a reddish brown. Occasionally some darker streaks are also apparent. The sapwood is paler than the heartwood, but there is no clear delineation between the two. This is a plain wood with an even, interlocked grain structure which can display a wavy type of figure on quarter-cut boards. Because of the mix of species referred to above, nyatoh is not always consistent in quality, weight, and working properties.

Top Grain when radially cut. **Middle** Grain when tangentially cut. **Bottom** Cross-section.

Source South-East Asia

Working properties

Weight (per ft³)	42lb (19kg)
Durability	Moderately durable
Bendability	Moderate
Hardness	Medium
Sawing and shaping	Take care
Splitting	Average
Gluing	Good

Properties of the wood

This timber, although variable, is slightly heavier than average. Drying can produce surface checks and distortion if care is not taken. Thicker material benefits from some predrying in thin stickers prior to artificial drying. The heartwood is only considered to be moderately durable and is best not used in damp or wet conditions. Treatment with preservatives is resisted due to the cellular structure of the wood. Some inclusion of silica will blunt tools rapidly if found. When absent, sawing and planing is relatively good, but some care needs to be exercized with the latter to avoid plucking out the finished surface. Adhesive properties are good. There should be no problems with splitting during fixing, but some predrilling might be useful. With effort, a good surface finish can be obtained.

Uses of the wood

Nyatoh can be an attractive timber and used as a general purpose, red hardwood. It can be machined for use in joinery, used in interior construction work for beams and rafters, and peeled for plywood manufacture.

Uses					Availability	Price
VENEER	PLYWOOD	FURNITURE	JOINERY	CONSTRUCTION		
	✓	✓	✓		✓✓	◆◆

Top Grain when radially cut. **Middle** Grain when tangentially cut. **Bottom** Cross-section.

PELTOGYNE SPP.

Purpleheart

Purpleheart is also known as **Amaranth**, **Purplewood**, **Palo Nazareno**, **Palo Morado**, **Coataquiana**, **Sakavalli**, **Koorooboooelli**, **Violet Wood**, **Purperheart**, **Amarante**, **Bois Pourpre**, **Pau Roxo**, or **Pau Ferro**.

This exotically named wood comes from trees growing in central and northern South America through Central America to southern Mexico. Trees can stand at heights of between 130–150ft (40–45m) or thereabouts. With some buttressing, apparent straight boles can be found up to 50ft (15m) or more. Interestingly, the heartwood is usually a dull brown when freshly cut from the log. This quickly changes on exposure, turning into a deep purple color. After time, the striking purple color diminishes and turns into a dark, purplish brown. The sapwood is clearly defined as a pale creamy light brown color. The grain is fairly fine and generally straight, mixed with some interlocking that produces a stripe on the quarter-cut boards.

Properties of the wood

Purpleheart is a dense and heavy wood when dried. Its heartwood is considered to be very durable. Drying is not too problematical, although there is a tendency for some pockets of moisture to remain in thicker material. Very sharp tools are required when working purpleheart, as it is extremely hard. Saws will often bind and burn in the cut and there can be a build up of a gum-like residue on all tools and around cuts. Planer blades chatter on the surface once their edge has gone off. Purpleheart definitely needs to be predrilled for fixings. A little work is required to ensure that adhesives are fully effective. This wood will stain and finish to a good quality surface.

Uses of the wood

At source, purpleheart is often used in construction as a structural timber. It has a good shock-resistant quality and therefore finds some use in tool handles and older style vehicle framing. It is also used for furniture making, flooring, and for turning smaller items.

Source Central and South America

Working properties

Weight (per ft³)	60lb (27kg)
Durability	Very durable
Bendability	Moderate
Hardness	Hard
Sawing and shaping	Difficult
Splitting	Poor
Gluing	Good

Uses					Availability	Price
VENEER	PLYWOOD	FURNITURE	JOINERY	CONSTRUCTION		
✓		✓		✓	✓	◆◆◆

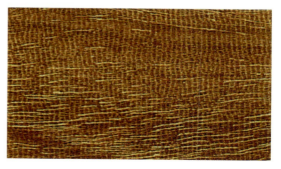

PENTACE SPP.

Melunak

The common English name of this wood is **Melunak** and it is also known as **Burmese Mahogany**, **Thitka**, and **Kashit**.

Melunak is made up of a number of species growing in South-East Asia and Indo-China. One species in particular, *P. burmanica*, is found in Myanmar. This species is the source of the woods with the other vernacular names above. In Malaysia, *P. triptera* is the most common and makes up the bulk of the commercially available lumber. The tree is a little over average height, at about 100–115ft (30–35m). Clear boles of 33ft (10m) or more long are produced. When freshly cut, the heartwood can vary in color from a pinkish brown through to a red brown. The sapwood is slightly lighter in color but is not always clearly defined. With a moderately fine interlocking grain texture, some stripe or roe-like figure can be visible on quarter-cut material. Occasionally, a white, mineral deposit is clearly visible within the cell structure of this wood.

Top Grain when radially cut. **Middle** Grain when tangentially cut. **Bottom** Cross-section.

Source Myanmar and South-East Asia

Working properties

Weight (per ft³)	42lb (19kg)
Durability	Moderately
Bendability	Moderate
Hardness	Medium
Sawing and shaping	Difficult
Splitting	Average
Gluing	Good

Properties of the wood

This wood is slightly heavier than average when dry. The heartwood is only considered to be moderately durable and, if required, treatment with preservatives is resisted. Care needs to be exercized during the drying process. If it is dried too rapidly, a high degree of surface checking will occur. Distortion can also be a factor. However, once dried to a suitable end use moisture content, it is considered to be stable. Often difficult to work, especially if the mineral deposits are present, melunak can cause saws to burn and planer blades to chatter. A reduced cutting angle will help to alleviate any surface plucking out due to the interlocked grain. Predrilling prior to using fixings is recommended. Adhesive properties are good and the wood stains relatively easily.

Uses of the wood

Melunak is not available in huge commercial quantities. Local uses include furniture, boatbuilding, and instrument making, such as carpenter's squares and straight edges. It is also used for general joinery.

Uses					**Availability**	**Price**
VENEER	PLYWOOD	FURNITURE	JOINERY	CONSTRUCTION		
✓	✓	✓	✓		✓✓	◆◆

Top Grain when radially cut. **Middle** Grain when tangentially cut. **Bottom** Cross-section.

PIPTADENIASTRUM AFRICANUM

Dahoma

The African hardwood **Dahoma** is also known as **Agboin, Ekhimi, Dabema, Toun, Atui, Tom, Bokungu, Banzu, Musese, Singa**, or **Mpewere**.

Dahoma is an African tree that is found predominantly in the west. It can grow to a substantial height of anything from 115–150ft (35–45m) tall. With a large bole, which is slightly buttressed at the bottom, long clear lengths of lumber can be produced. The heartwood and sapwood of this species are both clearly defined. The latter ranges from a light, golden brown through to a rather insipid darker brown. The grain can be slightly interlocking, providing a striped effect. When freshly cut the wood gives off an odorous, obnoxious ammonia-like smell. This can be irritating when you first begin working the wood, but it goes off after time. The sawdust of this wood can also cause irritation to the skin of some users, so care should be taken. It is advisable to wear long sleeves when working with it.

Properties of the wood

Of medium weight when dry, dahoma is considered to be durable. If preservative treatments are applied, then the heartwood is slightly resistant to these. Some care needs to be taken during the drying process, with high levels of shrinkage, distortion, and collapse all possible. The latter can sometimes be recovered, but if not, it will leave a rippled, washboard effect on the surface of the wood. Tools blunt easily when sawing and planing dahoma and quarter-sawn surfaces have a tendency to pluck out due to the interlocking grain. Dahoma screws, glues, and nails reasonably well, but some predrilling may be required. With the help of some filling a reasonable surface finish can be achieved.

Uses of the wood

More of a general purpose utility-type wood, dahoma has some uses in large structural applications where it can be used as a substitute for oak. Its odor and irritation factors tend to result in its use for flooring, truck beds, and some marine works.

Source Predominantly West Africa

Working properties

Weight (per ft³)	40lb (18kg)
Durability	Durable
Bendability	Poor
Hardness	Medium
Sawing and shaping	Take care
Splitting	Good
Gluing	Good

Uses					Availability	Price
VENEER	PLYWOOD	FURNITURE	JOINERY	CONSTRUCTION	✓✓	◆◆
	✓	✓	✓			

83

Top Grain when radially cut. **Middle** Grain when tangentially cut. **Bottom** Cross-section.

PLATANUS ORIENTALIS and P. HYBRIDA
London Plane

London Plane is also known as **European Plane**, **English**, **French Plane**, and so on, and the alternative name of **Lacewood**.

This tree grows across Europe and on into Asia Minor. The trees are fairly large by temperate standards, standing up to 100ft (30m) or more tall. Older trees can have large boles which will be clear up to about 33ft (10m). European plane is probably best known as a decorative, street-side tree. It is found in most capitals and large cities, lining streets and avenues. It also grows in woodlands and forests, but is not available in huge commercial quantities. When freshly cut from the log, the heartwood is pale creamy brown with no clear difference between this and the sapwood. The grain of this wood is straight, fine, and evenly textured. When cut on the quarter, it displays a distinct chink or short, feather-like figure. This wood is prized for its decorative uses and is often sold on the market as lacewood.

Source Throughout Europe and Asia Minor

Working properties

Weight (per ft³)	37lb (17kg)
Durability	Perishable
Bendability	Good
Hardness	Soft
Sawing and shaping	Take care
Splitting	Average
Gluing	Good

Properties of the wood

Plane is not considered to be a durable wood. With little difference between the heart and sapwood it is recommended that, in the unlikely event of it being used externally, it is treated with preservatives. It is a little less than average in weight when seasoned. Care when drying is important. Timber cut through and through will have a tendency to distort if the moisture is rapidly removed. Some predrying is advisable for all thicknesses prior to artificially drying. Working this wood can be a bit difficult at times. The dry lumber tries to bind on the saws when cutting. Sharp planing tools are required to avoid the surface plucking out, especially on quarter-cut material. It has good adhesive properties and should take fixings fairly well. It will stain and polish to a fine finish.

Uses of the wood

The lacewood lumber is probably the most prized and is used for decorative work in the solid, for veneers, and as an inlay. Plane wood itself is used for a variety of purposes, from simple furniture framing through to cabinet work.

Uses					Availability	Price
VENEER	PLYWOOD	FURNITURE	JOINERY	CONSTRUCTION		
✓		✓			✓	◆◆

Top Grain when radially cut. **Middle** Grain when tangentially cut. **Bottom** Cross-section.

POPULUS SPP.

Poplar

Poplar is also known as **Aspen** and **European Aspen**, **Black**, **Gray**, **White**, **Lombardy** and **Italian Black Poplar**, **Cottonwood**, **Eastern Cottonwood**, **Eastern Poplar**, and **Carolina Poplar**.

The poplar tree grows right through central North America, Europe and on eastward. In America, commercial quantities of poplar are mainly cut from *P. deltoids*, whereas in Europe there are probably around five or six different species, plus hybrids, drawn together and marketed as poplar. Larger growing species of this tree can reach heights of over 100ft (30m). With correct management clean, long boles can be produced. When freshly cut, the heartwood and sapwood are not clearly defined or distinct. The colors range from a pale creamy straw through to a pinkish, pale brown. The color of the wood can deepen closer to the core, where some darker brown streaking may be apparent. The grain is generally straight and free from knots.

Properties of the wood

This is a lightweight wood that is not considered to be durable. It dries fairly well and quickly, depending upon the mix of species. Some splitting will occur around knots if present and, in thicker material, some pockets of moisture may remain. Working poplar is reasonable, unless woolly material is found—occasionally the grain can be a little woolly and interlocked. Nailing and screwing properties are all good with little tendency to split. It has good adhesion. It will stain reasonably well but may occasionally be a bit patchy and it polishes fairly easily. Due to its lighter nature the finished surfaces can be susceptible to denting and marking.

Uses of the wood

Poplar is best used for internal purposes. It is often peeled for plywood production, split into small pieces for matches, and used as a general utility timber. In North America it is employed in household and kitchen furniture and is especially good when used for making blinds.

Source Throughout Europe and North America

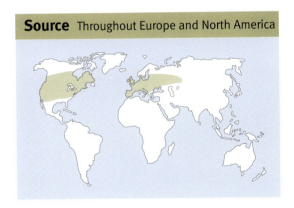

Working properties

Weight (per ft³)	29lb (13kg)
Durability	Perishable
Bendability	Poor
Hardness	Soft
Sawing and shaping	Take care
Splitting	Good
Gluing	Good

Uses					Availability	Price
VENEER	PLYWOOD	FURNITURE	JOINERY	CONSTRUCTION	✓✓	◆◆
	✓	✓	✓			

PRUNUS AVIUM

European Cherry

The common name of this hardwood is **European Cherry** and it is also known as **Gean**, **Mazzard**, or **Wild Cherry** and, sometimes, **Fruitwood**.

This tree is found throughout Europe and eastward. European cherry has many of the same characteristics of its American cousin. The tree tends to be shorter unless grown specifically in managed forest conditions. In the latter case, the overall height can reach something in the order of 66ft (20m). However, because it often grows alone, in mixed woodlands or in orchards, shorter trees are more common. This tends to restrict the lumber yield from the useable boles available. When cut from the log, the heartwood is a lighter version of American cherry. There can be some interesting variations in color with a tendency to a slightly greenish hue. The sapwood is clearly apparent and distinctly lighter. All goes slightly darker over time. The fresh lumber can also give off a rather pleasant odor. The grain is fairly tight but unlikely to be very straight.

Top Grain when radially cut. **Middle** Grain when tangentially cut. **Bottom** Cross-section.

Source Throughout Europe

Working properties

Weight (per ft³)	37lb (17kg)
Durability	Moderately durable
Bendability	Good
Hardness	Medium
Sawing and shaping	Satisfactory
Splitting	Poor
Gluing	Good

Properties of the wood

Not strong and only moderately durable, European cherry is slightly less than average in weight when dry. Care needs to be taken when drying to avoid too much distortion and warping. End cleating or strapping is a useful way to try and stop cherry's tendency to split. Shrinkage is about average. Due to the likely inclusion of wild and varied grain, sawing and planing can be difficult. Often the timber will pinch on saw blades, causing burn marking; a wider kerf is helpful here. Chipping out on the surface of planed material is also necessary, unless it has straighter grain. If care is taken with the finishing process, a smooth luster finish can be achieved on the show wood surfaces.

Uses of the wood

This cherry is not available in huge commercial quantities, which has tended to restrict its end uses. Providing it has been correctly dried for the appropriate end use it can have a number of applications for cabinet and furniture work, some joinery and moldings, paneling, carving, and turning.

Uses					Availability	Price
VENEER	PLYWOOD	FURNITURE	JOINERY	CONSTRUCTION		
✓		✓	✓		✓✓	◆◆

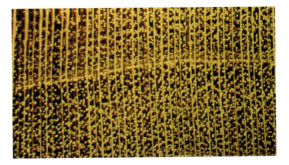

Top Grain when radially cut. **Middle** Grain when tangentially cut. **Bottom** Cross-section.

PRUNUS SEROTINA

American Cherry

American Cherry is also known as **American Black**, **Wild Black**, **Wild**, or **Rum Cherry**.

Although American cherry grows throughout the central band of North America, most of the commercial production of this wood comes from the eastern states. This is not a large tree, probably reaching a maximum height of 65–82ft (20–25m) in optimum growing conditions. With bole diameters of no more than 2ft (60cm) or so, the lumber produced is not wide. When freshly cut from the log, the heartwood varies from a rich red through to a darker reddish brown. This darkens on exposure and the narrow sapwood is clearly visible. In Europe, the wood is sometimes put through a steaming process that helps to produce a slightly darker, more unified color in the heartwood. The grain of cherry can be somewhat plain at times but does vary, with some darker streaking making it more attractive. On occasions, small gum pockets and pith flecks can be found.

Properties of the wood

Although weighing in at slightly less than average, when dry, American cherry is considered to be moderately durable. It can be susceptible to wood boring insect attack at times and should be preservative-treated if there is any risk of this. Drying can be problematical, with a fairly high degree of distortion and end splitting occurring if care is not taken. Once dry, the wood is fairly stable. Sawing and planing properties are good. Due to its inclination to split, predrilling is recommended prior to screwing or nailing. Cherry takes adhesives well and can be finished to a fine surface. Although it can be stained relatively easily, it is more valued for its natural coloration.

Uses of the wood

Cherry is widely considered to be one of the most handsome of woods. It is especially effective in furniture and for paneling. When used in high-quality cabinet work, matching with contrasting timbers is very effective. It is often used in boat trimming, flooring, for musical instrument components, and turns and carves reasonably well.

Source North America

Working properties

Weight (per ft³)	35lb (16kg)
Durability	Moderately durable
Bendability	Good
Hardness	Medium
Sawing and shaping	Satisfactory
Splitting	Poor
Gluing	Good

Uses					Availability	Price
VENEER	PLYWOOD	FURNITURE	JOINERY	CONSTRUCTION	✓✓	◆◆
✓		✓	✓			

87

PTEROCARPUS ANGOLENSIS

Muninga

Muninga has many other common names, among them **Bloodwood**, **Mukwa**, **Mninga**, **Ambila**, **Kajatenhout**, **Kejaat**, **Kiatt**, or **Kajat**.

This is an African tree that is found from the central parts of South Africa through to East Africa. It is a short tree in comparison to others standing, on average, around 66ft (20m) tall. Clear boles can be found at around 16–23ft (5–7m), but shorter ones are more common. When freshly cut, the wood gives off a faintly perfumed odor that disappears once dry. The heartwood is a pale, medium to dark golden brown with some occasional darker streaking. Over time it becomes a more uniform golden brown or reddish brown. The sapwood is paler in color and is clearly distinct from the heartwood. The grain is not often straight. However, the irregular interlocking grain makes for a fairly attractive surface. In some instances there are some white mineral deposits apparent, which can detract from the overall appearance.

Top Grain when radially cut. **Middle** Grain when tangentially cut. **Bottom** Cross-section.

Source Eastern and Southern Africa

Working properties

Weight (per ft³)	37lb (17kg)
Durability	Very durable
Bendability	Moderate
Hardness	Medium
Sawing and shaping	Take care
Splitting	Average
Gluing	Good

Properties of the wood

A lighter than average wood when dry, muninga seasons with little shrinkage, movement, or splitting. Some predrying of thicker stocks will help to speed up any artificial drying processes. The heartwood is considered to be very durable and resistant to treatment with preservatives. The inclusion of interlocking grain can make working muninga interesting. Some care needs to be taken to ensure cutters are sharp, especially when planing or molding the wood. Failure to do this may result in a woolly, plucked out surface finish. Nailing and screwing is relatively easy with predrilling needed near ends only as a precaution against splitting. It has good adhesive properties, due to the open-grained nature of the wood. It will stain well.

Uses of the wood

Muninga is an attractive, stable wood. This results in its use for high-quality cabinet and furniture work. At source it is peeled and used for plywood manufacture and as a decorative veneer. It also makes an attractive flooring material.

Uses					Availability	Price
VENEER	PLYWOOD	FURNITURE	JOINERY	CONSTRUCTION		
✓		✓	✓		✓	◆◆

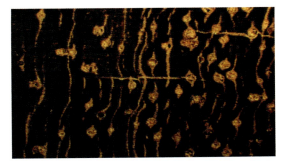

Top Grain when radially cut. **Middle** Grain when tangentially cut. **Bottom** Cross-section.

PTEROCARPUS SPP.

Padauk

The common English name of this hardwood is **Padauk** and it is also known as **African**, **Andaman** and **Burma Padauk**, **Vermilion Wood**, **Chanlanga-da**, **Muenge, M'bel, Mbeu, Corail, African Coralwood, Camwood, Barwood, Andaman Redwood, Mai Pradoo, Pradoo**, or **Amboyna**.

The Padauk tree grows right across Africa, through Indo-China and into South-East Asia. In each region a number of species are grouped together to form commercial quantities marketed under various names as above. Depending upon source location and local growing conditions, the trees can vary in height from around 65–100ft (20–30m) tall. Trunks are buttressed, so clear boles are obtainable in lengths of 23–26ft (7–8m). The freshly cut heartwood is a striking deep red through to a purple brown color with darker streaks. This darkens on exposure to a deep, uniform purple brown. The sapwood is clearly defined as a pale, grayish white. The grain is interlocked and can vary from medium coarse to coarse in texture.

Properties of the wood

Padauk is a heavier than average hardwood and the heartwood is considered to be very durable. Drying is difficult. Without care a high level of surface splitting and checking can occur. One prefelling solution that is believed to help is to girdle the tree. This involves cutting the bark right around the lower part of the trunk continuously. This effectively kills the tree, leaving it standing to dry before felling. The working properties of padauk are fairly good. Some plucking out of the surface when planing can occur. A lower cutting angle helps overcome this. The wood turns well and has good adhesive properties. Predrilling is essential. Staining is probably not necessary in most cases. With work and the judicious use of fillers, a fine finish can be achieved.

Uses of the wood

At source, the wood is used for a range of purposes, including construction through to framing and furniture. It can be employed for all joinery applications and makes an attractive, domestic flooring material.

Source Africa through to South-East Asia

Working properties

Weight (per ft³)	48lb (22kg)
Durability	Very durable
Bendability	Poor
Hardness	Hard
Sawing and shaping	Satisfactory
Splitting	Poor
Gluing	Good

Uses					Availability	Price
VENEER	PLYWOOD	FURNITURE	JOINERY	CONSTRUCTION	✓	◆◆
✓		✓				

PYRUS COMMUNIS
Pear

Pear is also known as **Fruitwood** when it is used in conjunction with apple, plum, and other woods from fruit trees.

Pear trees are not really grown for commercial lumber production, but the wood is interesting when it is available. Growing throughout Europe, the tree varies considerably in size and is subject to the local conditions and environment. On average these trees probably reach 33ft (10m) or so, but, on occasions, they may grow up to 66ft (20m). The fairly slim boles of this tree are not always straight and branching occurs fairly early. Narrow widths and short lumber lengths are the natural result. When freshly cut, the heartwood can vary from a light reddish brown through to some that might feature a slight purple hue. This all darkens to a more uniform color once exposed. There is no clear delineation between the heartwood and the sapwood, which is lighter. The grain is fine, even textured but irregular; some spiraling may have occurred during growth.

Top Grain when radially cut. **Middle** Grain when tangentially cut. **Bottom** Cross-section.

Source Throughout Europe

Working properties

Weight (per ft³)	46lb (21kg)
Durability	Perishable
Bendability	Moderate
Hardness	Medium
Sawing and shaping	Satisfactory
Splitting	Good
Gluing	Good

Properties of the wood

Pear wood is above average weight and slightly heavier than apple when dry. The heartwood is not considered to be durable and is best used internally. Drying pear can be difficult, producing a high level of warping if it is too rapid. Thicker stocks benefit from some predrying in thin stickers. Once the wood has reached a satisfactory moisture content it then remains fairly stable. Pear works fairly readily, but a reduced cutting angle when planing will help to avoid the irregular grain plucking out. Its adhesive properties are reasonably good. Easy to stain and polishes up to a fine finished surface.

Uses of the wood

The wood from pear trees is not commonly available. However, it can be used for a whole range of products from simple joinery through to fine cabinet work. It is good for musical instrument components. Pear is also a favorite with turners of small wooden items. It is sometimes used with apple, and occasionally plum, and termed "fruitwood."

Uses					Availability	Price
VENEER	PLYWOOD	FURNITURE	JOINERY	CONSTRUCTION		
✓		✓	✓		✓	◆◆

Top Grain when radially cut. **Middle** Grain when tangentially cut. **Bottom** Cross-section.

QUERCUS RUBRA and Q. FALCATA

American Red Oak

The common English name of this wood is **American Red Oak** and it is also known as **Northern Red**, **Southern Red**, **Spanish**, **Scarlet**, **Shumard**, **Pin**, **Nuttall**, **Black**, **Swamp Red**, **Cherrybark**, **Water**, **Laurel**, and **Willow Oak**.

Lumber for the commercial sales of American red oak is drawn from a number of different species. The trees are found throughout the eastern parts of North America. Old, mature trees can grow up to around 100ft (30m), but this is the exception rather than the rule. Bole lengths are not particularly long before branching. When freshly cut from the log, the heartwood has a distinct pinkish red/ reddish brown coloration. This fades away over time and can make it difficult to tell apart from other American oaks. The sapwood is distinct and a pale cream or gray color. As one would expect, the grain structure can vary considerably; it tends to be open with the growth rings apparent. Quarter-cut material does not have much figure due to the smaller ray structure.

Properties of the wood

The heartwood of red oak is not considered to be durable. Of average weight when dry, this wood can produce high levels of downgrade if care is not taken. The most common drying defects are surface checking, end splits, and honeycombing. The working properties of red oak are good, unless there have been problems in drying. Adhesive properties are average and, unless working near end grain, there should be no need to predrill for fixings. Staining, when required, usually yields satisfactory results and a good polished surface can be achieved with some work.

Uses of the wood

American red oak, with selection and care, can be used in similar applications to other oaks. The only major exception is cooperage, to which it is not suited. However, because it is not considered to be particularly durable, red oak is generally best used for internal purposes. These may include anything from basic construction work through to high quality furniture and cabinet work.

Source North America

Working properties

Weight (per ft³)	40lb (18kg)
Durability	Perishable
Bendability	Good
Hardness	Medium
Sawing and shaping	Satisfactory
Splitting	Average
Gluing	Take care

Uses					Availability	Price
VENEER	PLYWOOD	FURNITURE	JOINERY	CONSTRUCTION	✓✓✓	◆◆◆
✓	✓	✓	✓	✓		

QUERCUS ALBA

American White Oak

American White Oak has lots of other commonly used names, including **Northern White**, **Southern White**, **Chestnut**, **Post**, **Overcup**, **Bur**, **Chinkapin**, **True White**, **Swamp White**, **Swamp**, **Swamp Chestnut**, and **Live Oak**.

As is the case with red oak, the commercial production of white oak lumber comes from a number of species. In this case, *Q. alba* is probably the most important. White oak grows throughout the eastern parts of North America; distribution varies according to species. The trees are slightly shorter than red oaks, only reaching 82–90ft (25–27m) plus. With a fairly short bole before branching, long lumber lengths are rare. When freshly cut from the log, the heartwood is a pale, creamy color that darkens on exposure to a lighter brown. The sapwood is clearly distinct and can be quite wide. Like most temperate hardwoods, the grain is fairly open and coarse. Naturally, this does vary depending upon the area in which the tree has grown.

Top Grain when radially cut. **Middle** Grain when tangentially cut. **Bottom** Cross-section.

Source North America

Working properties

Weight (per ft³)	44lb (20kg)
Durability	Durable
Bendability	Good
Hardness	Medium
Sawing and shaping	Take care
Splitting	Poor
Gluing	Take care

Properties of the wood

White oak is considered to be durable. Because of the inclusion of high levels of tyloses, a foam-like structure found in the vessels, the heartwood resists preservative treatments. White oak is slightly heavier than red oak when dry. The drying process can be problematical if care is not taken. Typically, surface checking, end splitting, collapse, or honeycombing can occur. Some predrying of thicker stocks is recommended if possible. Predrilling is essential and nonferrous metals need to be used, in damp or wet conditions, to avoid the chemical reaction that leads to a dark staining. Adhesive properties are average. White oak takes a stain well and can produce a fine finished surface with care and some fillers.

Uses of the wood

White oak can be used both internally and externally for construction through to fine furniture and cabinet work. Its slightly harder nature also lends itself to use in both block and strip flooring. It is often employed in cooperage to make barrel staves.

Uses					Availability	Price
VENEER	PLYWOOD	FURNITURE	JOINERY	CONSTRUCTION		
✓	✓	✓	✓		✓✓	◆◆

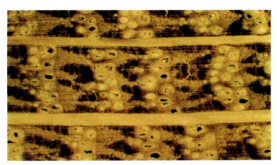

Top Grain when radially cut. **Middle** Grain when tangentially cut. **Bottom** Cross-section.

QUERCUS ROBUR and Q. PETRAEA
English Oak

English Oak is also sometimes known as **German**, **French**, and **European Oak**. Sometimes it is known in the United Kingdom as **Pendunculate**, **Durmast**, or **Sessile Oak**.

The two main species of oak identified above make up the majority of trees that grow throughout Europe, North Africa, and Asia Minor. European oak trees vary in height depending upon local growing conditions. On average they reach around 82ft (25m). Long bole lengths are not common, unless the trees are grown in managed forests. When freshly cut from the log, the wood gives off a fairly pleasant odor. The heartwood is a pale yellow straw-like color that darkens on exposure. The sapwood is lighter but often with no clear delineation. On occasions a partial or total darker brown color can be found in the heartwood. When present, this is selected out for use in furniture making. The grain is open and fairly coarse and, when cut on the quarter, displays high levels of figure.

Properties of the wood

Slightly heavier than average, when dry, this oak's heartwood is considered to be durable. Drying can be a lengthy and problematical process. To help avoid surface checking on thicker stocks, some predrying, on thin stickers, is recommended. Other drying defects include end splitting, distortion, and a fairly high risk of honeycombing and collapse. The working properties of European oak are good—it planes and molds well. With high levels of tannic acid naturally present in the wood, nonferrous fixings are essential if the typical dark blue/black staining that can occur is to be avoided. Predrilling is recommended when nailing and screwing. European oak stains well and will produce a fine finish when filled.

Uses of the wood

Traditionally, European oak has been used in structural building applications, externally for fencing, gates, and sidings. Its attractive figure results in extensive use for internal joinery, paneling, furniture, and cabinet work.

Source Throughout Europe

Working properties

Weight (per ft³)	44lb (20kg)
Durability	Durable
Bendability	Good
Hardness	Hard
Sawing and shaping	Satisfactory
Splitting	Poor
Gluing	Good

Uses					Availability	Price
VENEER	**PLYWOOD**	**FURNITURE**	**JOINERY**	**CONSTRUCTION**	✓✓	◆◆
✓		✓	✓	✓		

SHOREA SPP.

Dark Red Lauan, Meranti, and Seraya

This hardwood has several common English names, the most popular being **Dark Red Lauan**, **Meranti**, and **Seraya**.

The trees of the Shorea species grow throughout the countries of South-East Asia. Most commonly they are drawn together in commercial lots and marketed as dark red, light red, yellow, and white, followed by one of the colloquial names above. All are readily available, but the dark red grouping is probably best known. Depending upon habitat and local growing conditions, these trees can reach heights of over 210–230ft (65–70m) tall. Long, clear, straight boles are harvested up to 100ft (30m). The heartwood has a slightly reddish brown hue when first cut, which can vary depending upon local conditions. The sapwood is lighter in color and poorly defined. The grain is often rather boring, consistent, and uniform with partial interlocking. Some lighter inclusions of minerals or resins can provide a bit of character to this wood.

Top Grain when radially cut. **Middle** Grain when tangentially cut. **Bottom** Cross-section.

Source South-East Asia

Working properties

Weight (per ft³)	40lb (18kg)
Durability	Moderately durable
Bendability	Moderate
Hardness	Medium
Sawing and shaping	Satisfactory
Splitting	Average
Gluing	Good

Properties of the wood

Dark red shoreas are about average weight when dry. The heartwood is considered to be moderately durable. It is susceptible to attack by wood borers at source. This can be classed as pin hole —small clusters of holes about one millimeter in diameter—or shot hole, wider-spaced two or three millimeter-diameter holes. Distortion does occur during the drying process and there may also be some surface checking and end splitting in thicker lumber. All the dark red shoreas work reasonably well. Care needs to be taken with interlocked grain material to avoid a fluffy surface when planing. It has good adhesive properties and, with fillers, can produce a satisfactory finished surface.

Uses of the wood

This wood is used extensively on a local and export basis. The logs are peeled for plywood production and it is strong enough for light construction work. It is used for volume production of joinery, store and interior fittings. Its rather plain nature enables it to be stained to resemble other timbers.

Uses					Availability	Price
VENEER	PLYWOOD	FURNITURE	JOINERY	CONSTRUCTION		
	✓		✓	✓	✓✓✓	◆◆

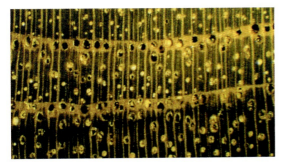

Top Grain when radially cut. **Middle** Grain when tangentially cut. **Bottom** Cross-section.

TECTONA GRANDIS

Teak

The common name—which is used internationally—is **Teak**. Wood from the Teak tree is probably one of the best known worldwide. It is found growing naturally throughout India, the Indo-China region, and now on through into South-East Asia. Commercial quantities of teak were sourced from Thailand originally, until logged out. During the last century, Indonesia has established sustainable teak plantations from where most of today's commercial lumber comes. The teak tree can stand up to around 150ft (45m). Old growth trees have shorter, clear boles while the plantation grown material would normally be harvested at a length of around 33ft (10m) or more. When freshly cut, the wood gives off a musky smell that diminishes but does not disappear. The heartwood is slightly greenish brown initially, with darker streaks. This all darkens down to a uniform golden brown over time. The sapwood is clearly distinct and is creamy white. This is a ring porous wood that has an open, straight grain.

Properties of the wood

Teak wood, when dry, is of average weight and density. The heartwood is considered to be very durable and resistant to attack by insects or fungi. Drying can be slow and moisture pockets can be found in thicker material. There is usually little or no downgrade produced in this process. The natural oils, providing the musky aroma associated with this wood, can make working the wood difficult. In most cases, tungsten carbide-tipped tools are highly recommended, to avoid losing a cutting edge too quickly. Adhesion is also affected by the oils. A light wipe over with turpentine prior to gluing is thought to help. Preboring is useful for fixing, and staining and polishing are satisfactory.

Uses of the wood

This is one of the most versatile woods available. Its natural properties lend themselves to a mass of end uses. Most commonly deployed in both interior and exterior furniture, it can also be utilized for anything associated with boatbuilding, joinery, flooring, decorative veneers, and such like.

Source India, Myanmar, and South-East Asia

Working properties

Weight (per ft³)	40lb (18kg)
Durability	Very durable
Bendability	Moderate
Hardness	Hard
Sawing and shaping	Take care
Splitting	Poor
Gluing	Take care

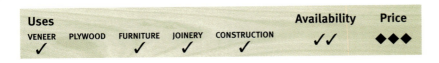

Uses					Availability	Price
VENEER	PLYWOOD	FURNITURE	JOINERY	CONSTRUCTION	✓✓	◆◆◆
✓	✓	✓	✓	✓		

TERMINALIA IVORENSIS

Idigbo

The common English name of this wood is **Idigbo** and it is also known as **Emeri** or **Framire** and a range of other vernacular names such as **Emil**, **Frayomile**, **Mboti**, **Bona**, **Cauri**, **Okpoha**, **Onhidgo**, **Ubir**, and so on.

This is an African tree found predominantly in the west. It is a fairly tall tree, reaching heights of up to 150ft (45m). It produces clear boles of 66ft (20m) or more. When freshly sawn from the log, the heartwood and sapwood, which is barely discernible, is a yellowish, light straw color with, on occasions, some pinker hues. The grain is fairly coarse in texture and can be shallowly interlocked. A distinct and prominent growth ring structure tends to give the wood a similar appearance to oak figuring. Idigbo contains a dye that, under wet conditions, will leach out and stain any surrounding areas a dark yellow. This chemical dye also reacts with ferrous metals if the wood is damp or wet. A black streaking or staining can cause significant disfiguration to the adjacent surfaces.

Top Grain when radially cut. **Middle** Grain when tangentially cut. **Bottom** Cross-section.

Source   West Africa

Working properties

Weight (per ft³)	37lb (17kg)
Durability	Durable
Bendability	Poor
Hardness	Medium
Sawing and shaping	Satisfactory
Splitting	Poor
Gluing	Good

Properties of the wood

Although only a medium weight wood, idigbo is considered to be naturally durable and should, under most conditions, not need to be treated with preservatives. However, it is not particularly strong and brittle heart can be a problem; these are shakes across the grain of the wood. On this basis, idigbo should not be used for structural purposes without careful inspection. Once dry, and there is generally little degrade in this process, idigbo is also very stable. It saws and planes fairly well with only slight surface plucking where interlocking grain is prevalent. It has good adhesion properties and, unless working close to end grain, should not need predrilling. A good finished surface can be achieved, but it can bruise fairly easily, due to its softer nature.

Uses of the wood

Idigbo has often been overlooked as a useful, commercial timber. Its properties lend themselves for use in both internal and external joinery, paneling, and furniture. As a replacement, it is a cheaper alternative to oak, due to the vaguely similar grain pattern.

Uses					Availability	Price
VENEER	PLYWOOD	FURNITURE	JOINERY	CONSTRUCTION		
✓	✓	✓	✓		✓✓	◆◆

Top Grain when radially cut. **Middle** Grain when tangentially cut. **Bottom** Cross-section.

TIEGHEMELLA HECKELII
Makore

Makore is also known as **Agamokwe**, **Baku**, **Abaku**, **African Cherry**, or **Cherry Mahogany**.

This is another West African hardwood that can grow to heights in excess of 130ft (40m). Boles are generally long, clean, and free of buttress, producing long lumber if required. When freshly cut from the log, the heartwood varies from a reddish brown through to a deeper purple brown. Makore has a natural luster, probably caused by the inclusion of silica, and the sapwood is clearly defined, being a creamy or pale yellow color. The grain is generally straight, with some wood showing signs of figure. This is likely to be a fine wavy or checkerboard effect with, occasionally, some darker streaks of color. Care needs to be taken when working this wood. The fine dust produced when sawing and planing this wood can cause irritation to the eyes, nose, and throat. In some cases it can cause or exacerbate other symptoms of ill health. Consequently, good extraction and protection are essential.

Properties of the wood

Makore is slightly above average in weight when dry. The drying process can take time, but no high levels of downgrade materials are reported. The heartwood is considered to be very durable and is extremely resistant to treatment with preservatives. Both sawing and planing can be difficult and all tools will need their edges regularly maintained. The silica content of this very hard wood quickly dulls the edges of all cutting and planing tools. Predrilling is recommended to avoid splitting, especially toward the ends of components.

Makore does have good adhesive properties and stains reasonably well. An excellent surface finish can be achieved with care.

Uses of the wood

This is a slightly heavy wood that is stable once dry. If the issues associated with the adverse health effects are ignored, makore can be used for a variety of end products. These include boatbuilding and marine uses, plywood manufacture, flooring, and cabinet work. This wood is more inexpensive than some options.

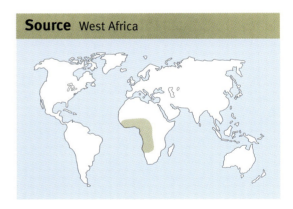

Source West Africa

Working properties

Weight (per ft³)	42lb (19kg)
Durability	Very durable
Bendability	Poor
Hardness	Hard
Sawing and shaping	Take care
Splitting	Poor
Gluing	Good

Uses					Availability	Price
VENEER	PLYWOOD	FURNITURE	JOINERY	CONSTRUCTION	✓✓	◆◆
	✓	✓	✓			

97

TILLIA AMERICANA

Basswood

The north American hardwood **Basswood** is also known as **Whitewood**, **Linden**, **American Linn**, or **American Lime** in the United Kingdom.

The Basswood tree occasionally grows to around 100ft (30m) tall but more commonly only reaches around the 66ft (20m) mark. With a high canopy, the boles can be straight and clear of branches for some length. The appearance of the wood is similar to lime, hence the use in the United Kingdom of the common name American lime. The creamy white sapwood merges into the light brown heartwood, which can feature some darker streaks. The grain is not distinct but fairly close. When freshly cut, a pleasant aroma comes off the wood; this dissipates over time. The lumber from this tree should not be confused with tulipwood (see page 68), another North American hardwood, and the tropical timber sesendok, both of which go under the vernacular name of basswood.

Top Grain when radially cut. **Middle** Grain when tangentially cut. **Bottom** Cross-section.

Source   North America

Working properties

Weight (per ft³)	24lb (11kg)
Durability	Perishable
Bendability	Poor
Hardness	Soft
Sawing and shaping	Satisfactory
Splitting	Good
Gluing	Good

Properties of the wood

Fairly light in weight, basswood dries readily with little or no movement and remains stable in use. It is classed as a nondurable timber, which is not often used in external applications. However, if preservative treatment is applied, it takes this easily and can be protected sufficiently for some outdoor uses. Basswood can be sawn and planed reasonably well and the close grain lends itself to certain end uses. Basswood will take stain and finishes easily. It has good adhesion properties and should not need predrilling.

Uses of the wood

Because it has similar properties to lime, a light, close-grained timber, basswood is often employed for pattern making and carving. This wood is popular with wood turners, as it turns well. Consequently, it is often used in craft related areas. Alternative uses are fairly diverse. For example, it has been cut for piano keys, small tool handles, plywood, moldings, and picture framing materials. Its lack of odor (after a period of time) means that it is often used in food containers and preparation boards.

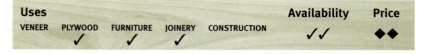

Uses					Availability	Price
VENEER	PLYWOOD	FURNITURE	JOINERY	CONSTRUCTION		
	✓	✓	✓		✓✓	◆◆

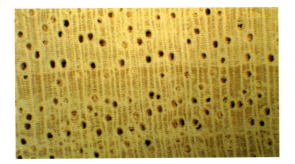

Top Grain when radially cut. **Middle** Grain when tangentially cut. **Bottom** Cross-section.

TRIPLOCHITON SCLEROXYLON

Obeche

Obeche is also known as **Wawa, Samba, Samba-ayous, Ayous, Arere, African Whitewood, Ewowo, Egin-fifen, Okpo,** and **Obechi.** Of these other names the most commonly found is Wawa. Obeche is an African timber found in many tropical forests. Although widespread, most of the commercial lumber produced comes from the western Africa region. The tree is one of the largest in the world, growing up to 200ft (60m) or more tall. The larger examples can have clear boles starting above buttresses at around 3ft (1m) in diameter, or more. The sapwood, which is wide, is hardly discernible from the heartwood, and is a light straw to creamy white wood when freshly cut from the log. Obeche lumber darkens slightly after exposure. The grain of this wood is fairly open, usually even and slightly interlocked. Quarter-sawn faces can show an attractive, fairly apparent striping. As a lightweight, fairly soft wood, obeche is easily worked with tools.

Properties of the wood

As a light-colored wood, obeche benefits from stacking on stickers as soon as it is cut from the log. If left close-stacked, there is a high possibility that surface staining or fungal attack will occur. This is a lightweight wood which dries easily and rapidly without significant shrinkage or distortion. Obeche is not rated as durable and external use should be avoided. Its strength-to-weight ratio is good, but obeche is not suitable for structural purposes. Although resistant to impact, the wood splits easily and cross-shakes are often apparent.

Some crumbling may occur near end grain and care needs to be taken to ensure cutting edges are sharp. It has good adhesive properties, with the joints more likely to hold than the wood itself.

Uses of the wood

Uses are fairly limited. However, because it takes stain well and is easily polished, it is often used as a substitute for more expensive timbers such as mahogany. Most commonly it is used as a foundation wood for veneering onto or as a core in plywood manufacture.

Source Predominantly West Africa

Working properties

Weight (per ft³)	24lb (11kg)
Durability	Perishable
Bendability	Moderate
Hardness	Soft
Sawing and shaping	Satisfactory
Splitting	Average
Gluing	Good

Uses					Availability	Price
VENEER	PLYWOOD	FURNITURE	JOINERY	CONSTRUCTION	✓✓	◆◆
	✓	✓				

ULMUS RUBRA and U. PROCERA

American and European Elm

Top Grain when radially cut. **Middle** Grain when tangentially cut. **Bottom** Cross-section.

The common English names are **American** and **European Elm** and it is also known as **Red** or **Nave Elm** in Europe and **Red**, **Brown**, **Slippery**, **Rock**, **American**, **Winged**, **Cedar**, and **September Elm** in North America.

Elm trees are readily found throughout North America and northern Europe. In parts of Europe, Dutch elm disease has devastated woodlands and forests in recent years, hence the collective approach to this review. Trees vary in size and shape, depending upon species. European elm can reach heights of 150ft (45m). Clear bole lengths are likely to be much shorter and, including North American elm, does not produce a great deal of long lumber lengths. The heartwood of commercially available elm tends to vary from a dull reddish brown through to a darker, brighter coloring. The sapwood is clearly visible and much softer in nature. The grain is open, coarse, and uneven, showing definite signs of interlocking.

Source   Northern Europe and North America

Working properties

Weight (per ft³)	40lb (18kg)
Durability	Perishable
Bendability	Good
Hardness	Medium
Sawing and shaping	Take care
Splitting	Good
Gluing	Good

Properties of the wood

A medium to light wood, elm is not considered to be durable and should be preservative-treated if used externally. The prevalence of interlocking grain tends to make the drying process interesting. Its lightness enables this to be fairly rapid, but a high level of distortion can result. Weighing down stacks of lumber while this process is followed sometimes helps. Working elm is generally reasonable, but the grain configuration, especially with dry lumber, can cause some saw binding. This is because the grain is extremely variable, which makes it one of the attractive features of this wood. A little care needs to be taken when planing to produce a good finished surface. Adhesion is good, and the grain helps stop end splitting when nailing or screwing.

Uses of the wood

Historical uses have been many. However, elm tends to be employed for furniture and show wood items such as paneling, flooring, internal joinery, and cabinet work, where its attractive grain can be appreciated.

Uses					Availability	Price
VENEER	PLYWOOD	FURNITURE	JOINERY	CONSTRUCTION		
✓		✓	✓		✓✓	◆◆

ALBIES ALBA

Whitewood

The widely available European softwood called **Whitewood** is also known as **Silver Fir** or **European Silver Pine** and, as whitewood, can be prefixed with the country of source.

This softwood is a true fir, and the species grows naturally throughout Europe; it is one of the trees that is often grown in plantation forests. The profile of the growing tree is somewhat like an open-branched, slightly pointed oval shape. Trees grow to heights of around 150ft (45m) under favorable conditions. Under careful management, the boles will be straight and free of branches to a reasonable height and, when felled, cut to regular lengths. There is very little difference between the heartwood and sapwood coloration. The wood is a pale creamy white with some light brown/orangey markings that reflect the difference between the early and latewood. The quality of the grain will depend on local growing conditions. When converted the lumber is graded into various general end use groupings.

Top Grain when radially cut. **Middle** Grain when tangentially cut. **Bottom** Cross-section.

Source Throughout Europe

Working properties

Weight (per ft³)	29lb (13kg)
Durability	Perishable
Bendability	Poor
Hardness	Medium
Sawing and shaping	Satisfactory
Splitting	Good
Gluing	Good

Properties of the wood

This is a light wood when dry that is not considered to be durable. Appropriate preservative treatments should be applied if it is to be used externally. It is not always artificially dried; this depends upon end use. However, when kiln drying whitewood, it can dry quickly with some warping, splitting, and shrinkage around knots. It works reasonably well, but needs sharp tools to maintain a good finish. Some break-out will occur around live knots and dead knots will often lose large chunks. Whitewood takes fixings well, has good adhesive properties and is often painted.

Uses of the wood

This whitewood has a wide range of uses. Poorer quality materials are selected for packing cases and pallets while the better wood is used for internal joinery. It is often sold for paper and pulp production and peeled for plywood manufacture. It is often mixed with European spruce and in this form is used for moldings, carcass work, telegraph poles, and turpentine.

Uses					Availability	Price
VENEER	PLYWOOD	FURNITURE	JOINERY	CONSTRUCTION		
	✓		✓		✓✓✓	◆

Top Grain when radially cut. **Middle** Grain when tangentially cut. **Bottom** Cross-section.

CEDRUS SPP.

Cedar of Lebanon

The common English name is **Cedar of Lebanon** and it is also known as **Cedar**, **Deodar**, **Atlantic**, or **Atlas Cedar**.

True cedar trees are found naturally growing through North Africa, the Middle East, through to India. *C. deodar* is commonly called *Deodar*, *C. atlantica* is called Atlantic or Atlas Cedar, and *C. libani* is called Cedar of Lebanon. The outline of the growing trees is an open, drooping-branched, conical shape. The wood from these three cedars is very similar and has been reviewed here as one. Although there is some distinct height variation between the species, and local conditions, the trees can grow, on average, to around 150ft (40m) or more. Often heavily branched, the boles are tapered. Harvested lumber is not likely to be long, and when freshly cut from the log gives off a strong, easily recognized, scent. The heartwood is a light brown and distinct from the paler sapwood. The difference between the early and latewood provides clear growth rings and the fairly fine grain is mainly straight.

Properties of the wood

Of lighter than average weight when dry, the heartwood of cedar is considered to be durable. The wood dries fairly quickly, but some care needs to be taken to avoid high levels of distortion. Working properties are reasonable; however, tools need to be sharp to avoid saws binding and some plucking out around knots. Cedar takes fixings well, but it is advisable to predrill closer to end grain. Adhesive properties are good and, depending upon the finish required, surfaces can be brought up to a reasonable quality.

Uses of the wood

These true cedars are not often available in large commercial quantities. At source they are used for structural and constructional purposes, such as in railroad ties, bridges, and houses, due to their reputation for toughness and longevity. Outside the countries of origin, most park-grown material will be knotty and suitable as a utility type of timber. Clearer-grained wood is suitable for joinery and molding work, in which cedar can be very decorative, at its best. Occasionally veneers are available.

Source North Africa, Middle East, and India

Working properties

Weight (per ft³)	35lb (16kg)
Durability	Durable
Bendability	Poor
Hardness	Medium
Sawing and shaping	Take care
Splitting	Good
Gluing	Good

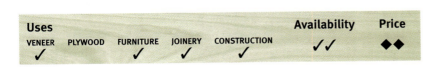

Uses					Availability	Price
VENEER	PLYWOOD	FURNITURE	JOINERY	CONSTRUCTION	✓✓	◆◆
✓		✓	✓	✓		

103

LARIX DECIDUA

Larch

This softwood is known both as **Larch** and **European Larch**. The Larch tree grows throughout Europe. It is one of the few softwood trees that is deciduous, shedding its needles in the fall. New, tender green growth sprouts in the spring. The overall appearance of the tree is conical with open branching. It can be quite tall, reaching heights of 150ft (45m). Depending upon age, growing conditions and management, branching can occur close to the ground or fairly high up the trunk. Trees which have not been managed will probably be fairly knotty. When harvested, the timber is cut into regular lengths. When converted to lumber, the heartwood is resinous and displays clear distinctions between the lighter-colored earlywood and the darker latewood. These growth rings are fairly wide and vary in color from a light to dark reddish brown. The sapwood is distinct and a paler color. In growth the trunks can spiral, producing a distorted grain.

Top Grain when radially cut. **Middle** Grain when tangentially cut. **Bottom** Cross-section.

Source   Throughout Europe

Working properties

Weight (per ft³)	35lb (16kg)
Durability	Moderately durable
Bendability	Poor
Hardness	Hard
Sawing and shaping	Take care
Splitting	Poor
Gluing	Good

Properties of the wood

Larch is one of the heavier and stronger softwoods that is commercially available. The wood is moderately durable, but should be treated with preservatives if used anywhere near ground level or in damp and wet conditions. It dries fairly rapidly when required, but will produce fairly high levels of waste from distorted boards, splitting around knots, and dead knot drop out. There is often significant shrinkage as well. Working the wood needs sharp tools and resins can build up quickly. Any wood with spiral grain can be difficult to saw and plane. Green wood is fairly easy to nail and screw, but dry wood will easily split, especially near end grain. In the unlikely event that the wood is to be polished or painted, some serious sealing will be required to stop the resins leaching through.

Uses of the wood

This wood is most likely to be used for external purposes. These range from simple fencing materials through joinery to weather boarding on buildings. It has traditionally been used as planking on wooden boats.

Uses					Availability	Price
VENEER	PLYWOOD	FURNITURE	JOINERY	CONSTRUCTION ✓	✓✓✓	◆

Top Grain when radially cut. **Middle** Grain when tangentially cut. **Bottom** Cross-section.

PICEA ABIES

Spruce

Spruce is also known as **White Deal**, **Norway** or **Common Spruce** and commercially as **Whitewood**, prefixed by **Baltic**, **Russian**, **Finnish**, and so on, according to origin.

This spruce comes from throughout Europe and the lumber produced is often mixed with other species and marketed as whitewood. It should not be confused with the American sitka spruce, *P. sitchensis*. The spruce tree is now one of the most popular plantation softwoods grown. The tree has a similar shape to larch, but with tighter branching. Young trees are harvested for sale as Christmas trees. It can grow up to around 150ft (45m) under favorable conditions. Branching occurs right up the trunk and is best cut back if better quality wood is to be produced. Spruce wood is a creamy white with little or no differentiation between the heart and sapwood. There is some slight color variation between the early and latewood. Knots tend to stand out against this pale background. The grain is often fine and straight.

Properties of the wood

Another lightweight wood, spruce is not considered to be durable. Drying the wood can be difficult. There is a fairly high level of shrinkage and distortion, especially in trees with spiral grain apparent. Surface checking and splitting can occur. Working the wood is reasonable, at least when it is free of knots. If sharp tools are used, planed and molded surfaces are normally ready to be painted as soon as they come off the machines. Staining on this wood can be patchy. Adhesion is good. Some pretreatment of resinous areas will be required if the wood is to be painted or varnished.

Uses of the wood

Poor quality material may be selected out for pulping, pallets, case-making, or carcasing. Better quality wood is used for a whole range of joinery products, including storefitting and moldings, etc. Top-quality timber grown in northern climes has a tighter grain, which is sought after for use in some musical instrument manufacture.

Source UK and throughout Europe

Working properties

Weight (per ft³)	29lb (13kg)
Durability	Perishable
Bendability	Moderate
Hardness	Medium
Sawing and shaping	Satisfactory
Splitting	Average
Gluing	Good

Uses					Availability	Price
VENEER	PLYWOOD	FURNITURE	JOINERY	CONSTRUCTION	✓✓✓	◆
	✓		✓			

PINUS PALUSTRIS, P. ELLIOTTII, *and P. CARIBAEA* Pitch Pine

The common English name of this softwood is **Pitch Pine** and the most familiar in this group are *P. palustris*, **Longleaf Pine**, and *P. elliottii*, **Slash Pine**. Also commercially available is *P. caribaea*, **Caribbean Pitch Pine.**

Within the different species identified above the most commonly available is probably *P. palustris*. The outline of the tree is rounded and open branched. They grow throughout the top half of South America, through Central America and up into North America. These are not tall trees, only reaching about 100ft (30m) high. Half of this can be clear and free from branching. When freshly cut the wood gives off a resinous odor that diminishes but remains with it. The growth rings are clearly defined. The lighter earlywood is a pale yellow brown and the latewood is a much darker, reddish brown. This contrast in colors can be an attractive feature. The sapwood is paler and is not clearly differentiated from the heartwood.

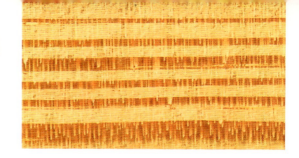

Top Grain when radially cut. **Middle** Grain when tangentially cut. **Bottom** Cross-section.

Source North, Central, and South America

Working properties

Weight (per ft³)	42lb (19kg)
Durability	Moderately durable
Bendability	Poor
Hardness	Hard
Sawing and shaping	Take care
Splitting	Average
Gluing	Take care

Properties of the wood

Of all the pine groupings, pitch pine is the hardest and heaviest; however, it is only considered to be moderately durable. Drying thicker lumber may be problematical, with surface checking an unfortunate feature. Due to the highly resinous nature of the wood, this can easily clog up saws and cutters when being worked. If tools are kept sharp, the process can be reasonably smooth. When fixing, some predrilling is recommended. The adhesive properties of this wood might be affected by the high resin content. Pitch pine will need sealing thoroughly before a satisfactory surface finish can be achieved.

Uses of the wood

At source, pitch pine is used for construction in both structural and nonstructural applications. It is often used in boatbuilding above deck and its hard-wearing properties make it a useful flooring material for both domestic and commercial use. Historically, it was used to make church and school furniture.

Uses					Availability	Price
VENEER	PLYWOOD	FURNITURE	JOINERY	CONSTRUCTION		
		✓	✓	✓	✓✓✓	◆

Top Grain when radially cut. **Middle** Grain when tangentially cut. **Bottom** Cross-section.

PINUS STROBUS, P. MONTICOLA, and P. LAMBERTIANA Yellow or White Pine

The generic common English names are **Yellow** or **White Pine** and the most familiar in this group is *P. strobus*, **Yellow Pine**. *P. monticola* is known as **Western White Pine** or **Idaho Pine**. *P. lambertiana* is known as **Sugar Pine** or **California Sugar Pine**.

This grouping of pines grows throughout the central band of North America, but is more prolific in the eastern states and along the eastern seaboard. The trees have a slightly conical outline and, as pines, can be very tall, reaching heights of up to 150ft (45m). The average height is probably about two thirds of this. Boles can be free of branching for 33ft (10m) or more. When cut, the sapwood is slightly discernible from the heartwood. The earlywood is a pale yellowish brown and the latewood a slightly darker straw brown; there is no striking difference between them. Resin pockets and canals are often clearly seen on sawn surfaces. The grain of this wood is soft, fairly straight, and even.

Properties of the wood

Yellow pine is at the opposite end of the spectrum from pitch pine, at about half its weight. The wood is not durable. It dries fairly rapidly and evenly with little or no distortion, but some care needs to be taken to avoid sticker staining. It is stable once dry. The wood works well, as one would expect, given its softness—sharp tools will give an excellent finish. No predrilling is required for fixings and its adhesive properties are good. On show wood faces, care needs to be taken to avoid resin exudations, which will spoil the look of the wood. Final polished surfaces can easily be dented.

Uses of the wood

Due to its stability, once it has been dried yellow pine has traditionally been used for pattern-making. Its lack of durability and softer nature determine mainly interior end use. In furniture and cabinet work it is usually a secondary wood, often being used in items like window blinds and paneling. It also has uses in musical instrument components, moldings, and light joinery products.

Source Predominantly North America

Working properties

Weight (per ft³)	24lb (11kg)
Durability	Perishable
Bendability	Poor
Hardness	Soft
Sawing and shaping	Satisfactory
Splitting	Poor
Gluing	Good

Uses					Availability	Price
VENEER	PLYWOOD	FURNITURE	JOINERY	CONSTRUCTION	✓✓✓	◆
		✓	✓			

PINUS SYLVESTRIS

Redwood

Redwood is also known as **Scots Pine**, but is generally marketed and sold as **European Redwood**, with this generic name often prefixed with the wood's country of origin.

Of all the pines commercially available, this is the most common and prolifically used softwood. It grows throughout Europe and has been successfully introduced worldwide. The Scots Pine tree, from which the redwood lumber is cut, has a slightly rounded profile with open layers of branches. Depending upon local growing and management conditions, the trees can reach heights of up to 150ft (45m). The boles are usually free of branching for maybe half of this. When cut, there is clearly a difference in color between the early and latewood. The former is a light brown and the latter a darker, reddish brown. There can be some marked differences in how tight or open the growth rings are. The sapwood is apparent. The grain can be fairly even, resinous and both live and dead knots can show on all faces.

Top Grain when radially cut. **Middle** Grain when tangentially cut. **Bottom** Cross-section.

Source UK and throughout Europe

Working properties

Weight (per ft³)	33lb (15kg)
Durability	Moderately durable
Bendability	Moderate
Hardness	Medium
Sawing and shaping	Satisfactory
Splitting	Average
Gluing	Good

Properties of the wood

Redwood weighs in about halfway between pitch and yellow pine. It is not considered to be a durable wood and therefore should be treated with preservatives for external use. There is a tendency for the wood to be attacked by a blue-staining fungi when it is wet. Some dipping or spraying with an appropriate antistain solution is therefore recommended. Alternatively, the wood should be dried as quickly as possible. Drying can be rapid and produces little downgrade if care is taken. Redwood has excellent working properties, provided tools are sharp and any resin build up is carefully removed. It takes fixings well, can be stained without difficulty and produces a satisfactory surface finish.

Uses of the wood

Redwood is extensively used in joinery, for moldings, turnings, and all kinds of constructional work. It is often peeled and used as plywood faces and cores. In fact, there are not many applications for which this wood cannot be used.

Uses					Availability	Price
VENEER	PLYWOOD	FURNITURE	JOINERY	CONSTRUCTION		
			✓	✓	✓✓✓	◆

Top Grain when radially cut. **Middle** Grain when tangentially cut. **Bottom** Cross-section.

PSEUDOTSUGA MENZIESII

Douglas Fir

Douglas Fir has a range of other common names, including **Columbian** or **British Columbian Pine** and **Oregon Pine**, **Red** and **Yellow Fir** and **Douglas Spruce**.

Douglas Fir is indigenous to North America. Although called fir, and often pine, it is a different species. For many years it has been successfully grown worldwide in both managed conditions and as a park or garden tree. The profile of the tree is conical and slightly open branched. In old growth forests, Douglas Fir can reach heights of up to 200ft (60m). Well over half the bole will usually be clear and free of branches and the lumber produced can be free of knots. When cut, there is only a slightly discernible difference between the heartwood and sapwood, which is slightly lighter. The growth rings are clearly apparent, with the earlywood a light brown and the latewood a darker, orangey brown. When cut on the quarter this produces a straight, stripy grain. This is a resinous wood and can have some ducts and pockets visible on surfaces.

Properties of the wood

This wood is slightly heavier and stronger than redwood and is considered to be moderately durable. Although it dries without too much downgrade, thicker lumber benefits from some predrying to help avoid surface checking. Shrinkage is not significant, but there can be some subsequent movement in situ. Working Douglas fir requires sharp tools. They can be dulled fairly rapidly and resinous build-ups need to be avoided. The wood has a tendency to split and therefore predrilling for all fixings is recommended. Douglas fir has fairly good adhesive properties and can be brought up to a satisfactory finished surface.

Uses of the wood

Douglas fir has an established market for top-quality internal and external joinery, moldings, and paneling. It is straight, free of knots, and the grain lends itself to use in structural applications. The wood is often laminated into beams and peeled for plywood manufacture. Some material can be used successfully for flooring.

Source North America

Working properties

Weight (per ft³)	35lb (16kg)
Durability	Moderately durable
Bendability	Poor
Hardness	Medium
Sawing and shaping	Satisfactory
Splitting	Poor
Gluing	Good

Uses					Availability	Price
VENEER	PLYWOOD	FURNITURE	JOINERY	CONSTRUCTION	✓✓✓	◆
✓	✓	✓	✓	✓		

SEQUOIA SEMPERVIRENS

Californian Redwood

This famous softwood is known as **Californian Redwood** and is also referred to as **Sequoia**, **Redwood**, or **Coast Redwood**.

This is a large, extremely tall tree in its natural habitat, which is the western seaboard of America. Californian redwood has been successfully grown elsewhere in the world as a decorative parkland tree. It can obtain heights of up to 300ft (90m) or more. The Californian redwood tree has a slightly elongated oval, open branched profile, with a distinctly tapering bole. Boles can be free of knots for about one third of the height of the tree. Felling these trees is controlled and only limited commercial quantities become available annually. It has a thick bark, which is recovered and used in the production of filters and fiber boards. When cut from the log, the wood itself is fairly straight-grained, with some distinction between the early and latewood. These range from a light brown to a darker, reddish or purple brown. The sapwood is distinct and an off-white color. There is no evidence of resin.

Top Grain when radially cut. **Middle** Grain when tangentially cut. **Bottom** Cross-section.

Source Western North America

Working properties

Weight (per ft³)	26lb (12kg)
Durability	Durable
Bendability	Poor
Hardness	Soft
Sawing and shaping	Take care
Splitting	Poor
Gluing	Take care

Properties of the wood

Although this is a lightweight, not particularly strong wood, the heartwood is considered to be durable. Drying Californian redwood is relatively easy, with end splitting being the only major problem if handled with care. Once dry, it is fairly stable in use. Sharp tooling is required to ensure ease of sawing and planing. Some binding may occur on saws and chip bruising of planed surfaces will happen if the waste is not cleanly removed. With its tendency to split, predrilling for fixings is highly recommended. The adhesive properties of this wood are not good and some glues will stain the surfaces adjacent to joints. A satisfactory finished surface can be achieved, but it does dent rather easily.

Uses of the wood

The natural durability of Californian redwood lends itself to lightweight uses in which this property is a distinct benefit. Consequently, it is often used for both external and internal joinery, paneling, door and window manufacturing.

Uses					Availability	Price
VENEER	PLYWOOD	FURNITURE	JOINERY ✓	CONSTRUCTION	✓	◆◆

Top Grain when radially cut. **Middle** Grain when tangentially cut. **Bottom** Cross-section.

TAXUS BACCATA

Yew

The common English name of this popular softwood is **Yew** and it is also known as **English**, **Irish**, **European**, or **Common Yew**.

Yew trees grow naturally throughout Europe, North Africa, the Middle East, and on into India. It is now recognized that there may be some varieties within the species. For example, English yew tends to have a short bole with a rounded, slightly pointed canopy, in which the branches grow more horizontally. Irish yew has an oval profile in which the branches generally grow vertically. However, the wood from both, when it is available, is of a very similar nature. Because the trees are not often tall or wide the lumber produced is generally short and narrow. Irregular growth patterns lend themselves to the attractive color variations in the heartwood growth rings. This can vary from a bright orangey yellow through to a dark purple brown. The sapwood is clearly distinct and an off-white, cream color. The grain is often interlocked and wavy. It is fine and tight giving a smooth feel to the finish.

Properties of the wood

Yew is just above average weight when dry. The heartwood is considered to be durable. Drying yew is often not as traumatic as it might first appear. It dries rapidly with little distortion and only some extension of existing splits. The conditions of growth may affect the levels of downgrade. Working with yew requires sharp tools. If interlocking grain is prevalent, there could be some binding on saws and chipping out of planed surfaces. Predrilling for fixings is essential and a wipe over with mineral spirits some time before gluing will help with adhesion. Due to the fine-grained nature of the wood, a fine finished surface can be achieved.

Uses of the wood

Yew can be a very attractive wood to work with. Lumber and burrs can be sliced to produce extremely decorative veneers. The smaller sizes tend to see the wood used for craft-orientated products, because it turns and carves well. Some solid woods are used in smaller cabinet work and yew was traditionally used to make English longbows.

Source Europe, North Africa, and into Asia

Working properties

Weight (per ft³)	42lb (19kg)
Durability	Durable
Bendability	Good
Hardness	Hard
Sawing and shaping	Take care
Splitting	Poor
Gluing	Take care

Uses					Availability	Price
VENEER	PLYWOOD	FURNITURE	JOINERY	CONSTRUCTION		
✓		✓			✓	◆◆

THUJA PLICATA
Western Red Cedar

This widely available American softwood is called **Western Red Cedar** and is also known as **Giant Arborvitae**, **British Columbia Red Cedar**, and **Red Cedar**.

Western red cedar trees naturally grow throughout the central band of North America and have been successfully introduced to other countries worldwide. In the latter case this is both for commercial use and, in parklands and so on, for decorative use. The profile of the tree is conical with a slight resemblance to an arrowhead. In its natural habitat, this is a tall tree, reaching heights of at least 250ft (75m). Wide boles can be free of branching for up to one third of this height. When freshly cut from the log, the wood gives off a distinctive and pleasant peppery/spicy odor. The growth rings are apparent, with some color variation between early and latewood. This ranges from a pinkish straw brown to a slightly darker reddish brown. The sapwood is clearly distinct and an off-white color.

Top Grain when radially cut. **Middle** Grain when tangentially cut. **Bottom** Cross-section.

Source North America

Working properties

Weight (per ft³)	22lb (10kg)
Durability	Durable
Bendability	Poor
Hardness	Soft
Sawing and shaping	Satisfactory
Splitting	Average
Gluing	Good

Properties of the wood

This is probably one of the lightest, commercially available softwoods when dry. The drying process is fairly rapid and uneventful for thinner stocks, but not so easy with thicker materials. The heartwood is considered to be very durable, lending itself to external uses. Western red cedar is fairly brittle and some care needs to be taken when working it. It saws and planes reasonably well with sharp tools. Good waste clearance while planing is important if chip denting is to be avoided. It nails and screws well but does contain chemicals that react with nonferrous metals, causing some staining. It has good adhesive properties and produces a fine finish, albeit easily dented.

Uses of the wood

Western red cedar's natural durability has enabled it to be used for shingles and shakes for both roofing and sidings. In most cases the wood is cleft rather than sawn for these end uses, thus making it less susceptible to water ingress. This durability also lends itself to the use of the wood for external joinery, claddings, etc.

Uses					Availability	Price
VENEER	PLYWOOD	FURNITURE	JOINERY	CONSTRUCTION		
			✓		✓✓	◆◆

Top Grain when radially cut. **Middle** Grain when tangentially cut. **Bottom** Cross-section.

TSUGA HETEROPHYLLA

Western Hemlock

Western Hemlock is also known by a range of other common names, including **West Coast**, **Pacific Hemlock**, **Hemlock-Spruce** or **Western Hemlock-Fir**, **Grey Fir**, or **Alaska Pine**.

Western Hemlock is found growing naturally up the west coast of North America and is also found in Asia. It has successfully been introduced elsewhere as both a commercial plantation tree and a decorative tree. The profile of the tree is conical with horizontal, open branching. It can grow up to heights of 200ft (60m). The boles are wide and branching naturally occurs fairly low down unless managed. When cut from the log, the wood is rather pale in comparison to some. Growth rings are apparent, with the earlywood being a light brown and the latewood a slightly darker brown with a reddish hue. The sapwood should be discernible in most cases and is a little lighter. The grain is normally straight, even textured, and has no pronounced scent. The wood is nonresinous but some thin, darker streaking may be traumatic resin ducts.

Properties of the wood

Western hemlock weighs about the same as redwood when it is dry. The heartwood is not considered to be durable. Drying this wood needs a little care, to avoid surface checking. Thicker material can dry a lot more slowly, due to the difficulty with removing the moisture from the core of the lumber. The wood works fairly well with the appropriate tools. Some care when sawing is required, to avoid back surfaces breaking out and spelshing. When cross-cutting, support immediately under the cut will help to alleviate this problem. Predrilling for fixings is not necessary unless close to end grain. The wood has good adhesive properties. A satisfactory surface finish can be achieved ready for sealing or painting.

Uses of the wood

Logs are often peeled for use in plywood manufacture. In the solid wood the better quality material gets used for internal joinery, moldings, and trims. Poorer quality material ends up as packing cases, pallets, studding, and joists.

Source Western North America

Working properties

Weight (per ft³)	30lb (14kg)
Durability	Perishable
Bendability	Poor
Hardness	Medium
Sawing and shaping	Satisfactory
Splitting	Average
Gluing	Good

Uses					Availability	Price
VENEER	PLYWOOD	FURNITURE	JOINERY	CONSTRUCTION	✓✓	◆◆
		✓	✓			

Tools and the workshop

All woodworkers need tools and a place to work their wood. It takes time and expense to build up a good collection of trusty woodworking instruments, but there is a lot of enjoyment to be had in the process. A reliable and comfortable workshop setting is vital, as well. You should feel at home in the place you are working, with plenty of space and everything you need conveniently to hand. This way you will work most effectively. The following pages give advice on what you need and how to get it.

Setting up a workshop

Setting up a workshop from scratch needs some careful and logical planning so that you make the best use of the space available and end up with the workshop you want. Not everyone can aspire to the roomy ideal pictured opposite, but a good floorplan will ensure maximum comfort and use of space.

Above right The more space you have in a workshop, the better. Over a period of time you will accumulate more and more tools and might want to graduate to some heavy-duty machinery.

Planning your workshop

Start off by drawing how you would like your workshop to look, bearing in mind the available space. Mark positions for windows, doors, lights, and sockets. Cut cardboard shapes scaled to represent your bench and machinery. When you have marked the workflow directions, find the right places for your cutouts, allowing space for working as well as paths, doors, and windows.

If feasible, a long, thin workshop is probably best, as it allows you to plan the workflow through the workshop. Separate working areas are handy, as is a storage area for raw materials first in line. These could be followed by static machinery such as saws and planes and, finally, an assembly and finishing area. Ensure there is lots of natural light, if possible. Otherwise, allow for plenty of lamps or strip-lights placed strategically over workstations.

Supply of essential services

A cold water supply to a sink will help when mixing glue or cleaning up. Make sure that there are plenty of electrical sockets and place these behind benches and at waist height on walls. Overhead sockets help minimize the problem of trailing cables. If a dedicated extraction system is to be installed, think about where the ductwork will go and ensure that the isolation blast gates are fitted to each machine inlet port. Extraction bagging units should go outside, possibly under a simple roof structure, to avoid the inevitable leakage of dust.

Comfort in your workshop

Consider your neighbors. If you plan to use heavy, noisy machinery at odd hours, you can minimize the potential for complaint by opting for noise insulation (such as double-

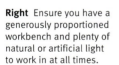

Right Ensure you have a generously proportioned workbench and plenty of natural or artificial light to work in at all times.

glazed window units which also retain heat). A wood-burning stove, which will provide heat in winter, might also be a good solution for waste disposal—both of excess wood and any other flammable materials that you might use regularly in your workshop. If this is not possible, think about alternatives—and certainly when it comes to heating. Long hours standing at a bench

on a concrete floor can be uncomfortable. You may find a wooden floor more congenial, if you have the option when you are setting up your workshop, and even old rugs or carpet scraps are better than unforgiving cold, hard concrete.

Storage

After settling on a spot for your main workbench, rack up the most frequently used tools close by. Perhaps you can store large hand and powered tools in cupboards underneath and create racks in front (as long as they don't obscure the light) to hold chisels, screwdrivers, hammers, and other smaller tools. Additional cupboard and racking space can be located around the workshop.

Workshop security

If you are working with powered tools, set up a bell system to warn you of any visitors, lock the workshop door, and put up a sign to keep children out. Always make sure that someone knows you are in your workshop and how long you intend to be there—and that they can get in if necessary. Isolate electrical equipment before you leave and keep a first aid kit handy.

Above Set out your woodworking tools in a logical fashion, with everything close to hand and easily obtainable.

Left A woodburning stove is good for both heat and disposal.

Essential workshop equipment

Everybody has their favorite tools and particular way of working—after all, a big part of woodworking is innovation—but there are certain essential items which no woodworker should be without. Of course, there is still plenty of scope for choice and personal preference, but this is what you will definitely need.

Above right A good workbench and vise are minimum requirements.

Workbenches

A workbench generally becomes the focal point of the workshop. Think carefully about its size and shape before rushing off to buy or make one. Consider what you will be making. Large joinery items, like stairs, doors, and windows, require plenty of work surface; less is needed for furniture or cabinet making. Depending upon how tall you are, a comfortable working height will be between 30–35in (800–900mm). You should be able to stand comfortably, working at the vise, for longish periods without getting backache. To control your tools correctly you will need to be above them, working down and away.

Workbench care

Always keep your workbench clean and tidy, removing dried glue, oil, or paint spills promptly, as these will mark your projects. Regularly sanding and cleaning the top and lightly waxing afterward is good practice. If the top is damaged, consider reskinning it with an additional layer of good-quality ply.

Vises

These are vital pieces of equipment. They range from simple bolt- or clamp-on types that wind in and out to hold the workpiece in place, to sophisticated ones incorporating a "dog"—an adjustable vertical stop—against which the workpiece can be placed. Vises should be fitted with timber protectors or pads over the metal faces to avoid damage to pieces that are being worked.

Integral bench stops

Adjustable integral bench stops against which work can be pushed and held are useful. Some are located at the end of the bench while others appear at strategic points. A hold fast can be fitted to the workbench, also, to secure different shapes and sizes while you work on them.

Bench hooks

These can fit over the edge of your bench, into the vise or the jaws of a workmate. They are

Right A 7in (175mm) woodworking vise.

Far right A standard portable bench hook.

excellent for holding small- to medium-sized pieces of wood while cutting across the grain.

Miter blocks

Cutting miters is easier with a miter block. These can be simple, one-sided items or of a box construction to give better saw stability. The boxes are available ready cut, but you can make your own for site work. If more sophisticated guides are required, consider a metal one that will clamp your workpiece in place. For really accurate miter sawing, a specialist miter saw system allows you to swing the saw blade from side to side into preset locations. They can also be set at rightangles, potentially doing away with the bench hook.

Other guides for cutting miters

The simple bench hook can be marked and cut out for this or you can make a guide with two legs for use in a vise or workmate. For gripping thin pieces of wood, you might modify your

bench hook (see illustration right). A similar device can be made with a couple of pivoting jaws fitted to a board or directly to your workbench. For repetitive length cutting by hand, set up a bench hook with an adjustable stop.

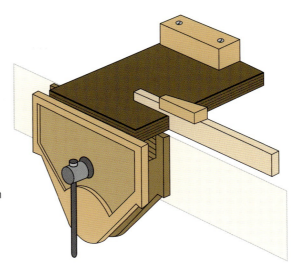

Sawhorses

If you are working with upholstery, a pair of sawhorses can accommodate larger pieces of timber or sheet materials that a workbench may not be able to handle. Sawhorses are simple to construct and, in their basic form, take up little space. You can make different types of sawhorse with useful additions (see illustration below).

Above A bench hook with a wedge for holding thin material.

Below left A diagram showing how to make a basic sawhorse.

Below A sawhorse can be height adjustable for ease of use.

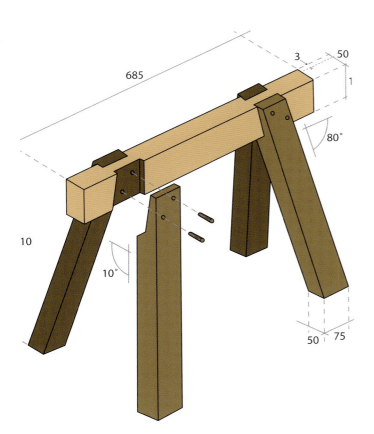

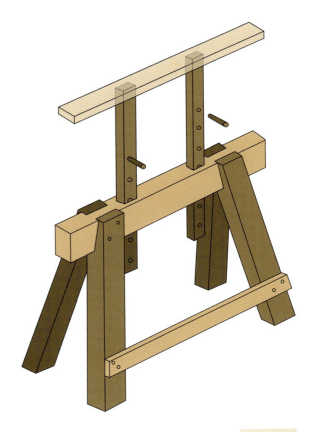

Tool starter kits

It is wise to be selective and take time over your choice of tools. Naturally there will be some that wear out, break, or get lost, but there is no reason why many should not last for years, providing you look after them. Always buy the best quality you can afford and, when in doubt, go for well-known brand names.

Above right Start out with a basic toolkit and build it up over time.

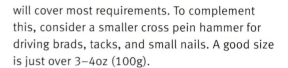

Getting started

Buying secondhand is a cost-effective way to begin a tool collection. However, unless you know where they come from, do not buy powered tools in this way. Alternatively, buying new tools should not break the bank if you keep your eyes open for special offers. Below are some ideas for a reasonably priced basic starter kit.

Saws

You will probably need two or three saws. A universal hard-point saw with six to eight, or possibly ten, teeth per inch (tpi), or points per inch (ppi), is useful for ripping down material and, if you are careful, cutting across the grain. A 10 to 14 tpi tenon saw with a brass or metal back is essential and, for curved shapes, a coping saw is useful. Saw "keeps" for protecting blades are a good idea.

Above A selection of different woodworking saws. From top to bottom: tenon saw (1); dovetail saw (2); reversible offset dovetail saw (3); offset dovetail saw (4); bead saw (5).

Hammers

A claw hammer can both draw and drive nails. A mid-weight one—around 10–12oz (280–340g)—will cover most requirements. To complement this, consider a smaller cross pein hammer for driving brads, tacks, and small nails. A good size is just over 3–4oz (100g).

Chisels

Start with three or four bevel-edged chisels with impact-resistant plastic handles. Sizes to include are quarter, three-eighths and half inch (six, 10 or 12 millimeters) and, if you can stretch to it, an eighth and three-quarters of an inch (three and 18 millimeters). Remember, you can make a bigger hole with a smaller chisel, but you cannot make a small hole with a big chisel. Try to pick a range from one supplier that you can easily add to so you end up with a matching set. For sharpening, you will need an oil or wet stone, preferably a combination one with fine and coarse grades of abrasive.

Screwdrivers

Two or three screwdrivers will cover most needs—a small to medium and a large straight tip for slotted

Right Hammer (1), chisel (2), and screwdrivers (3).

screws. A medium-sized "Phillips" or "Pozidrive" will deal with most other types of screws. The best handle is smooth, wooden, and slightly elliptical.

Drills

Go for a small hand drill and a brace or an electric drill, unless you can afford them all. If that is the case, it might be best to opt for the electric version at the outset and add the others later. It also depends on the type of work you are doing. If you go for the electric drill, get one with a range of speeds for cutting into different materials. You will need accessories, as well. Universal High Speed Steel/HHS bits are essential and come in various sizes, while countersunk and plug-cutting bits are also useful.

Planes

A simple smoothing plane with a two or two-and-a-half inch (50 or 60 millimeter) wide blade is a good starting point, taking into account the width of your oil or wet stone.

Squares and rules

A combination square that can be used for try and miter squaring is a good choice. Some include spirit levels and a scriber. You must, at least, have a traditional try square for marking out. One that is five or six inches (100, 125 or 150 millimeters) is the best option to go for. The cheapest steel retractable tape measure that is six feet (two meters) long should suffice for most jobs. A steel rule of six or twelve inches (150 or 300 millimeters) is useful for finer measurements.

Odds and ends

You can make a bradawl from an old screwdriver by grinding or filing a sharp point onto it. A nail punch can be made from a nail measuring four or six inches (100 or 150 millimeters); you simply file off the tip. Old hacksaw blades make excellent marking and cutting knives. To make the handle, wrap tape around a couple of strips of wood each side of the blade. Pliers or preferably pinchers are also useful.

Above This handy screw holder is made from an old piece of board with jelly jars attached to it. The jars are see-through, so it is easy and handy to select the screw you want.

Above Try to mount your tools on the wall within easy reach.

Below Manual hand drill (1); smoothing plane (2); carpenter's try square (3).

Sharpening and setting

If you are planing, sawing, drilling, or using a router, you may need to sharpen or touch up a cutting edge. Depending upon the type of edge, you may require a range of files, stones, and a grinding wheel. The files will be specific to the job. Stones are used to hone the final edge and grinders to create the basic angles.

Above right A wet grinder is invaluable for precision tool sharpening.

Above A selection of sharpening stones.

Right Sharpening different drill bits. Clockwise from top left: auger; spur; dowel; flat.

Stones and grinders

There are a number of different sharpening stones and types of grinder that are designed to help the woodworker keep his or her tools in peak condition. The following is a brief selection of the best.

Originally made from a natural Arkansas stone, **oilstones** can also come from manmade silicone carbide or aluminum oxide. The range of grit size is good and they are available as individual stones. Some small stones are available for sharpening shaped cutters.

Waterstones should be soaked before use but never have oil applied to them. They have a large range of grit sizes. Waterstones work and cut quickly, although smaller grit sizes produce the finest finish.

Although they are expensive, **diamond stones** are very useful and will last a long time. Due to their hardness, diamond stones can sharpen TCT, tungsten carbide-tipped tools and router cutters.

The most common type of grinder is the **dry stone grinder**. These machines are single- or doubled-ended and take wheels made from various abrasive materials. With a double-ended machine you may wish to have a coarse, quick-cutting wheel on one end and a finer wheel on the other. Take care when using these; they can easily overheat the cutting edge of the tool, which could affect the ability to keep an edge, or resist chipping.

A **wet stone grinder** (see illustration above) will eradicate the problem of overheating the cutting edge. Wheels are mounted vertically or horizontally and run in a trough of water or have a drip feed from above. Being drenched

continuously cools the surface of the wheel. Always wear safety glasses, goggles, or a face shield whenever you are using a grinder.

Sharpening drill bits

Drill bits often get damaged. Usually a set of small files can restore an edge. You will probably need a range of sizes and cuts—coarse for filing out large imperfections and fine for touching up. Some small diamond stones could also sharpen bits with wings.

Auger and spur bits should be sharpened from the original angles. This needs to be done by hand, unless you have a special wheel for your grinder. Some of the adapted dowel bits can be sharpened on a grinding wheel, providing

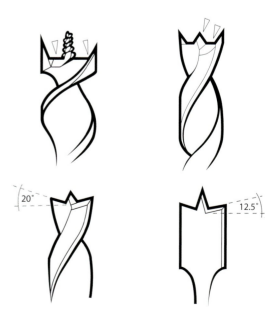

you have a square corner to fit. Getting the right curve to the edge on the inside of Forstner bits can be difficult, unless you have a cone-shaped grinding wheel. Flat bits can be sharpened on a grinder, provided you maintain the original angles. Remember to provide some clearance to the side cutting edge to prevent them from burning during use.

Engineers' twist bits are always breaking and are thrown away or reground if long enough. The recommended cutting angle is 59 degrees, which can easily be reproduced. As you grind the end, turn it away from the wheel to provide clearance. If you wish to play around with the cutting angle, then do so.

Sharpening and setting saws

Sharpening saws comes with practice. The key is to have the right tools and take your time. Depending upon the materials being cut and the quality of finish required, you might reduce or increase the set. Certainly, for rip sawing it would not be appropriate to have too fine a set. Tenon and dovetail saws can be effective with little set and are more accurate. With new saws, it is reasonably easy to follow the manufacturer's angles when touching up.

Before sharpening

Your first job is to buy the appropriate tapered file to fit the shape of the saw tooth to be sharpened. You will need a jig to support the sides of the saw blades (often called "chops") that will hold the blade while you work on it. Make sure there is enough room below the two loose pieces to take a back saw. For sharpening, the teeth should protrude ½in (12mm) and be supported throughout the length being worked on. Before sharpening, the saw may need "topping out" to level off the tips of the teeth so that you have a straight row when finished. This can be done in the chops. Run a mill file lengthways down across the tips of the teeth until they are straight. Never take off more than you need to. Then use a sawset to bend the teeth out from the saw blade to create the kerf. Sawsets are available to buy. Particularly handy are those that come with a magnifying glass.

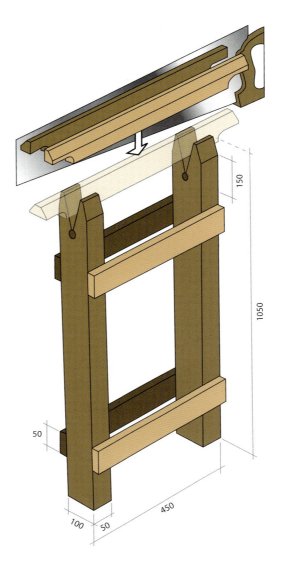

Left A set of saw "chops." These are especially useful when they are fully adjustable, like these. If you make your own, build them to the dimensions given in the illustration, in millimeters.

Above Sawing with a blunt saw is hard work and you will never make a neat cut with dull saw teeth. Make it a habit to sharpen all your saw blades on a regular basis.

Sharpening

Fit the saw firmly into the chops. Do a bit at a time if the jaws are not long enough to do the whole blade in one go. Mark the top of the saw chops' jaws with the appropriate angles to guide you when filing. Simple pencil lines at 45 and 65 degrees should suffice.

Every other tooth should be sharpened from in to outside, with two or three strokes of the file. Do not stretch, move your body, or the chops. Mark with a bit of chalk the last tooth sharpened so that you do not lose your place. When you have done one side, turn everything around and do the other.

Sharpening should now be complete. Most setting mechanisms relate to the number of

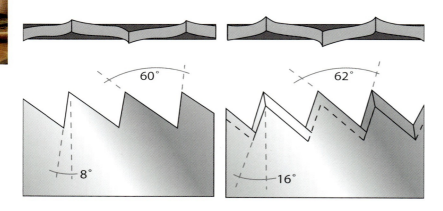

Above Ripsaw teeth (left); cross-cut saw teeth (right).

Sharpening chisels and plane irons

Regrinding

The principle is basically the same for these cutting tools. If the blades of your chisels and plane irons are blunt, regrind them on a dry or wet grinder at an angle of about 25 degrees. For general-purpose use, the most important thing is to get a straight edge. Be careful not to overheat the cutting edge of the tool when grinding it and keep it cool by regularly dipping it in water. You can tell when you are about right with the angle of sharpening as you will notice "spark out" along the top edge. This occurs when the grinding stone is fully in contact with the surface it is working on, and is characterized by small sparks flying away from the top edge. The tool is most likely to overheat at this point, so take care. With chisels, it can help to mark a line on the back as a guideline to work to on the tool rest. If you are at all unsure, consider buying a special guide attachment for your grinder to make life easier.

tpi; more for less and less for more. Your tool should identify the number of teeth and a position at which it is to be set. The setting process can be carried out in the chops or on the bench. Select alternate teeth and apply the setter. It will push the tooth out by a predetermined amount. Exert the same amount of pressure each time; if the handles should be closed then shut them. Swap round and do the other side, marking where you got to with chalk, as this saves redoing some of the teeth.

Right Sharpening cross-cut saw teeth (top); sharpening ripsaw teeth (bottom).

Far right A "topping out" device.

Honing

Honing starts on a coarse grit stone unless you are touching up an edge. The honed angle should be about 30 degrees. The aim is to create a small flat at the tip of the ground edge. Lubricate the stone throughout the process. Place the ground blade face down to the stone

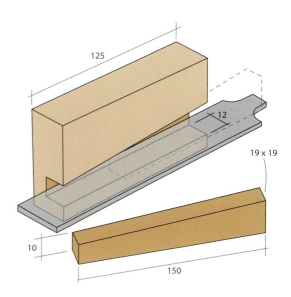

and make contact right across it. You can tell if you have the correct contact by slightly lifting the back end and letting it go; with your fingers positioned at the front it should rock back into place. To get the 30 degrees, lift the back of the blade or top of the handle slightly. You are effectively lifting the blade so that it rides on the front leading edge and will be close enough for most jobs.

Start to run the blade alternately back and forth and in a figure-eight. This will help maintain a flat surface on the oilstone and hone the edge evenly. Keep checking the edge. It should not take many circuits to create the small flat. Turn the blade over and, holding it flat against the oilstone surface, rub in a circular motion to remove the burr. Always finish with a stroke away from you. Repeat the process on a finer grit stone to finish off. If a tiny burr remains, gently draw the cutting edge through a piece of gash wood to remove it. If you are not confident about maintaining the honing angle, buy a jig.

Sharpening and caring for router cutters

Care

Use a solvent or, if necessary, an abrasive cleaner to remove resin build up. If the cutter has a guide roller, take it off. If you have time, soak everything overnight in solvent and clean the dirt off using a stiff bristle brush. Store in a box away from moisture to avoid rust.

Sharpening

You can only hone flat cutting edges and for this job you will need a range of small diamond stones. Opt for a fine grit, as this will ensure the best results. Holding the cutter firmly on the bench, position yourself in such a way that you can stroke the flat under-face with the diamond stone. You can protect the cutter from damage by resting it on stiff foam or something similar. Remember that the cutter is balanced, most likely with two cutting edges. To maintain this balance accurately, without damaging your router bearings, count the strokes that you make for the first side and then repeat the same number on the second side. Two or three strokes should be enough in most cases, but check the cutting edge as you go to see how you are doing. When you have finished, the cutter should be clean and bright. If you accidentally knock chunks out of your router cutters, buying new ones is probably cheaper than getting them reground professionally.

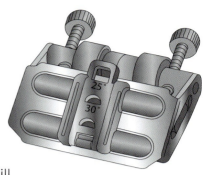

Above An adjustable angle guide.

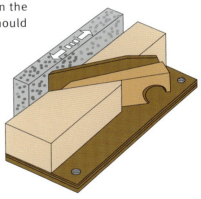

Below A homemade static guide.

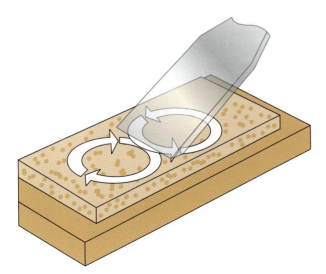

Left Honing in a figure-eight pattern (far left); removing the burr (left).

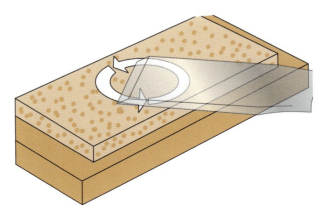

Hammers and other driving tools

Generic hammers that do a variety of jobs, and special types for specific tasks, are widely available to the woodworker. The handles may be made of wood, synthetic material, or steel. Although wooden and synthetic handles may provide better shock resistance, metal ones are stronger and last longer.

Above right Hammers and nails remain a mainstay of woodworking.

Below A selection of wooden-handled hammers: cross-pein hammer (1); square-headed cross-pein hammer (2); pin hammer (3); square-headed pin hammer (4); claw hammer (5).

Below right Removing a nail with a claw hammer.

What to look for in a hammer

If you prefer a wooden handle on your hammer, opt for hickory. It is strong, flexible, and shock-resistant. However, always check that the timber grain is straight, as short angles across the grain could lead to a break over time. If a wooden handle becomes loose, submerge it in water for several days. The wood will swell and tighten against the head socket.

Using a hammer

Balance is important when using a hammer. Unless you need a specialist hammer, go for a heavy one. Extra weight will enhance your driving power, reducing the number of blows required to drive nails home. To maximize efficiency, provide control, and maximum striking force, grip the hammer at the end of the handle farthest from the head. To start a nail, tap it lightly in place, and then follow with clean, strong strokes, swinging from the elbow. Always watch the nail, not the hammer-head, when you are hammering, as otherwise you will probably miss.

Types of hammer

Claw hammer

The eponymous claw is useful for pulling out nails and straightening bent ones that you are driving in. To avoid damage to delicate surfaces, put a piece of gash wood between the head of the hammer and the object from which the nail is being drawn.

Claw hammers are available in various shapes, weights, and sizes. Choose according to how much work you expect to do with the

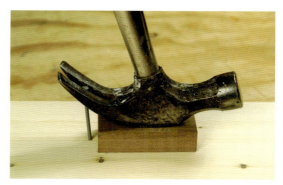

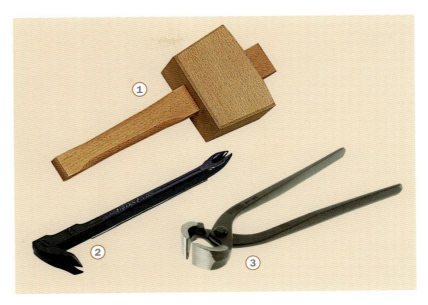

hammer, although the comfort factor is also important. If you plan to use it a lot, a heavy claw hammer of around 18oz (500g) is about right. For lighter use, anything from 10–14oz (280–390g) should be sufficient.

Ball-pein hammer
The pein is the end of the head opposite the striking surface and, in this hammer, is rounded. These hammers are mainly useful for metal basing.

Cross-pein hammer
The wedge-shaped pein can be used to start or set nails. Once started, the head is turned round to strike and drive the nail home. There are some variations, but the pattern usually adopted is called the "Warrington." A lightweight version drives in smaller pins and tacks.

Carpenter's mallet
The traditional mallet has an elongated head, with all its faces slightly tapered so that contact is always at rightangles to the tool being struck. This is a simple tool that can be made or adapted. If the head breaks, you can replace it with one made from a tight-grained wood such as beech, apple, or hickory. If you are working with chisels, this tool will do less damage to their handles than a hammer.

Carver's mallet
This mallet is also unlikely to damage other tools. Its entire circular face can be used with less likelihood of a chisel deflecting if a mishit occurs. Carvers' mallets normally come in two

sizes: lightweight for controlled tapping and cutting and heavyweight for bulk waste removal, stop, or stab cuts. The heads are often made from Lignum Vitae, because of its weight-to-size ratio, or long-lasting properties.

Lump hammer
A lump hammer drives wedges and does other heavy jobs. It also adds extra weight when putting up studding or knocking together tight joints. Remember to protect decent faces with softer, gash stock.

Cabriole hammer
The Cabriole hammer has evolved from and for the upholstery trade. With their small, curved heads, these hammers strike and drive home the tacks used to secure webbing and materials. If a mishit occurs, the smaller head should do less damage to show-wood. Some are magnetized so that tacks can be picked up and started quickly. Most have drawing claws to remove bent or misplaced tacks.

Veneer hammer
Technically not a hammer, but nevertheless named so, this tool is used to work and squeeze out excess glue from between the veneer and the ground, base material. The working end of the tool should be smoothly rounded to prevent damage to veneers.

Above left Using a cross-pein hammer to start a pin.

Above A carpenter's mallet (1); double-ended nail pullers, for extracting nails (2); pincers, for lighter-weight nail extraction (3).

Braces, drills, and boring tools

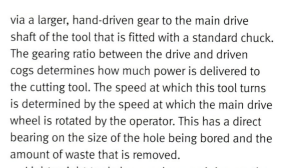

Boring tools come in all shapes and sizes. They are fitted with a drill/bit chuck and have a mechanical action that rotates the fitted tool to make a hole. Although largely superseded by modern powered drills, hand-held boring tools are useful for jobs requiring great control and accuracy.

Above right A hand drill is often useful for precision work, when a slower drilling speed might be advisable to avoid damage.

Braces

Braces are driven by muscle power. Hole size and depth are only limited to the strength of the operator and the tools used. Braces employ the cranked handle system without gears. Ratchets, cranks, and special angles enable the operator to reach into and drill in awkward spaces. A brace should have a free-moving, probably wooden, ball head for comfort, enabling the tool to turn without causing friction against the body. At the business end of the tool, there will be a three- or

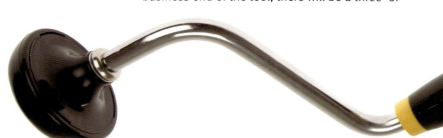

Above A standard carpenter's brace, with a full-size handle.

four-jaw chuck to take the drill bit. These chucks are self-tightening, if one hand holds the chuck tight while the other rotates the tool shaft. Reverse this action to remove a drill bit.

The sweep of the brace's action determines its size. Most braces have a ratchet incorporated into the action, enabling the user to operate the brace with short strokes—which is especially useful in confined spaces.

Hand drills

Sometimes referred to as "wheel braces," hand drills come in different shapes and sizes (see illustration above right). The power is transmitted

via a larger, hand-driven gear to the main drive shaft of the tool that is fitted with a standard chuck. The gearing ratio between the drive and driven cogs determines how much power is delivered to the cutting tool. The speed at which this tool turns is determined by the speed at which the main drive wheel is rotated by the operator. This has a direct bearing on the size of the hole being bored and the amount of waste that is removed.

Lightweight tools have only one pinion on the drive wheel; this is fine, providing nothing too hard or big is drilled. However, with the larger hand drills, opt for a double-pinioned version, because the extra drive power will enable bigger holes to be bored.

Drill bits and other boring tools

Some of these numerous tools are used in hand drills and braces, others for powered tools and some for both. Brace bits have a tapered square shank at the bottom to fit into the jaws of the chuck, while others have a universal chuck that can take round-shanked bits as well.

Twist and dowel bits

Twist bits are straight-shanked, with two cutting edges, in the form of spiral grooves, with a point ground on the sharp end. Dowel bits are of similar design, with a lead point and a couple of spurs ground onto the sharp end, so a clean hole can be cut in face and end grain.

Forstner bits

These tools cut clean holes. With a central lead point and edge cutters that are sharpened and shaped to the diameter of the required hole, they cut the outer circle before removing the central waste. They are ideal for fitting kitchen door hinges and similar jobs.

Flat bits

Flat bits are used in powered drills. They usually have a long lead point with two cutting wings to the sides. The cutting edges of the wings can be at rightangles to the shank or ground with a small angle to create a cleaner outer edge cut. Flat bits come in a variety of different sizes.

Auger bits

Various patterns are available on these drill bits, some of which are used in powered tools. "Multispeed" auger bits can be used in both powered and hand tools.

Countersink bits

Countersink bits are made for all types of drill. Many different patterns are available, including those that are manufactured for use with a twist bit. The countersunk tool is center bored and a twist bit is threaded through it. A grub screw holds the countersink in place and, when in operation, a pilot hole and countersink recess are drilled out in one go.

Below Wheel brace with enclosed gearing (1); joist brace (2); wheel brace with enclosed gearing and pistol grip (3); corner brace (4).

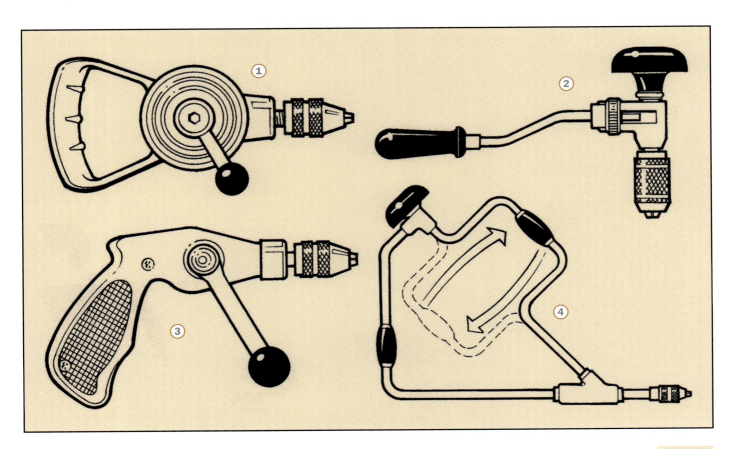

Screwdrivers

Every workshop should have a range of screwdrivers for different jobs, including straight and cross-head drivers. The advantage of cross-head drivers is that they are supposed to provide better grip when driving in screws. This is true, provided the driver is accurately matched to the size of recess.

Above right Screwdriving by hand reduces the risk of damage to the piece you are working on, especially if you are using softwood or the work has a fine finish.

What to look for in a screwdriver

Apart from the tip fit, the most important part of a screwdriver is the handle. In most cases, occasional use should not be a problem, whatever the material and type of the handle. However, if you are using a particular screwdriver frequently, the handle should be smooth and comfortable, as otherwise you will get blisters. If possible, opt for soft-textured handles, avoiding hard, ridged, plastic ones, which can slip.

Using a screwdriver

It is important to take up the right stance when using a screwdriver. Having positioned the tip of the screwdriver into the screw head recess,

Below A selection of straight and cross-head screwdrivers.

Below right Different versions of straight and cross-head screwdriver tips.

your wrist and forearm should be in line with the direction of drive. Extra body weight can then be added to help drive the screw home. Be sure to keep everything in a straight line as you apply more pressure.

Whatever the job you are screwing into, it is nearly always a good idea to predrill pilot screw holes—a small one for the tip and a larger one for the shank of the screw. You need to take more care when driving home lighter metal screws. One way to avoid breakages is to drive a same-sized steel screw in first. This cuts the track and enables the softer-metaled screw to follow and tighten up the joint. To lubricate the screw (so that it can be easily removed in the future), apply a small amount of grease, oil, or soap to the screw beforehand.

You can also get extra purchase on screw slots by modifying the driver's tip; a slight hollow in the end or a number of notches cut into it can sometimes transfer power more efficiently (see illustration below right).

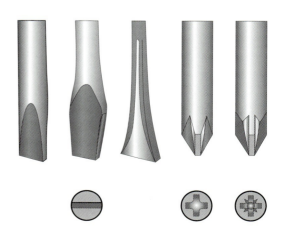

Types of screwdriver

There are many different types of screwdriver available for woodworking. Here is a brief selection of the best.

Cabinet screwdriver

The cabinet screwdriver's slightly bulbous handle, combined with its straight strong shaft, will easily drive home most straight-headed screws. This type of screwdriver is available with wooden, resin, or plastic handles.

London pattern screwdriver

Similar in shape to the cabinet driver, the London pattern screwdriver has the handle slightly flattened on both cheeks. The drive shaft is also made up from a flat piece of steel.

Short screwdriver

A short, stubby driver is useful for getting into tight corners. It can be used in conjunction with pliers to make a short, right-angled driver.

Ratchet screwdriver

Ratchet screwdrivers are available in both straight and cross-tip design. They usually come with the ability to set the ratchet for drive, withdraw, or fixed positions.

Yankee screwdriver

With a special double-spiral shaft, these tools drive screws home extra quickly. Once the tip of the driver is located in the screw head recess, a pumping action turns the shaft and drives the screw home. Modern versions also work like a ratchet; the shaft can be closed up and the tip locked off. Take care, though: an over-enthusiastic action might cause the tip of the driver to slip and cause damage.

Cross-tip screwdrivers

These come in three main types: Phillips, pozi-, and super-drive, plus variations to suit particular screw-head designs. All should provide extra purchase on the screw head if matched correctly.

Above left Always match the size of the slot to the width of the tip.

Above Some screwdrivers feature interchangeable heads.

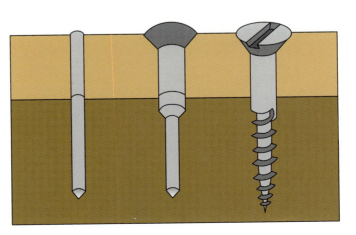

Far left Hollows or nicks in the tip of a screwdriver can actually be an aid, on occasion.

Left Always match the right type of screw with the right type of screwdriver.

Saws

Although many different types of saws are now available, the rip and cross-cut saws will do the bulk of your workshop work. However, it is vitally important to ensure that you are using the right saw for the job. Otherwise, it is all too easy to create unsightly cuts or to damage both the wood and your tools.

Above right Always use the right saw for the job in hand.

Selecting the right saw

Smaller saw teeth produce a finer cut and bigger ones cut faster and remove more waste. Ripsaws have larger teeth because they are used for cutting down the grain of the wood. Cross-cut saws need smaller teeth to avoid tearing, as they cut across the grain. You should also consider the shape and sharpening features of the saw you intend to use. Traditional ripsaws cut on the long, forward stroke, producing a smooth cut on the top surface but resulting in some break-out of the wood fibers on the back. If this break-out (or "spelshing"), causes a problem, you must support the component being cut on the underside. Cross-cut teeth also cut on the forward stroke, but remove less waste and there is less potential for spelshing. On modern saws the teeth can cut in both stroke directions, which is ideal for general use but less so for more specialized jobs.

Below A range of different sized saw teeth.

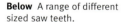

The other factor affecting the efficiency of the saw cut is the "set" applied to the teeth. This refers to how the teeth are alternately set (or slightly bent) to one side or the other of the saw blade. Simple or specialist tools can achieve this, creating a cut that is wider than the saw blade, facilitating free movement within the cut as it is made. The width of this cut is called the "kerf." A saw with a wide kerf, for example, will take more effort to cut through the component because it removes more waste; this is why it is always important to select the right saw for the job.

Types of saw

There are many different types of hand saw available for woodworking, all with specific

purposes and designs. Here is a brief selection of the best and most useful.

Hardpoint saw

With fewer people able, or willing, to sharpen and set a traditional saw, these are growing in popularity. During the manufacturing process each tooth is shaped, set, and sharpened. The tips are hardened to provide a longer cutting life—up to five times that of a traditional tool. Although hardpoint saws are a relatively low-cost buy, their tips are too hard to resharpen. Once they are blunt, they are no longer of any use.

Bow saw

A straight, detachable blade is mounted into the frame at the bottom and tensioned by twisting a piece of string at the top of the frame to tighten it. Modern variations include threaded wing nuts and lever actions in metal frames. These are rarely used for delicate work, although smaller bow saws with wooden frames are an alternative to a coping or fret saw, depending upon the type and size of blade used.

Ripsaw

With three to six teeth per inch of blade, these are not for fine work, but cut quickly if maintained and sharpened regularly.

Cross-cut saw

Used for cutting panels, these may have anything from six to ten teeth per inch of blade. The blade does not need to be so long because slightly shorter, more careful strokes should be taken while cutting.

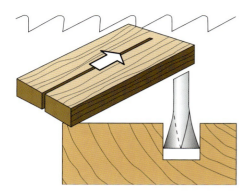
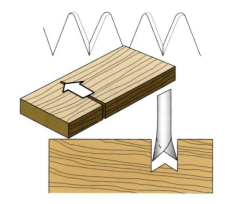

Left The ripsaw cuts along the direction of the grain (far left), whereas the cross-cut saw cuts across it (near left).

Pull saw

These cut on the pull rather than the push stroke. With the cut reversed, there is no need to have the blade strengthened along the back, and this gives the saw a wider range of uses. It also means that the thinner steel that is used in the blade creates a finer cut. Longer, larger pull saws are available with bigger teeth for rapid cutting.

Tenon saw

Tenon (or "back saws") are vital for simple joint making. Made from lighter-weight steel, the blade is strengthened with a strip of thicker metal, usually brass, folded over both sides of the top edge. The finer blade and smaller teeth, around 10–12 teeth per inch of blade, produce more accurate cuts.

Dovetail saw

A mini version of the tenon saw, these are even finer, with anything from 14–18 teeth per inch of blade. The set on the dovetail saw's teeth should be slight so that you can make accurate cuts in fine, detail work with very little wastage of wood resulting.

Gent's saw

With its small teeth, anything from 18–24 teeth per inch of blade, the gent's saw does finer, small-cut jobs.

Reversible saw

This saw has a cranked handle and a detachable, or pivoting, reversible blade, enabling the blade to be offset to both left and right for use in tight corners.

Above Various types of woodworking saw: ripsaw (1); cross-cut saw (2); tenon saw (3); traditional pattern dovetail saw (4).

Veneer saw

With its short, thin blade, the veneer saw's cutting edge is rounded for easy penetration into thin material such as veneer. These saws are often cranked with teeth on both edges of the blade so that they can be used both ways, working against a straight edge. With little set and a similar tooth count to the gent's saw, the veneer saw is used for fine work.

Inlay saw

A small version of the gent's saw, with a thin blade and fine teeth, this little saw is used for slicing thin strips of wood to size for fine cabinet and inlay work.

Flush cutting saw

This saw has been designed with the set off to one side, so that it can be used up close to a surface without causing damage to the wood it is being used upon. It is commonly used for trimming off dowels and pegs in joints. With a thin blade, the teeth of this saw are sharpened and shaped to cut on the pull stroke.

Coping saw

This saw can cut in any direction if it is turned or adjusted to do so. Its fine blade can cut tightly curved shapes. With a hole drilled in a workpiece, the blade can be threaded through and remounted to make a cut.

Fret saw

A larger version of the coping saw, the fret saw has a deeper frame. Delicate cuts can be made towards the center of a workpiece. However,

Below right Various types of saw: dovetail saw (1); bead saw (2).

Right Handsaws like this coping saw can be used for delicate, intricate work.

this saw is not for heavy-duty use, because the blades can easily distort or break. It is a good idea to keep a few spare blades to hand if you plan to use a fret saw on a regular basis.

Pad "keyhole" saw

This hole-cutting saw has a retractable blade that can be set at a little over the thickness of the material being cut. If shorter strokes are used, this should extend its life.

Compass saw

This saw cuts curves and shapes away from the edge of a workpiece. A hole is drilled first and the saw is used to enlarge and cut an internal shape.

Floorboard saw

One among several specialist saws, this has a rounded cutting point that enables a cut in a board to be started from the middle outward. Once through the floorboard, the saw is then reversed, with short strokes used to cut to each edge. An ingenious and adaptable addition to the hand saw collection!

Metal cutting saws

A large frame hacksaw will cope with most metal-cutting jobs (see the illustrations below). It can cut forwards, backwards, and sideways, depending on how the blade is loaded in the frame. For smaller, more awkward jobs, consider a padsaw or junior hacksaw. Even better may be a mini hacksaw that uses standard blades that can also be used in a large frame hacksaw.

③ ④

Above and left Various types of saw: coping saw (3); fret saw (4);compass saw (5).

⑤

Left The cleverly adapted floorboard saw (6).

⑥

Far left and left There are times in woodworking when you need a saw that will cut through metal.

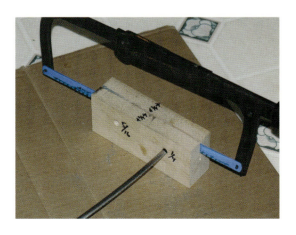

Chisels

If you are planning to make joints, you need a basic set of chisels. There is a huge choice available so, before deciding what to buy, it is a good idea to identify how you will use them, how many you will need and how much you wish to spend. If you plan to use your chisels regularly, always buy the best that you can afford.

Above right Chisels must be kept really sharp to be effective.

Below A square-edged chisel (left); a bevel-edged chisel (right).

Choosing a chisel

There are two universal, basic shapes of chisel blade—square- and bevel-edged. Square-edged chisels cut holes and remove waste in bulk. Bevel-edged chisels get into corners and create angled joints like dovetails. Both can be used for paring but, depending on handle design, some are more comfortable to use than others.

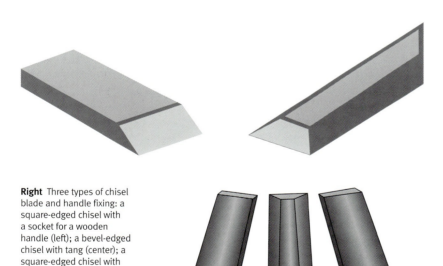

Right Three types of chisel blade and handle fixing: a square-edged chisel with a socket for a wooden handle (left); a bevel-edged chisel with tang (center); a square-edged chisel with tang (right).

Chisel blades

The choice of blade width, thickness, angle of cut, and shape of chisel shank is endless. European chisels have a blade running the majority of their length, with a short tang or socket to fit into the handle. The increasingly popular Japanese chisels have a shorter chisel body and a long shank. Cheaper chisels are made from drop-forged, high-carbon, or alloy steel, while top-quality versions come from hand-forged steel that is worked and beaten into shape.

Handles

The shape and construction of the chisel handle is important. The choice of wood or plastic depends on your budget, but striking chisels need handles made of shock-resistant wood (such as ash, beech, hickory, and box) or shatter-proof plastic resin. The wooden handle of a mortise chisel, for example, has strengthening ferrules at the striking end and where the tang fits into it. Apart from those with plastic handles, most other chisels have a ferrule at the tang end only. For hand work, a smooth handle is best, as otherwise you could end up with blisters.

Types of chisel

There are many different types of chisel available for woodworking. Here is a brief selection of the best.

Mortise chisel

These heavy-duty, square-edged chisels cut mortise holes. The blades are thick and do not snap off when used as a lever to remove the waste cut. Start with a few key sizes and build toward a full range.

Firmer "register" chisel

This multipurpose square-edged chisel can be used for paring and cutting light mortises. The name derives from the thicker blade, which is considered to be firmer, providing greater strength and control.

Paring chisel

Paring chisels can be square-edged or, more usually, bevel-edged. Although not for striking, these general-purpose chisels are used for a variety of jobs and come in a range of lengths and widths.

Skew chisel

Skew chisels are usually handed so that the cutting edge can reach right or left into tight spots. The blades are square- or bevel-edged with non-striking handles.

Pocket chisel

These short, handheld chisels (available in square- and bevel-edged versions) clean out small recesses like hinge sockets. Short versions are often called "butt" chisels and fit comfortably into the palm of the hand.

Corner chisel

This cleans out joint corners or trench ends. The right-angled blade is sharpened from the inside.

Cranked chisel

If you are hand cutting trenches across the grain, the cranked handle of this square- or bevel-edged chisel is useful. Your hand remains above the workpiece while the business end is cutting parallel with the surface.

Swan-neck chisel

A swan-neck, or "lock-mortise" chisel cuts and scoops waste out of a deep mortise hole, often made while fitting a lock. It is not readily available, but if you come across one secondhand, it might be worth adding to the tool kit.

Drawer lock chisel

This chisel is a light, striking tool with a pair of cranked cutting edges at each end of a bar. The cutting edges are set at opposing angles and the chisel is struck, without too much force, on the elbow to make the cut.

Gouge

Two basic types of gouge are available. The first—called an out-cannel gouge—is sharpened on the outer cutting edge, while the other—an in-cannel gouge—is sharpened on the inner cutting edge. The former cuts and cleans out hollows in a workpiece while the in-cannel gouge trims out the shoulders of a rounded socket joint. Be sure to familiarize yourself with the difference, as their functions really are quite different.

Carving chisel

Carving chisels feature cutting shapes that range from flat, through slight to more extreme-dished, to shallow and deep gouges. You will also find sharp- and rounded-bottom vee gouges, spoon, dogleg, and bentback shaft shapes. Some of these tools are sharpened in-cannel and some out-cannel.

Above The unusual drawer lock chisel is used specifically for cutting out key holes in drawers.

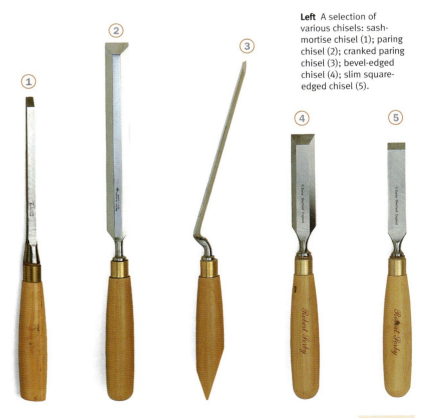

Left A selection of various chisels: sash-mortise chisel (1); paring chisel (2); cranked paring chisel (3); bevel-edged chisel (4); slim square-edged chisel (5).

Planes

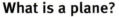

Every workshop needs at least one hand plane and these broadly fall into four types—bench, block, rabbet, and plow planes. You will almost certainly use a bench plane, but whether you need the others depends on what you are working on. As ever, take your time before over-investing in tools you might not need.

Above right A hand plane allows you to take your time on the job.

What is a plane?

The bench plane is based on the tool that was patented by Leonard Bailey in 1858. This type of fixed-cutting angle bench plane, with its adjustable depth of cut assembly, is adopted in some form or other across all metal rebating, block, and molding planes that are in use in woodworking today.

Using a plane

When using a bench plane, it is important to have a sharp blade, set the shaving thickness correctly, and adjust the depth of cut to suit the wood being worked. The angle at which the blade is held in the body of the plane, on the frog assembly, is commonly 45 degrees. There will be different angles offered on the smaller planes, depending upon what they are intended to be used for.

The standard grinding angle for the planer blade is usually 25 degrees. This should be honed to a razor-sharp edge at 30 degrees.

Once the blade is sharp, you should set the cap iron in the correct position. For softwood this should be back further from the leading edge of the blade. Bring it forward for finer work and most hardwood. The range will probably be from about two millimeters down to less than half a millimeter. Take care not to damage the cutting edge when setting the cap iron and placing this in the frog assembly.

With the blade and cap iron mounted in the frog, wind the whole assembly so that it protrudes below the face of the plane body. To set the cut square, invert the plane and adjust, by sight, using the lateral lever. Once this is done, draw the blade up to where you think a suitable cut can be made and try it out. Any fine adjustments can then follow.

Below left The frog assembly of a standard bench plane.

Below center Cutting angles for planes.

Below right Adjusting the blade of a plane.

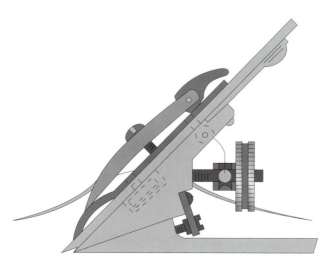

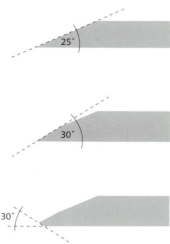

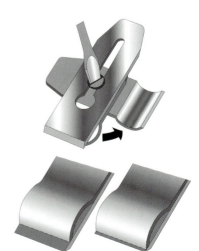

Troubleshooting

Occasionally, once you have set up your plane, it may not work as well as you feel it should do. There could be a number of reasons for this. If the blade appears to be moving when the plane is in use, check that the cap iron is firmly fixed and/or tighten the lever cap by adjusting the central screw. This should secure the blade more firmly. If there is still a problem, take the whole assembly out, strip it down, and remove any bits of waste that might have become trapped in the frog. Having cleaned it up, put everything back together and try again. Sometimes shavings will get between the cap iron and the blade. There may be resin or something else on the cap iron or the blade might be out of true. Take these two elements apart and clean them up gently with some steel wool and light oil. If the blade is slightly dished, try flattening it by tapping the center. If it does not improve, you may need a new blade or cap iron.

With new, metal-bodied planes it is important that the sole plate is level. Sole plates are usually flat, but some makers groove them to reduce friction in use. Check if the sole plate is true with a straight edge, running it both across and down its length. If it is slightly out it is possible to rectify the problem yourself, but it is probably best to return to the supplier and ask for a replacement. If that is not possible, the alternative is to take it to an engineering works and have them regrind it.

Left An exploded view of the assembly of a standard hand plane.

Left Alternative names for different lengths of bench planes. This table attributes common names to different lengths of bench planes and the variations between the United States and Europe over the last two centuries.

	United States		Europe	
	19th century	20th century	19th century	20th century
16 in	Jack	Fore	Jack	Fore
18 in	Fore	Fore	-	-
20 in	Fore	-	Trying	Jointing
22 in	Jointer	Jointer	Trying	Jointing
24 in	Jointer	-	Long	Jointing
26 in	Jointer	-	Long	Jointing
28 in	Jointer	-	Jointer	Trying
30 in	Jointer	-	Jointer	Trying

Types of plane

There are many different types of plane available for woodworking. Here is a brief selection of the best and most useful.

Try or trying ("jointer") plane

The largest group of bench planes, these are available with both metal and wooden bodies and their lengths range from 20–30in (500–760mm). The try plane produces long, flat surfaces, trimming uneven ridges down to the flat surface required.

Fore and jack plane

The fore plane is a compromise between the try and jack plane. It is usually about 16–18in (400–450mm) long, and can be used instead of, or as well as, the try or jack plane. Used for roughing down and general planing work, Jack planes are around 14in (350mm) long.

Smooth or smoothing plane

These are used to finish off a surface. They are the shortest of the bench planes, measuring 6–12in (150–300mm) long. Blade width can be anything from 1¾–2½in (44–65mm) wide.

Scrub plane

This plane can remove large amounts of waste quickly. Its purposely ground convex blade makes alternate diagonal cuts across the grain. Avoid using this plane on interlocked grain stock, as it will tear out the wood.

Scraper plane

This tool offers an alternative to hand finishing with a scraper. Usually used on hardwoods, it can produce a fine finished surface.

Block plane

This small plane is held in one hand and used for fine finishing work both with and across the grain.

Shoulder plane

Available with a wooden or metal body, this is mostly used with one hand. The blade is matched to the same width as the body so it can trim square shoulders on joints like tenons.

Bull-nosed plane

This has the blade width right to the edges of the body. Because the blade is set at the front of

Above Scraper plane.

Right Jointer plane (1); jack plane (2); metal smoothing plane (3); wooden smoothing plane (4).

the tool, it is used to get close to corners when cleaning up.

Rabbet plane
This plane has a blade the full width of the body which, in use, is run against a fixed batten or strip of wood to create the rabbet. Some come with thin, preformed cutter blades that are thrown away after becoming blunt.

Rabbet and fillister plane
These are usually metal-bodied and may have a second throat so that the blade can be moved forward to form a bull-nosed plane. Incorporated into the bodies of both these planes is an adjustable fence, so that the width of a rabbet can be set and worked off an edge. A depth stop on both versions ensures that the finished rabbet is the correct size.

Plow plane
The plow plane cuts grooves and small rabbets using a range of width blades. Available in both wood and metal bodies, the position of the groove is set using a side fence and the depth with a stop.

Combination planes
With the appropriate blades, these planes can form other joints and beads.

Multi-plane
The versatile multi-planes are supplied with a range of different-shaped blades for molding. With the correct blades they can rabbet and groove.

Compass plane
This plane finishes off both internal and external curves. Usually mounted in a metal body, the sole plate can be flexed and adjusted to match the desired curve.

Router plane
Humorously know as the "old woman's tooth" this plane is the precursor of the modern, powered router. It has now largely been superseded by the power tool, but some woodworkers prefer to use this plane, believing that it gives them more control, as is the case with many hand tools. With a cranked blade set centrally in a wooden or metal body, this plane can clean out housing joints and hinge recesses.

Above Rabbet plane.

Above Router plane.

Left Block plane (1); combination plane (2); shoulder and bullnosed planes (3); plow plane (4).

Spokeshaves, draw knives, adzes, and scrapers

This is a mixed collection of useful cutting and finishing tools. Some of these tools have a very long and interesting history. Types of adze—a form of axe—have been used since the Iron Age. Spokeshaves, draw knives, and scrapers are all basically variations on the theme, which have evolved over the centuries.

Above right A set of traditional carpenter's spokeshaves.

Spokeshaves

These were once used for shaping cart and wagon spokes (see the illustration above). The modern, metal-based versions are like a bench plane with a similar, but smaller, blade assembly. If used correctly they can shape a component very quickly.

Flat sole

These can create simple chamfers, rough down a component, or smooth off convex curves. Always work with the grain when smoothing convex curves. The work should be planed from the crown down in one direction first, turned, and worked down in the opposite direction to finish.

Below A modern flat sole spokeshave.

Below right A modern round sole spokeshave.

Round sole

With a rounded sole plate, this cuts concave shapes and is ideal for internal curves. It can only be matched, depending upon the arc of the curve, by a compass plane.

Chamfer

This is a flat-sole shave with additional miter guides (called fences) fitted to each side and set at 45 degrees to the cutting blade. The shave produces an accurate 45-degree chamfer.

Half-round

This specialist shave has a concave body, sole, and a blade to match and is used to produce rounded sections.

Radii

Only buy this if you plan to use it regularly. It is used just to plane and produce hollows.

Combination

These combine the benefits of a flat and half-round shave in one tool. Also available are other unique, combination shaves, designed to produce flat or convex work and, when turned over, will plane concave faces.

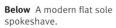

Left A selection of old adzes, in this case used for finishing oak wine barrels.

Draw knives

One of the oldest groups of shaping tools, draw knives have a cutting edge that is usually drawn toward the user to make the cut.

Flat, straight blade

This simple blade usually measures around 10in (250mm). The blade is forged from one piece, with handles set at rightangles to the blade.

Flat, curved blade

Often with slightly splayed handles, this knife has a flat blade that is curved toward the user.

Curved blade

This has a dished, slightly curved shape, enabling the user to cut shallow hollows.

Push knife

With straight or curved blades, the handles are in line with the blade so that the user can operate in both directions.

Inshave

This is a more specialist tool, measuring around 6in (150mm) across, with a tightly curved blade. It is commonly used for shaping chair seats and scooping out large bowls.

Scorp

A one-handed, smaller version of the inshave, with a tightly curved cutting edge, the scorp scoops out recesses and smaller bowls.

Adzes

Adzes date from ancient times but today are most often used for hollowing out chair seats.

Scrapers

A scraper is the cabinet-maker's main finishing tool. A piece of flat steel, it has a fine cutting edge—a burr—burnished onto it. This edge can clean off thin slivers of wood, glue, and so on.

Below left A one-handed inshave (left) and a scorp (right).

Below A modern gouge-shaped adze.

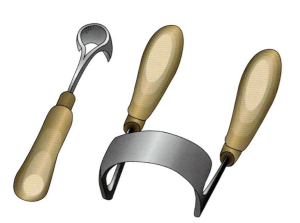

Files, rasps, and surforms

Every workshop should have a selection of files, rasps, and surforms. These tools are invaluable for the rapid shaving and balling off of waste wood, offering varying degrees of finish, although never very smooth. Files, rasps, and surforms are all classified by their degree and depth of cut.

Above right A selection of traditional files and rasps.

Files

The range of files includes flat, half-round and shaped files—from small, needle files to large, single-handled files. A set of needle files will help you make adjustments to small metal work, while the tiny, double-ended riffler files reach small spaces. Larger wood and metal files range from 5–6in (125–150mm) in length up to 12in (300mm) or more. Very rough cutting files are called bastard cut files and range through to fine double cut. Often, a piece of abrasive paper wrapped round a file helps finish off a shape, and can improve the quality of the surface.

Below Various types of cut patterns on files: double (left); single (center); rasp (right).

Rasps

Rasps are not a tool for fine finishing. However, if you need to remove shaped waste fairly rapidly, one of these will come in handy. Rasps come in similar sizes and shapes to the larger files. These tools have their surfaces covered with teeth of a uniform size that enable them to be used with or across the grain. Some are finer than others. The teeth are formed by punching out uniform, short spikes all over the surface. These teeth are sharp and can remove waste more rapidly than a file; they cut on the forward stroke. However, they can damage the surface of the workpiece if not handled with care. It is also a good idea to ensure that your rasp has a handle to avoid the spikes ripping your hands. The cutting teeth are graded, working, once more, from a rough, bastard cut through to a smooth rasp. Standard shapes of rasps are flat, half-round, round, and triangular. The most versatile of all these tools is the half-round rasp.

A number of "Japanese" saw rasps are available on the market. These are blades made up with a cutting surface resembling an open lattice work that allows the waste to drop through, away from the cutting face. These are often supplied with two cutting faces, rough on one side and smoother on the other. Other variations also include tools that have specifically been designed to be used in a powered hand drill or jigsaw. These rasp cutters need to be used with care and control, as otherwise they can easily damage the workpiece. Don't forget the rifflers mentioned in the files section above: these small tools use a similar cutting face to the standard rasp.

Surforms

Surforms are the big brothers of the rasp and are a modern tool that has been developed from them. Surforms are designed to produce rapid cuts and shapes in wood. Put simply, they are made from thin sheets of steel that have been perforated to create cutting teeth. Normally the cutting action with a surform is away from the user but, if required, most can be turned round to cut on the pull stroke. Some smaller tools are made specifically to cut in this direction. The perforations should be big enough for the waste to work its way through to the back of the cutting face. However, unfortunately this is not always the case. In particular, when working with wet or resinous wood, surforms can clog up. In use it is always a good idea to keep a look out for this. A sharp, occasional tap of the surform on the workbench might just clear the clogging before it becomes too much of a problem.

The cutter blades on surforms are made up in different shapes and sizes. Most are made in a standard format to fit into some form of frame or handle assembly. The larger tools have blades that are replaceable once they have worn out. Out of choice it is always a good idea to buy a surform tool body into which you can fit different or replacement cutting blades. Sometimes the framed versions will have reversible handles to enable the cutting action to change from, say, like that of a plane to that of a file. Shapes are usually flat, half-round, and full-round.

Surforms are used as a roughing down tool. This might be for creating internal shapes on furniture that will be finished off with some other tools or, possibly, for cutting waste away before final carving. Like rasps, surforms are not for creating finished surfaces on fine furniture or for the faint-hearted! Flat and half-round surforms are handy for quick waste removal and a round one is particularly useful for enlarging holes. Carvers will find the surform useful, as will chair-makers, for roughing out components. Having the advantage of not being very expensive, two or three of these tools will always find some use in the general woodworker's toolbox.

Above A modern metal-bodied flat file surform (top) and a modern round file surform (bottom).

Below A selection of old carpenter's files, rasps, and surforms.

Squares and bevels

Your most essential workshop tools will be try and miter squares, combined into a one-piece tool or bought in different shapes and sizes. These are handy for marking out when completing accurate projects. You can make your own squares by picking some suitable timbers and ensuring they are correctly assembled.

Above right For precision marking out, use a square and a workplan.

Try square

A try square ensures that components or internal and external frames are square. If large enough, it can also be used as a straight edge and, if so designed, can also mark miters. As this tool can affect the quality of, say, your jointing, it must be precisely set at 90 degrees. To do this, ensure that you have a flat, straight piece of wood, present the try square, and mark a line across the grain. By turning the square over and bringing it up to the previously marked line, you can see if it is accurate. If not, make adjustments to the square as necessary.

There is a large range of different try squares on the market and traditional styles come in a variety of sizes. If you can afford it, it is a good idea to have two or three different squares of different sizes to hand. You will probably get most use from one with a 12in (300mm) blade.

Carpenter's square

Made from one piece of steel, this large square is often called a "layout" or "rafter" square. It is used to set the angle of rafters and other setting out procedures during the construction of buildings and must be totally accurate. It comes in various sizes, although one arm is generally about 24in (600mm) long and the other 15in (400mm). You really only need to invest in one of these squares if you are planning lots of large-scale work or roof constructions and so on.

Miter square

The marking blade of this tool (which is not actually square) is set at 45 degrees so that internal and external miters can be marked and checked during assembly. Test for the accuracy of this angle by using a protractor.

Right A carpenter's square (1); a medium-sized standard try square (2); a carpenter's miter square (3).

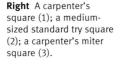

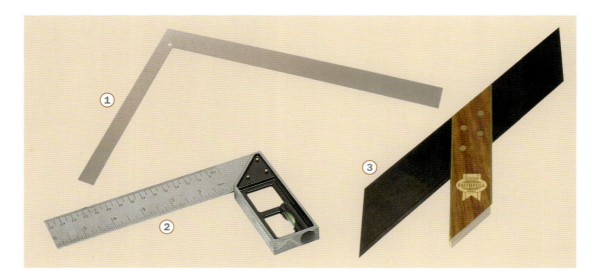

Multifunction ("combination") square

Able to perform a number of different functions, these squares normally incorporate a spirit level, and may be used as try and miter squares. Sometimes they even feature attachments or integrated parts so that the user can mark both the face and the edge in just one setting. These tools are very useful for many different tasks.

Dovetail square

Dovetail squares can help with cutting joints. The angle of slope usually differs slightly between different woods. Most softwoods, and soft hardwoods, need a more acute angle of cut in their joints than hardwoods in order to provide stronger joints overall. Set the slope on a softwood dovetail square at one-in-six and at one-in-eight for a hardwood dovetail square.

Sliding bevel

With a split handle, folding blade, and locking mechanism, the sliding bevel can mark out any angle consistently. It is also used for setting fences on machines and has long been a popular tool with boatbuilders and shipwrights, who have traditionally used this tool for marking out angles on boat decking. With care, the sliding bevel can even be used to mark out dovetails. Opt for one which features a fully recessed locking mechanism, as this will not get in the way when you are marking out; the adjustable blade is normally secured with a short brass lever or wing nut, and it is best if this is tucked out of the way where it cannot cause any damage to workpieces. A middle-sized bevel with a 6–8in (150–200mm) blade is a good starting size. Larger sliding bevels can be used to mark out sheet materials.

Above left Marking out using a wooden-handled try square.

Above A mini dovetail square.

Left A selection of various squares and bevels: a try square (1); a sliding bevel with a locking lever and adjustable blade (2); a miter square (3).

147

Marking and measuring

This section deals with all the other woodworking tools that are used for marking out and measuring. It also incorporates most of the remaining small workshop tools that are commonly used by the woodworker. These are vital aids of which you can never have too many. The good news is that they are largely inexpensive to buy.

Above right Tape measures come in many different forms.

Below A selection of woodworking rules, from top to bottom: a wooden four-fold rule; a plastic four-fold rule; a steel rule; a metal straight edge.

Rules

Rules, whether made of metal, wood, or plastic, must be accurate. A couple of metal ones of six inches and 12 inches (150 and 300 millimeters) in length will be useful. They should begin the incremental measurements from one square end and be marked in millimeters and inches.

Straight edges

These check how straight or flat an item might be, but they are also useful for marking out. They are available ready-made, but you can make your own from a section of wood, ensuring that the straight edge is flat and straight. Hanging them from a hook helps avoid distortion.

Tapes

Retractable metal, plastic, or fabric tapes are available, but the lightweight metal ones are good for marking long lengths. Take care of the hook, so it does not become bent and affect your measurements. Apply some light oil occasionally to keep the tape retracting easily, remembering to wipe off the excess.

Marking knives

Sometimes a knife is better than a pencil for marking out on wood. A knife mark can be used as an index point when working with chisels and fine saws. If the knife is held vertically, run its flat or beveled face against the try square (for example); otherwise, joints may vary.

Scratch awl

This sharp tool is good for marking plastics and laminates, such as kitchen worktops, and can also be used as a marking tool for wood.

Marking gauge

This marks lines down the length and across the

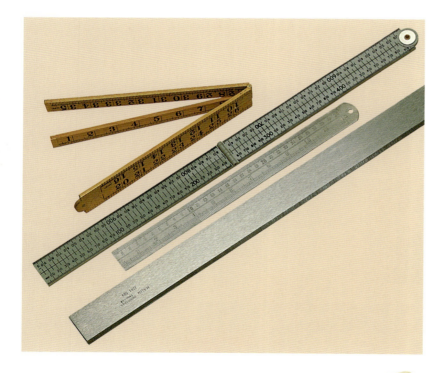

Right A standard marking knife.

grain. Be careful when using across the grain because the fibers might tear.

Mortise gauge
This gauge has two points and a mechanism that enables the user to mark parallel lines in one go.

Cutting gauge
Designed for marking across the grain as it cuts rather than tears, this gauge has a small, sharpened, pointed knife set into the head.

Punches
These are useful for center-marking before drilling and for knocking nails and pins below the surface before filling.

Bradawl
The quickest way to start a screw in soft wood is to push the pointed end of a bradawl into the wood and turn. Usually made from round steel, a bradawl can be used for marking a center for a drill bit or a piece for the lathe.

Compasses
Marking circles requires a compass and these come in various sizes and shapes. A carpenter's compass will be a large, angled, hinged frame made in the traditional style, usually with spikes in each leg to position and mark.

Spirit levels
For general woodworking, two spirit levels (a long and a short) are useful. Check for accuracy by viewing the bubble in the level in one position and turning it round to see if it is in the same place.

Calipers
Calipers are handy for measuring inside bowls and thicknesses if turning is being contemplated. In a similar vein, a vernier gauge is also an accurate measuring tool that can be useful to the average woodworker.

Odds and ends
There is a whole range of other measuring and marking tools. A pair of "winding sticks" can check that a wider component is flat. A "pinch stick" helps ensure that a project is square. Others gauge the height that a saw or cutter protrudes from a workpiece, and so on.

Above A marking gauge (left), mortise and marking gauge (center) and cutting gauge (right).

Below A square-headed nail punch and a heavy-duty ribbed box level.

Below A selection of bradawls with tips of varying sizes.

Cramps and clamps

Cramps or clamps—what should they be called and which one is which? This is often the subject of much debate in woodworking circles, but for the purposes of this book we call the smaller holding devices "clamps" and the larger ones "cramps." The key thing to bear in mind is what each one actually does.

Above right A collection of large pipe and bar cramps.

Below A standard sash cramp (1); a standard "C" clamp (2).

Below Sash cramps in use on a job.

Sash cramps

Traditional sash cramps are made from a flat steel bar, a T-shaped steel section, or a box section. The flat-bar sash cramps do most framing jobs, although T-bar cramps are generally better for heavy-duty work. Extension bars can accommodate longer jobs or, with the sliding tails removed, two cramps can be bolted together to create a more accommodating version of the same thing.

Pipe and bar cramps

These cramps come as a head and tail set which fits onto a rectangular section of wood or a predetermined size of pipe. Mostly, the heads and tails that fit onto the wooden bars will be held in place with a pin through the bar, enabling a range of different-length cramps to be made up if required. Pipe cramps usually have a cam or one-way clutch action holding the tail, and often, the head in place. Generally, a lightweight set of these is mounted on a ½in (12.5mm) pipe and a heavyweight set on a ¾in (19mm) pipe.

"C" clamps

So-named because they look like the capital letter "C," these clamps are immensely strong and also fairly versatile. The cast-metal body and screw-head assembly allow pressure to be placed at any point that they can reach. The maximum jaw width of a "C" clamp is usually 12in (300mm). There are many different brands of "C" clamp available on the market.

Bar clamps

These clamps tend to be mounted on some form of bar section. The tail stop is fixed, or forged from the bar itself, and the head slides, allowing the head to be positioned close, or right up to, the work and tightened into place. However, be careful if you choose to use this type of clamp, as they can distort easily.

Quick clamps

Most quick clamps can be used one-handed. The most common type is based on a pressed-steel body, similar to a mastic gun, enabling the operator to hold the workpiece with one hand and ratchet up the clamp with the other. Extremely heavy pressure can be exerted on a joint using these clamps. Some bar-clamping systems have a quick-clamp facility and shorter ones can be used in the same way.

Odds and ends

Many other cramps, clamping tools, and systems are also widely available and range from simple frame cramping assemblies and nylon web strapping systems to specialist clamping tools for, say, tightening up floor boards. If you are not sure which one to use, consult your local dealer.

Above A standard bar clamp.

Left A one-handed quick clamp.

Left Several "Solo C" clamps being deployed simultaneously on a big job.

Adhesives and glues

Adhesives and glues have always been important in woodworking, but no more so than in recent years. This is because the technology behind them has developed exponentially in the last few decades, resulting in a wide range of versatile fixing substances that offer incredibly strong bonds.

Above right There is a lot of choice, but select your adhesive carefully.

Below Many brands of adhesive are internationally available.

Right Properties and uses of different adhesives.

Specialist adhesives

Before discussing the more common glues and adhesives, mention must be made of two specialist types. One is available in a tube that fits into a mastic gun and fixes baseboards, architrave, wall cladding, and so on, sometimes even without the need for other types of fixing. This type of adhesive can bond wood, masonry, and metal in any combination and is rapid setting. It can be readily obtained from most hardware stores.

The second is expanding foam, which grows to around 30 times its liquid size. Useful for "second fix" tasks, it can also be used as a gap filler for heat and sound insulation. Make sure there is somewhere behind the joint for the excess to go, using a knife to clean up after the foam has hardened. The foam comes in tubes with a dispensable nozzle. As these clog up quickly, keep some spare nozzles or use an applicator gun that can be purged with the right cleaner.

General-use adhesives

There are a lot of different general-use adhesives on the market and many of these are of use to woodworkers. The bonding process with these comprises two parts. The first is the adhesive's ability to penetrate the structure of the components being jointed. This mechanical part of the process will form small "keys" into the adjacent faces. The second part is the adhesive's strength in sticking to the material. Under the right conditions, the resulting bonds should be stronger than the materials they are jointing.

Animal glues

The most common animal glue is hide or "scotch" glue, made from boiling up cattle parts such as horns and hooves. This glue is a favorite of furniture makers and has been for many years. The glue is easy to apply and has a reasonable shelf life. It is also reversible; applying controlled

	Water resistance	Rigidity	Curing time	Dry color	Gap filling
Animal glues	Poor	Excellent	6 hours	Brown	Poor
Elmer's Glue	Poor	Poor	2 hours	Clear	Poor
UFR adhesives	Excellent	Excellent	8 hours	Cloudy	Good
Epoxy resin adhesive	Excellent	Excellent	30 hours	Clear	Excellent
Polyurethane adhesive	Excellent	Good	4 hours	Cloudy	Excellent
Contact adhesive	Excellent	Poor	20 mins	Cloudy	Poor

heat with an iron and a little water will loosen most joints enough to part them. Scotch glue is often used for fixing veneers.

Elmer's Glue (Polyvinyl Acetates)

These are commonly available water-based adhesives that dry clear and fairly hard. Types are available for both interior and exterior use. The drying time depends upon the local temperature but will normally be long enough to put together complicated structures. The rapid-drying versions are useful when gluing together components in a particular order.

Urea Formaldehyde Resin (UFR) adhesives

UFR is a combined white-powdered resin and hardener that dries into a cloudy glass-like substance that can be cut or planed. It forms a rigid joint and is ideal for structural use. Beware of face-surface contact, especially when staining. Residual glue will seal the grain completely and stop stains penetrating the wood, leading to a light tidemark around joints. UFR curing times relate to the temperatures in which they are applied, so do remember this when using UFR in summer.

Epoxy resin adhesives

These adhesives are ideal for waterproof joints in exposed locations. They come in two-part kits, with hardener and resin mixed together before application (always follow the manufacturer's mixing instructions). The chemical reaction between the two creates heat and is fairly rapid, so you may need to test to see how much time you have before the joint becomes inflexible; this is especially important with larger projects.

Polyurethane adhesives

A relative newcomer to the market, polyurethane adhesives can bond a whole range of materials, apart from wood, and can be used both in- and outdoors. They are probably as strong as the epoxy resin described above, with the advantage of being one shot with no need to mix. Polyurethane adhesives actually react and harden when exposed to moisture (although do not permanently immerse them in water). Most manufacturers will therefore recommend that you slightly dampen the joining surfaces of very dry timber before application. Once applied, this adhesive often effervesces slightly.

Contact adhesives

Most contact adhesives allow various different types of materials to be bonded, although they are not ideal for structural wood-to-wood jointing. When using these glues, spread both joining surfaces with the adhesive, wait a predetermined time and then press the two together. The best types of contact adhesives incorporate a time-delay mechanism, allowing for some maneuvering to take place before the parts finally bond together.

> ⚠ **Caution**
> Take care when using adhesives, avoiding contact with your eyes or open wounds. Some of the chemicals in them can cause skin reactions and rashes.

Below Some adhesives can be applied with a glue gun.

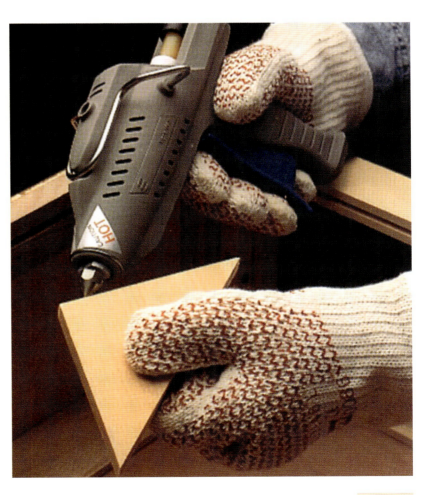

Power tools

Thanks to technological advances, nowadays most electric power tools are available without a cable, which makes working in many situations much easier and quicker. However, there is still a case for retaining powered tools with cables: they are powerful and efficient and you won't run out of batteries at a critical moment.

Above right Practice with power tools before beginning actual work.

Below An electric chain saw and a circular power saw.

Selecting power tools

Your choice of power tools should reflect how and where you might use them, and your budget. Often, a combination of different tools and power sources will do the trick. Pneumatic systems are also available for operating a range of tools and, with a small compressor, are worth considering for high-volume production.

Unless specifically mentioned, the following information refers to electric power tools that are both cable- and battery-operated.

Saws

There are a number of different types of power saw available for woodworking. Here is a brief selection of the best.

Chain saw

Great for chopping down trees, a gas-powered or electric chain saw can also cut through big boards quickly and efficiently. Do take care when using these tools, though, preferably getting some training before taking them on.

Circular saw

The average blade diameter of a circular saw is around 6in (150mm). Small diameter saws are good for cutting floorboards, for example. A cable- or battery-operated mid-range machine is fine for occasional use and lightweight work. If you want the tool to run for longer, go for a larger one. Most are direct power-driven from the electricity supply, but some advanced battery pack models with larger blades are available.

Whatever its size, a circular saw is driven at rightangles to a flat sole plate. There will be some form of depth of cut adjustment mechanism. Most sole plates are hinged on one end and have a slide on the other so that they can be set to different thicknesses. There are a number of accessories that will turn a handheld circular saw into a fixed table saw.

The saw should be held firmly and steadily fed into the workpiece to be cut. A retractable blade guard will automatically uncover the blade to start the cut, springing back after the cut is made. DON'T fix it up out of the way. If you put the saw down as it slows, with the

blade exposed, the tool will react violently and unpredictably and you could be hurt.

Jigsaw

The jigsaw is invaluable for cutting internal and external curves, ripping down and across the grain and cutting sheet materials. The range of cutting capacities depends on the power of the tool, the blade length, and the type of material being cut. The usual capacity is around 2–3in (50–75mm). Larger ones are available, but avoid using them on hard material.

A flat sole plate forms the main working surface. This should be able to be canted for angled work and you may find your tool has a side fence. The stroke of the blade, the amount of movement up and down to create the cutting action, should be adjustable, depending on the blade and what is being cut. Check the recommended stroke before starting.

Jigsaw blades come in many shapes and sizes. Those with large teeth are for softer materials, medium-sized teeth for harder materials, and fine teeth for metal

Reciprocating saw

Used for cutting wood, metal, softer construction blocks, and pipe-work, this saw mimics the hand saw's action by reciprocating a blade, in line with the body, back and forth. With a small sole plate placed against the workpiece, they make a quick cut.

Alligator saw

This is a lighter-weight alternative to the reciprocating or chain saw. Two blades are set side-by-side and move in opposite directions creating the cutting action. On site, an alligator saw is useful for cutting softer building material. It is less dangerous than a chain saw, has longer blades than a reciprocating saw, and creates more waste because of its blade design.

Miter saw

Simple hand-operated miter or chop-off saws have a circular saw blade that cuts on a downward stroke. The position of the blade can be set at rightangles to the back fence or adjusted through various angles to the left or right of center. A compound miter saw enables the operator to set the tool to cut a combination of angles in two planes that allow, for example, a cornice joint to be made.

More sophisticated saws are designed around a sliding mechanism, increasing the width of cut. The saw blade body is drawn toward the user and lowered into the workpiece. The cut is made on a backward stroke.

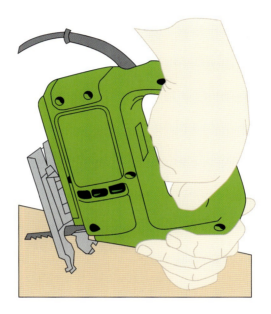

Left The jigsaw features a flat plate that can be canted down so that the saw can cut into work at an angle.

Below A miter saw.

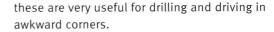

Above A cordless drill.

Above A cordless angle drill.

Below A cordless screwdriver.

Drills

With the design of the keyless chuck, options for drilling and screwing became far greater, and now special quick-release or hexagonal tool chucks are also available. Overall, you may need two or three different tools to cover most eventualities. For straightforward, occasional work, opt for a medium-powered drill with a keyless chuck. For a lot of site work, consider a low-voltage option with a transformer, which offers protection against the dangers of cable damage.

General purpose drill-drivers

The wattage rating indicates the power of a drill. Below 600 watts will do for light use, while anything up to 800 watts is sufficient for most jobs. Battery-operated drills range from 12–14 volts and above. The really expensive tools start at 18 volts and can reach over 30 volts.

Ideal options include a reversing facility and a variable speed or range of speed adjustment.

Heavy duty and percussion drills

Those with battery packs of more than 18 volts in capacity will probably include a useful percussion facility. For heavy-duty masonry drilling, a cabled tool with a power rating of over 800 watts is best. With these larger-cabled tools the chucks are keyed or have a hexagonal quick change-over system.

Angled drills

These are based on a lightweight general-purpose capacity with a small chuck. The important consideration is the width between the top of the head and the jaw of the chuck. The shorter this is, the tighter the space the drill can be fitted into. You may have to shorten a set of bits to accompany a drill like this, but these are very useful for drilling and driving in awkward corners.

Screwdrivers

Most general-purpose powered drills can be used as a screwdriver as well, especially those with a variable-speed trigger. Some manufacturers have designed smaller, lightweight tools specifically as screwdrivers. These are battery powered with smaller-capacity units, and most should be left on permanent charge for use at any time.

Sanders

Sanding is a notoriously long and tedious task, so powered sanders are a godsend. However, you will still need to hand-finish some corners, shapes, and delicate work. Three main types are available (see below), but you can also add specialist sanding tools, such as flap and flail attachments, to your powered drill. These are fine for intricate work and flap-sanding attachments will do for flat surfaces, while a mini-drum sanding kit (available in various diameters) cleans up small, inner curves and circles.

Try to avoid inhaling fine wood dust when you are sanding. Not only can it cause irritation, but wood dust is also, to a degree, carcinogenic. Be sure to operate an efficient dust extraction system and wear a partial, or full-face, respirator.

Detail (or delta) sanders

Operating an orbital route (see orbital sanders below), these are good for final finishing off in tricky corners due to their ability to sand right up to an edge, depending upon how the abrasive sits on the sole plate. There are options to change the shape of the sole plate and the type of attachment.

Orbital sanders

These are often referred to as "finishing sanders." This is because their operating pattern produces a fairly fine finish. The pad, or sole plate, of the sander is driven in a tight elliptical pattern with forward and sideways movement. When using coarse abrasives, a swirling pattern can clearly be seen. To avoid this, work down from a coarse

Far left Using an orbital sander.

Left Using a power sander.

to a fine grit. The sander's speed is usually stated as orbits per minute. Top-end rates will be around 25,000 orbits per minute, while slower, or variable, speed options are available to allow for different types of materials to be worked.

Most square- or rectangular-shaped orbital sanders take a standard width of abrasive that is cut from a large roll. Alternatively, you can buy the more expensive precut sheets to fit your sander.

Random orbit sanders

These tools run on a random elliptical sanding pattern that leaves little or no marking on the working surface. They can be effective, removing waste rapidly, when fitted with a Velcro-type system and punched-hole abrasives.

Belt sanders

Belt sanders are used for bulk waste removal before the workpiece is finished with an orbital or random orbital sander. A fabric-backed abrasive belt is wrapped and stretched around two rollers, one of which is driven. Between the rollers is a flat sole plate that is placed on the surface of the workpiece while sanding.

It can be difficult to avoid digging into the surface when using a belt sander. Practice will help, but using a sole plate attachment will prevent this from happening.

Smaller sanders

Smaller, narrow-belt sanders (also called "power files") are available. These take belts from ½–2in (13–51mm) wide. Some have long noses to reach into tight spaces.

Planes

Handheld planes remove the sawn surfaces of timber before you finish off with something else. Some have handy attachments for rabbeting; others can be inverted in a stand to use as a surface planer, while optional accessories turn some heavy-duty models into a thicknesser.

Cut and motor size

The width of cut generally comes in two main sizes: 2½–3¼in (65–80mm). Wider industrial versions remove more waste and so require more effort to control.

In terms of motor size, something in the region of 500–600 watts will tackle occasional jobs, but for regular use aim for 750 watts with a "soft-start" motor control system to extend the life of the machine. Cutter block rpm will also vary, probably between 10,000–20,000 rpm.

Lighter machines usually have a maximum depth of cut of 1/16in (2mm) while industrial versions, with up to ¼in (5–6mm) depth of cut, have proportionally larger motors.

Above A detail sander.

Above A belt sander.

Left Using a power planer.
Below An electronic planer.

Routers

With the mass of jigs and attachments available, a router is one of the more essential and versatile workshop tools.

Router motors

These can be classified into three groups: light, medium, and heavy/industrial use. Motors of up to 600–700 watts fall into the first group while those with 800–1200 or 1300 watts belong to the medium group. Anything higher can be classed as an industrial rating.

Router operation

Most routers have a swivel or dial speed control that is set at the required level before starting work. It is important to set the correct rpm for the cutter mounted in the router and this should be indicated in the manufacturer's instructions. A range of 10,000–20,000 or more rpm is common.

The internal measurement of the collet relates directly to the shaft size of the cutter, which is ¼–½in (six, eight or 12 millimetres). Most have a self-locking mechanism that works as you tighten the collet nut. Logically, routers that accept ½in/12mm collets can take smaller ones, but not vice versa. Opt for a router that accepts

Above A router base plate adapter enables greater precision and adaptability.

Right A portable woodworking router.

a larger collet if you require total flexibility. However big the cutter, the shaft should always be inserted at least three-quarters of its length before the collet is tightened.

A router must feel comfortable—not too heavy if you are hefting it about but not so lightweight that it judders. If possible, deal with trailing cables by hanging them over a shoulder or suspend them above you.

Dust extraction

Modern routers are supplied with a plastic shield and dust extraction port to stop too much dust landing on the user. Opt for a good-sized extraction port; one that is too small will easily clog.

Plunge routers

These cut internal slots, grooves, and holes but you should ensure that the pillars, or legs, fit correctly into their housings. Check for wobble and play. Ideally, the pillars should be polished or chromed. The return spring needs enough guts to pull the router out of the workpiece when pressure is released. The plunge mechanism requires a lock so you can use it as a fixed plate if you wish. Some manufacturers make a dual-purpose router with two bodies. The cutting head and motor fit into a plunge- or fixed-base body for total flexibility. The fixed base is best for repetitive and fine, precision freehand work, because the center of gravity is lower.

Side fences

Most side fences are fitted to the router on a pair of round bars. These are locked to the base plate and the adjustment is made on the outboard side. Better routers have a fine wheel adjustment facility. The surface of the fence that runs adjacent to the workpiece should be smooth enough to generate little friction.

Router base plates

These are often round or, more commonly, elliptical in shape, with two parallel straight sides. For precision routing, base plates should be securely fitted with a smooth surface at rightangles to the motor drive/cutter shaft. Its outer circumference must be exactly centered to avoid slight discrepancies in molding size during

use. Heavy router work requires the base plate to be run up a batten or guide. The center hole should be big enough to allow the collet and large cutters to pass through. If not, there should be a removable section to allow this to happen. Some jigs require extra projection beyond the base plate, so this center hole clearance is important.

Left An angle grinder.

Jointers

There are two types of dowel jointers—round and flat.

Round dowel jointers

These are used in the mass production of furniture or for smaller projects, potentially offering an alternative to traditional joints. Various sizes are available, with chamfers around each end and grooved up their length. The grooves let out the excess glue. If specific diameters of ready-made dowels are not available, you can make your own from long lengths of round dowel, remembering to run at least one small saw cut up the length of each dowel to allow out excess glue.

Flat dowel jointers

These are often called biscuit jointers because of the shape and size of the dowel joints they produce. Most are made from compressed beech, and should have the grain running across the short width rather than down the length.

Biscuit jointers utilize a small, circular saw attached to a power tool body to cut various-sized slots to suit the appropriate dowel. When choosing a jointer, bear in mind that a heavy tool, which might be stable in use, will eventually become tiring, although a light tool may move around in use.

The Domino

This jointing tool combines the benefits of round and flat dowels into one machine, creating strong joints. It uses oval-shaped, solid wood dowels of various thicknesses and widths. A special cutter fits into the main body of the tool and it both rotates and moves from side to side, creating an elongated slot with rounded ends. Like the biscuit jointers, two opposing slots, when fitted with the special dowel, form the joint.

Nailers and screwers

It is worth considering dedicated power tools if you plan to do a lot of nailing and screwing. For use in the workshop, pneumatically operated tools are best, as they are fast and efficient.

Above A coil system nail gun.

Other miscellaneous kit

Battery-pack combination sets

One of the combination, battery pack sets of tools could be useful for a smaller workshop or for general on-site work.

Small angle grinder

The metal cutting blade on a small angle grinder can be useful for cutting off old nails and screws. An angle grinder can also be fitted with other discs, rendering it highly versatile.

Vacuum cleaner

A vacuum cleaner is an essential piece of kit for any woodworker, even if a workshop has a dedicated dust extraction system.

Left A flat dowel or biscuit jointer.

Woodworking techniques

Although as woodworkers we all have our own preferences and particular ways of doing things, there are certain fundamental principles and techniques in woodworking which should always be followed. This chapter lays these out one by one and offers a series of supporting tips and ideas designed to help you improve your woodworking skills. Hopefully, this information will contribute towards the invaluable library of knowledge that is your own personal woodworking experience.

Sawing techniques

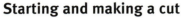

Holding a saw correctly is vitally important. In most cases, a firm grip with the index finger pointed in the direction of cut is the right way, but always try out any new saws for fit before buying. If they feel uncomfortable then consider something else. Remember, you can only work happily if your tools feel right.

Above right The correct way to hold a saw, with the index finger pointing down the handle in line with the cutting action.

Starting and making a cut

To start a cut, you might find it easier to draw the saw blade toward you rather than away from you. This technique is especially useful with thinner saw blades. Once a small groove is established, you can then revert to conventional sawing techniques.

Another technique when starting a cut is to use the thumb of your free hand to guide it. However, if you do this, make sure that your thumb is cocked up high enough to avoid being cut by the saw teeth. If you are working to a line, always cut on the waste side, so that the final component can be finished to size.

The sawyer needs to be in a comfortable position to make a true cut. A cutting angle of around 45 degrees should be fine, working off a saw horse, in a vise, or on a bench. Take even, consistent strokes; the cutting action is always

away from you unless you are using a pull saw. If you deviate from the line at all, correct this by applying slight sideways pressure, during the cutting stroke, to the left or right.

When nearing the exit from the cut, use your free hand to support the falling piece, providing it is not too large. With bigger sections, you may need help from another pair of hands.

When cutting smaller sections or narrow strips of thin sheet materials, try using your free hand to slightly lift the waste piece as the saw cut progresses. This should provide the blade with enough free action to make the cut.

If you have to make a cut that is out of the normal cutting range, it is often possible to reverse the saw and cut away from yourself. Some traditional saw handles have special notches cut out to allow your fingers to wrap around the handle for better control.

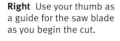

Right Use your thumb as a guide for the saw blade as you begin the cut.

Far right Holding thin material like ply apart will ease the cut as you saw through it.

Far left Sometimes it is possible to reverse the saw in the cut.

Left Using a sawhorse can make cutting easier.

You can use larger frame saws for ripping and cross-cutting, providing they are fitted with the right blade. If you are doing shaped work, try fixing the workpiece into a vise or clamping it to the side of your bench. This will keep your hands free to concentrate on the trickier cutting that the shaping will doubtless involve.

Sawhorses can be very useful, both in terms of supporting work and giving you better sawing access. If their height and position are suitable, they should help you carry out an extensive range of ripping and cross-cutting jobs.

When using fret or coping saws on thin materials, you may need to provide support underneath the cutting point to make the process easier. For this, you could use a simple jig, fixed into a vise or screwed onto the workbench, or just an underlying board on a sawhorse. Try to avoid cutting into the support.

Left Support thin material on a sawhorse to ease the cut.

Below left Placing a wedge in the end of a cut helps free the blade.

Tips for success

- Reversing the blade in a coping saw can sometimes be helpful. In effect the saw is converted to a pull saw, and the blade is in tension rather than compression. This should result in fewer breakages.
- On a finely set saw blade, some candle wax rubbed onto its cheeks helps reduce friction while cutting.
- Look after your saws. Protect the cutting tips with a plastic sheath (known as a "keep") or something similar. Lightly oil them when not in use. Always keep them sharp and ready for action.
- Sometimes when ripsawing (cutting down the length), the board being cut will close up and pinch on the saw blade. You can keep the cut open simply by inserting a small wedge.
- Cutting sheet materials can be difficult, especially if they are thin. An easy way to stop the sheet flopping about, and pinching on the saw blade, is to support it each side of the cut with a couple of planks of wood placed on a pair of sawhorses.
- Through cuts with a saw will produce fine whiskers (spelshing) on the opposite side, away from the cut. To avoid this, use a bit of gash stock underneath to support the object piece while it is being cut.

Planing techniques

Planing is one of the essential woodworking techniques that requires practice and application to learn to a good standard. When setting up a workpiece for planing, inspect the wood to ascertain the general direction of the grain. Always plane with the grain if you can, to avoid tearing the wood fibers.

Above right The correct planing action on the edge of a workpiece.

The right way to plane

When planing, either by hand or when using a machine, you dress (plane up) the workpiece in a series of set sequences. You start on one face. If the workpiece is slightly cupped you should plane the dished face flat, level, and straight first. This is marked and the first edge is squared off this face, followed by the second edge, also squared off the first face. Finally, the workpiece is brought to thickness and finished off.

When smoothing or jointing, try to maintain the right positioning and movement through the planing action. Initially, the emphasis is on pushing the plane from the rear and down on the front. As the stroke progresses, this alters on exit to downward pressure at the rear and a forward push at the front. Practicing this movement will help to ensure straight planing.

Always use the right plane for the job. A smoothing plane will not be much good for straightening edges that are to be jointed. Conversely, the quick removal of waste requires a smoothing or scrub plane.

When you are edge-planing thin material, it is easy to rock the plane and this can make it difficult to finish off properly square. To counteract this problem, hold the plane steady, using some of the fingers of the leading hand which should run up underneath the first finished face.

Wider pieces of wood need a combination of different cuts to level them off. Begin by working the face of the workpiece with strokes that alternate slightly across the grain, from one side to the other. Finish off by planing down the direction of the grain.

Right The correct planing action on the face of a workpiece.

Far right Use the right plane for the job.

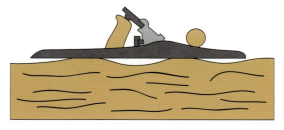

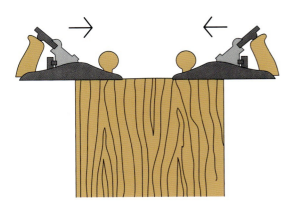

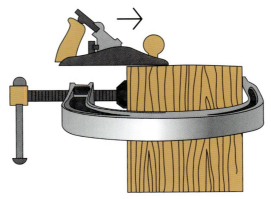

Far left On end grain, work from the outside in...

Left ...support the exit point with a clamped bit of waste.

Use the sole plate to check progress during this flatting process. Lay it on its side, at a slight angle, at rightangles to the direction of grain.

Getting a good, clean cut on end grain can be difficult. If you work one way across the grain it will break out on the exit side. The correct way is to work the end from both sides until the finish is achieved.

Narrower pieces of end grain work might need a slightly different approach. A piece of gash stock can be clamped to the exit edge to ensure that the break-out is minimized.

The alternative method of cleaning up end grain is with a shooting board. The workpiece is held firmly by hand and the plane "shoots" up the board to clean it off. Providing the support stop is at rightangles to the side, a perfectly square end can be cut.

You can make simple shooting boards yourself. They are also useful for cutting miters and to achieve this you only need to set the supports at 45 degrees.

Tips for success

- Wooden planes improve with age. The more they are worked the less friction they appear to have when moving over the workpiece.
- Rub candle wax onto a metal sole plate to ease friction.
- You can produce a smoother, more consistent rabbet when using a rabbeting plane by starting at the farthest point and working backward.
- Take care of your planes and always keep the blades sharp. Never put a plane sole plate down on any surface.
- A bit of gash stock on the bench will keep the cutter free, or always turn it on its side to protect it.
- When putting the plane away after use, draw the blade up clear of the sole plate. If it is not to be used for a while, take the blade assembly apart and lightly oil it. You can put it all back together when next you use it.

Below Two shooting boards—one for tidying miters (bottom).

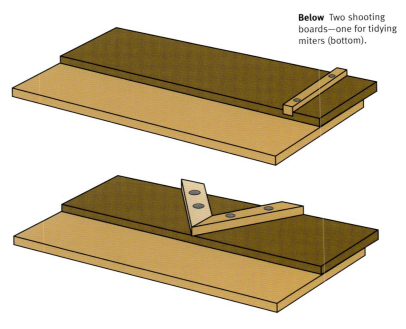

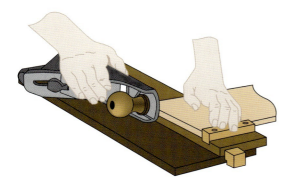

Above Use a shooting board to make end-planing easier.

Chiseling techniques

Chisels are used for a variety of different woodworking tasks and there are several basic techniques that need to be perfected. In joint-making they are particularly useful for removing waste wood and for paring components down so that they will fit together tightly and accurately.

Above right With practice, your chiseling will become perfect.

Right Vertical paring with a chisel.

Far right Using a bevel-edged chisel.

Using a chisel correctly

Always work the chisel away from yourself. It is easy to make a slip and a sharp tool will slice through flesh without any difficulty.

The ideal position for making a horizontal cut is when your forearm is parallel to the floor. This allows you to apply the maximum amount of cutting force with the least effort; all your body weight should be behind the cut. Guide the chisel with your free hand. For greater force, strike the butt end of the chisel with the ball of your hand.

For vertical cuts by hand, make sure that you are able to get your shoulder right over the end of the chisel. Once more, if you are in the right position, your body weight will help the cut to be made. As you grip the chisel, your thumb should be in between your shoulder and the butt end of the chisel. Guide the chisel with your other hand by slipping the blade in between your index and middle finger. If more effort is needed, strike the handle with a mallet.

Trenches across the grain are cut in three stages. The first is to cut down the edges to the right depth with a fine saw. To remove the bulk of the waste you need to work from both sides to the center. To finish off, work again from both sides to bring the bottom of the trench level.

Mortise holes should also be cut in stages. Make the first cut, with the flat of the chisel away from you, just inside the final end mark. Turn the chisel round and make another cut just behind the first and lever the waste out. Continue in this way until you have nearly reached the other end of the mortise slot. Do not yet cut down the end marks. Continue this

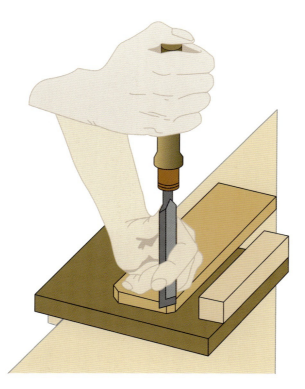

process a layer at a time until the required depth has been reached. With through mortises, work from both sides into the middle. When the bulk of the waste has been removed, trim the ends true and square. To remove bulk waste quickly, and for big mortise holes, you may like to make some drill holes first, as this will make life easier. Once that is done, follow the above procedure.

When making framing joints with beads, molds, or rebates, cutting a miter to join these sections in the corner helps to make a neat joint. A simple chisel miter jig will help the process along. You can easily make one of these yourself.

Tips for success

- Paring chisels are designed for use by hand and should not be struck.
- If you have to strike a chisel, always use a wooden mallet, never a hammer head, as this will damage the chisel.
- If you can afford it, buy a wet grinder for sharpening your chisel blades. It is the most efficient way to achieve a really sharp edge on your tools. Alternatively, a combination grinder incorporates a standard, high-speed dry abrasive wheel with a wet stone facility on the other end.
- The side edges of some chisel blades are quite sharp. To avoid cutting your fingers when paring, take the edge off them slightly with an oilstone.
- At times it can be useful to have a spare set of inferior-quality chisels that you can be forgiven for abusing slightly. If there is any chance of cutting into a stray nail or screw, for example, these are the ones to use.
- Chisels and gouges should be kept sharp to cut efficiently and reduce the amount of effort required to work them. Always buy the best quality you can afford, as they will last longer and keep their edges better.
- When putting a chisel down after use, try to keep the cutting edge up and away from any other items.
- Store chisels in plastic covers or in rolls.

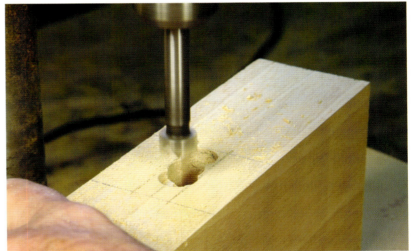

Above Cutting out a mortise: making cuts with a chisel (top); drilling out as an alternative (center); finishing off (bottom).

Turning techniques

Entire books have been written on the subject of wood turning, lathes, and their associated tools, jigs, and accessories. There is not enough space to cover the subject in detail here, but the following is all the basic information that the wood turner needs to get started, at the very least.

Above right Rapid waste removal with a gouge on the lathe.

The art of turning

With practice, the wood turner is able to cut continuously, creating streams of shavings flying over his or her shoulder. This only happens if the lathe is set up correctly and is operated at the right working height. The ideal position is for the center line of the lathe to be in line with the tip of the cutting tool and the elbow of the operator, whose forearm should be parallel to the floor.

You must also be comfortable and in the right position to create shaving streams. Try standing as close to the lathe as possible, with the tool handle tucked into the side of your body and held in place with your forearm. Your feet should be slightly apart, and you should not be leaning either backward or forward. This stance should enable you to swing the cut from left to right. On longer pieces, you may have to stop and reposition yourself. If this is the case, carefully work over each finishing point to avoid any high spots where you overlap.

Grip the cutting tool firmly in your leading hand. The other hand controls and guides the tool during the cutting process. For rough cutting, employ the overhand grip. This is very useful, as large gouges enable swathes of waste to be removed quickly.

For delicate finishing and bead work, use an underhand grip. Putting your thumb on the top of the cutting tool helps you to retain better control for those fine, fiddly bits.

Cutting between centers (cylinder work) is fairly simple. With the workpiece mounted, select your tool. If you are using a gouge, for example, rest the blade on the workpiece with the heel running directly on it. The gouge cannot yet make a cut. To start the cutting procedure, raise the back end of the handle slightly until the tip engages on the workpiece. Rock the tool into the cut as you travel one way and rock it back to go in the other direction. Gradually increase the amount of pressure you exert as the cut progresses.

Right Fine cutting on the lathe.

Far right Keep your thumb firmly on top of the cutting tool.

Bowl work on a face plate follows two distinct working sequences. Having mounted the blank from which you are going to make your bowl, work on the outside first to bring the whole thing into balance as quickly as possible. Your stance should be identical to that when turning between centers. Rough down the shape carefully. A "dig in" at this point might reduce the eventual size of the workpiece if it has to be cut out, so this is to be avoided at all costs.

Having shaped the outside of the workpiece, consider the cutting field for the middle. The rest should be placed so that the tool can follow the center line when cutting. The area of cut is from the center to the nearest edge.

When face-plate working, the removal of waste and final shaping should take place from the outside toward the center. This way you will be working on the down side edge only. Remove bulk waste with a gouge and carefully use a scraper for final finishing.

Tips for success

- Practice makes perfect. So, when starting out, don't get straight into trying to turn a finished project or a new shape such as a bead. Practice on odd bits of softwood or other gash stock. Go for the real thing only once you get the hang of how you need to control and operate your tools.
- Your lathe should have a variable speed control, set to faster for small work and slower for larger pieces. This reflects the peripheral speed of the workpiece as it rotates. If the revolutions per minute, (rpm) is, say, ten, the outer, cutting point on the smaller pieces travels a lot less distance than a large one. Practice will tell you how fast to go for the size of the workpiece being turned.
- When polishing your work, you can save time by leaving it in the lathe. Applying oils, waxes, polishes, or seals can be done quickly and easily. You can do any subsequent rubbing down, burnishing, or polishing with the workpiece in motion. For best results, you may need to adjust the rpm slightly.
- Prepare your blanks before they are mounted in the lathe. Thick chunks for bowls should be marked out and the corners cut off and rounded on a bandsaw or by hand, if possible. Items turned between centers can also have their sharp corners removed. By preshaping slightly, a lot of hard waste removal is done off the lathe.

Above left Rough down the shape carefully, avoiding dig ins.

Far left A finished piece: a turned bowl.

Left The finished turned lamp project on pages 224–7.

Veneering techniques

Wood veneers are covered in some detail in the general introduction to this book, on pages 20–21. Like wood turning, the art of veneering could fill an entire book. Here is an introduction to the basic techniques required to make a start in this ancient and fascinating area of woodworking.

Above right Wood veneers stored in a case for safe keeping.

Choosing wood and creating veneers

The key to any veneering project is to get the base material (the "ground") correct. If it is going to split, shrink, or react adversely to the veneer fixed to it then your previous work will be wasted. Sheet materials made up from plys, chipboard, or fiber board can be used successfully and these should all be sized with a diluted application of glue.

A solid wood ground is the traditional base for a veneer. It is best to avoid hardwoods like teak and oak, as one is naturally oily and the other too open-grained. A tight-grained, light-colored hardwood or a clear-grained softwood are both suitable. Any knots, pitch pockets, and other similar defects need to be cut out, plugged, and fixed with the same grain orientation. End grain plugs will eventually stand out, disfiguring the finished surface.

It is important that whatever material you decide to use is dry. It is best to make up solid wood grounds from strips, but do ensure that the end grain orientation is alternated to compensate for any potential movement.

Shaped grounds are interesting challenges. They can be made from stable, solid wood but this is wasteful and expensive. If you wish to do

this, however, remember to keep the scraps, as they can be used as cauls and will match the shape exactly. Steamed and laminated sheets can also be used and, once made, they should be strong and very stable. The two traditional ways of making shaped grounds are via wood bricks (using small pieces of wood that are joined like a brick wall and then shaped once the adhesive has cured), or coopered to shape, with each strip being produced with the appropriate angle on their sides and then joined like a barrel.

Once the grounds are ready, you can start veneering. Remember that both sides of the item must be veneered, to balance the ground and ensure there is no movement. Use the best stuff on the face and anything else on the backside. The veneer should run at rightangles to the grain of the ground to provide further stability.

For smaller projects it is probably best to use a veneer hammer. This is not a hammer in the true sense of the word—it is used to squeeze out excess glue from between the veneer and the ground. For this to work properly, the veneer should be perfectly flat. Therefore, you will need to do some preparation first. The veneer should be slightly dampened with some sized glue and then placed between two flat planks, each lined with waxed paper. These should be clamped up and weighed down overnight. By morning they should be flat and true. But beware: it is very difficult to remove bubbles left in the veneered surface after it has been attached. So, if the first flattening session does not work properly, try again until you get it right.

Below Different methods of preparing "grounds" for curved veneering.

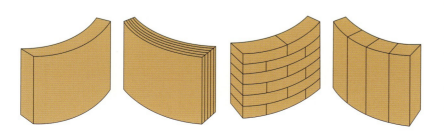

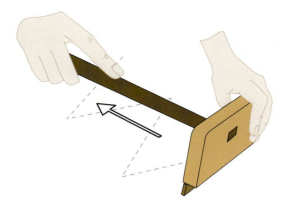

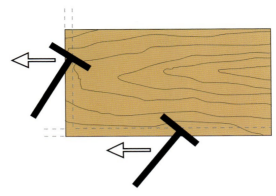

Far left Start the veneer hammer off in a zigzag pattern.

Left Apply the veneer hammer all over the surface.

Once the adhesive is on, apply the veneer hammer all over the surface, from the center out, in a zigzag, overlapping pattern to ensure total coverage, remembering to wipe excess glue off the hammer as you go along. Not doing so might affect the quality of finish. If the veneer overlaps the edge then make sure that part of the hammer remains in contact with the main workpiece. Use it diagonally over the edges, otherwise you may break the veneer and ruin the job.

Another way of applying the veneer is by using cauls. These are two flat or shaped plates that fit each side of the assembled workpiece.

Once you have applied adhesive to the individual components, they are tightened into place to hold everything steady whilst the glue sets. Ensure that you allow sufficient time for the glue to cure before removing the cauls.

Animal glue is generally regarded as the best adhesive for veneering, because it remains flexible during the position stage. The glue is heated and starts to cure as it cools. If necessary, the process can be reversed by warming it up slightly with an iron. Other proprietary products specifically designed for fixing veneers are also available.

Below Applying a veneer using cramps (top) and cauls (bottom).

Tips for success

- Make sure that any animal glues are fresh for veneering. You can reheat them once or twice, but doing this too often might lead to loss of integrity.
- Take care when cleaning up a project after applying veneer. It is all too easy to scrape or sand through the veneer and expose the ground.
- Always store veneers carefully. Set aside a special place where they can be weighed down and kept flat. Alternatively, construct a sealed box in which they can be stored safely (see image at top of opposite page). Make sure they don't move around and get broken.
- If you want to see the effect of matching your veneers, hold a mirror to the surface at rightangles. You will then be able to clearly see what it will look like when it is in place.
- Do not use pens or inks to mark out on the veneer faces. These can be difficult to remove and may stain lighter woods.
- Prepare your veneer patterns well in advance so that the assembly process is smooth. Do a dummy run to see how long it takes and ask for help if necessary.

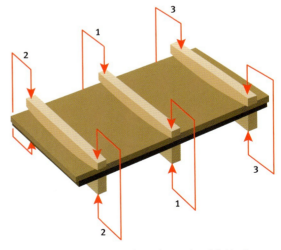

Arrows denote cramps; numbers show order of tightening

Bearer

Caul

Veneer

Groundwork

Bearer

Gluing techniques

The different types of adhesives and glues that are suitable for woodworking are covered on pages 152–3. Here, we consider the techniques required for applying them effectively. Adhesives have become ever stronger over the years, and if not applied in the correct manner they can ruin your work.

Above right Apply glue carefully and avoid excess.

Using glues effectively

The first point to take into account is which type of adhesive to use. For some jobs, a delayed adhesive action will be helpful. Where structural components, or joints under stress, are married together, glue that sets rigid is probably required. If a simple adhesion is required, then one of the more flexible glues might be suitable. Think through the various aspects associated with your project and choose your adhesive accordingly.

One of the most important points to make at this juncture is that the joints being fixed together need to be well made. Adhesive alone will not bridge and join large gaps successfully. If they are visible, wide, glue-filled joints will also look awful. Straight-edge or face joints should be exactly that—straight. Mortise and tenons, dovetails, and other cut joints should be snug fits. Dowels need to be gently pressed home (not driven with a hammer!), or they will become less effective.

When joining wood together, the simple principle is to work the glue into the adjacent structures to form a joint that is often stronger than the original material. When edge jointing, apply glue to both adjoining faces and "rub" the glue into the surfaces by working the boards back and forth. This helps to create a good, tight joint and squeezes out any excess glue. Socket joints need to be worked in and out to achieve the same result.

Gluing-up complex projects with multiple joints needs planning. It may not always be the most obvious sequence that has to be used. When making chairs and tables, with lots of frames, rails, or odd shapes, the gluing-up process may take two, three, or more attempts to get everything up together. Plan the sequences and have a dry run for each stage. Consider the time factors involved. Will you have enough time to glue and make the joints before the adhesive starts to go off? A hot, sunny day is

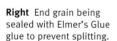

Right End grain being sealed with Elmer's Glue glue to prevent splitting.

Far right Think carefully about the suitability of the adhesive you plan to use.

- Never use too much or too little glue. Too much may interfere with the joint seating and too little will affect its strength. Apply to one or two surfaces as directed by the manufacturer.
- How deep the adhesive penetrates into the wood surface will not only depend upon the grain structure but also how dry it is. If the wood is wet, the adhesive may "float" on the surface and not bond. Always make sure the jointing faces are clean, grease- and dirt-free and also dry, unless otherwise instructed by the manufacturer.
- UFR adhesive hardeners are activated through contact with moisture. Although shelf life is claimed to be quite long, always reseal the tub immediately after use. A small amount of dampness will start to have a detrimental effect. Store in a cool dry place; I keep mine in the study. When buying, always check the dates on the bottoms of containers and buy the newest rather than oldest stock.
- Although not recommended for more than short periods, you can leave the top off a container of Elmer's Glue without too much detrimental effect; all that happens is that it thickens. However, do protect it from frost, because that will have an effect upon its ability to bond.
- Always have a dry run prior to actually gluing up your components. There is nothing worse than finding out halfway through that one or two pieces do not quite fit!
- Never release the clamp pressure on a glued-up project unless you are confident that the adhesive has cured. If you want to speed things up a bit, then store in a warm dry place overnight. If the items are not too big, bring them into your house for a while.

not always the best time to be gluing. Cold days will normally, depending upon the adhesive, give more time to get everything up together. A dry run will also identify where you might need some help to simply hold a piece or two for a short time. If no help is to hand, you will have to be resourceful and maybe make up some simple support jigs instead. Making frames, in stages, also requires that you get each section square or set at the correct angle. Two chair sides that don't match when the cross rails and stretchers are put in place will wobble. It can be cured by equalizing the legs to fit firmly on all four but, to the discerning eye, the seat or back rails might look out of line.

Having tried out the joints for fit, you should have a good idea of how many clamps and cramps you will need for the job. This is another factor that will affect the gluing-up strategy. For simple frame and flat surface work, lay out the clamps ready with some packing pieces. More complex shapes and sections may need to have additional bits left on or specially shaped packers made so that pressure can be applied to the joints to pull them up together. Choose your packing materials carefully. Make sure they are softer than the object pieces so that they don't dent any surfaces. Some woods, like oak, will mark if they get wet or damp. Using water-based adhesive alongside a metal sash clamp can often cause a staining reaction that might take some work to remove. Old, neutral paper placed in between will help avoid this.

Check out the earlier section on glues and adhesives on pages 152–3 for the fine detail on which glues do what in woodworking. Additionally, in the panel above you will find some more tips that you might find useful.

Above left Apply glue liberally to both mortises and tenons.

Left Some gluing-up jobs can be extremely complex.

Joinery

There is a subtle difference between a carpenter and a joiner, although most woodworking craftsmen are trained in both disciplines. The former "carps" the wood to produce structural work such as roofing, while the latter "joins" the wood to produce nonstructural items. In this section we examine joints and associated items—known collectively as joinery. Strong joints are essential for good project making, so it is important to learn how to make them early in your woodworking career.

Types of joint

The key to any successful project, apart from the quality of the work, is choosing the right joint. It is not always necessary to use the most complicated type if a simple joint will achieve the desired outcome. Sometimes the joint itself becomes a feature and, in this case, much more care is needed in its preparation.

Above right A well-made wood joint will last for many years.

Introduction

Joinery can only be produced if the wood to be worked is of a suitable quality, the joints are made accurately, and the final item is finished off to an acceptable standard. The joiner needs a practical understanding of geometry and proportion and should be able to visualize how all the components are to be assembled in the finished piece.

A useful joinery technique for the general woodworker is the practice of making full-size drawings of the project in hand. By doing this, construction details can be defined, joints positioned, and angles calculated. A little effort taken to prepare working drawings will save time later and will avoid costly mistakes.

Types of joint

Wood joints are generally grouped together into a variety of different types as follows.

Dry joints

Dry joints are made so that they can be altered easily and as necessary. They allow movement in adjacent components or are fixed with nails or screws. Most dry joints are associated with flooring and wall coverings.

Glued joints

Glued joints are to be fixed permanently or, if animal adhesives are used, can be released and reset if required (as in much furniture making). The disadvantage with glued joints is that, in the majority of cases, once they are made they cannot be easily disassembled.

Framed joints

Framed joints are used in the construction of a frame, hence their name.

Below A dry corner halving joint and mitered halving joint.

Below right A dry edge-to-edge joint, using round dowels.

Plowed/grooved and tongued joints

These joints are used where some shrinkage is expected but the gap is still bridged sufficiently to stop dust passing through. The grain of the tongue, or fillet, runs in the same direction as the two adjacent pieces.

Other joints

Angled joints connect components at different angles on various planes while dovetail joints are in a group on their own and are considered later on in this section.

Dry joints

As previously indicated, most dry joints are associated with flooring and wall coverings.

Plowed/grooved and tongued joints

These are used where some shrinkage in the wood is expected but the gap is still bridged to stop dust passing through. The grain of the tongue, or fillet, in these joints runs in the same direction as the two adjacent pieces.

Fillet joint

The fillet joint is used in thicker flooring to enable individual lengths to be raised without disturbing others.

Rabbet joint

The rabbet, or half lap, joint is often used for

heavy-duty flooring on trucks. It allows for secret fixing if required and replacement is fairly easy.

Beveled tongued and rabbet joint

This is a strong profile used in flooring in which secret nailing is required. Each piece is placed over the previous one when it has been fixed in place.

Beveled tongued and groove joint

A basic joint for flooring, this can be secret-nailed, but will probably be double-nailed in the traditional way.

Top A fillet joint.

Above A half lap, rabbet joint.

Far left A loose tongue joint.

Bottom left A beveled tongued and rabbet joint.

Below A beveled tongued and groove joint.

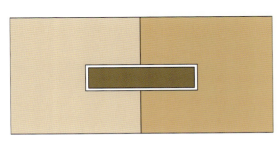
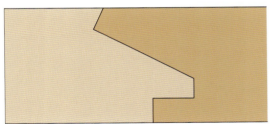
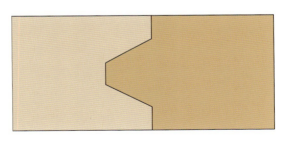

Right A tongue and lip joint.

Far right A tongued and edge joint: single tongue.

Below right A tongued and edge joint: double tongue.

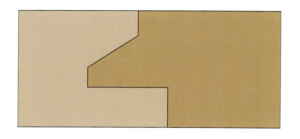

Tongue and lip joint

Similar to the beveled tongued and rabbet joint, the tongue and lip joint does not reduce the width of the board as much and so provides better surface coverage.

Horizontal wooden sidings, weatherboarding, or paneling can all be made up from a number of different profiles. In most cases the design of the joint, and how it is fixed, enables movement to take place as the boards seasonally change size as weather conditions alter.

Glued joints

In these examples, the term "glued joints" refers to edge jointing to make up wider or thicker boards. A proprietary adhesive should always be used to ensure that the integrity of the joint is maintained.

Rubbed edge joint

The rubbed edge joint is a simple, basic joint that relies on the adhesive being worked into the wood structure on the adjacent faces. By

rubbing these faces back and forth before final positioning, the adhesive is worked into the wood and forms keys. These joints are ideal for simple, light projects.

Tongued and edge joints

These joints utilize a cross-grained tongue to improve the strength of the joint. Once more, the adjacent faces should have adhesive applied and be worked together before final fixing.

Loose and fixed tongues

These joints should be made up in two ways. The grain of the first, a feather tongue, should run in the same direction as the two joining pieces. This should not be used for structural purposes. The grain of the second, the cross tongue, should run at rightangles to provide extra strength in the joint.

Dowel joints

Dowel joints can provide an edge joint with extra strength. As a rule of thumb, they should be placed about 12in (300mm) apart. Premade dowels are available in various sizes from any hardware store.

Biscuit joints

Also called flat dowel joints, these are a quick and efficient way in which to make a joint. They

Below A cross tongue (top); a feather tongue (bottom).

Far left A dowel joint.

Left A forked tenon joint.

can be used for edge, end, and side jointing, and mitering if the wood is thick enough. Biscuits come in a range of sizes to suit most projects.

Framed joints

Most of these joints are based on a mortise and tenon principle. The actual choice of joint will depend upon the end use of the project in hand. The mortise—female—joint should always be cut first. The tenon—male—joint can then be made to fit tightly and snugly into it.

Simple tenon

This is formed by cutting down two cheeks and trimming off the shoulders.

Haunched tenon

This is often used as a through tenon that is then wedged in place. The haunch enables more wood to be left on the outer extremity of the mortise, so that it can be wedged without breaking.

A pair of tenons are used when wide components are to be jointed and are haunched to reduce them in size.

Stump tenon

This has a thicker section at the base of the main tenon. It enables more cross-strain to be placed on the joint if the frame comes under pressure.

Forked tenon

A simple joint, this is used when connecting cross-sections to rails. The shoulders are slightly beveled to ensure that a tight joint is created when it is closed up.

Double tenon

This joint is used when the material to be jointed is very thick. Haunches may or may not be employed. Thick, wider materials may be jointed with a pair of double tenons.

Barefaced tenon

This joint may or may not be haunched and is often used when the tenon component is thinner than the mortise component section.

Fox tenon

A fox tenon joint is used when internal wedging of a joint needs to take place, to stop it coming apart. The mortise hole is slightly widened at the base. Slots are cut into the tenon and small, slim wedges inserted. When the joint is closed up the wedges force the tenon apart and lock it into the mortise hole.

Far left A haunched tenon.

Left A double tenon.

Below A barefaced tenon.

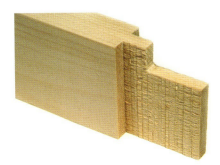

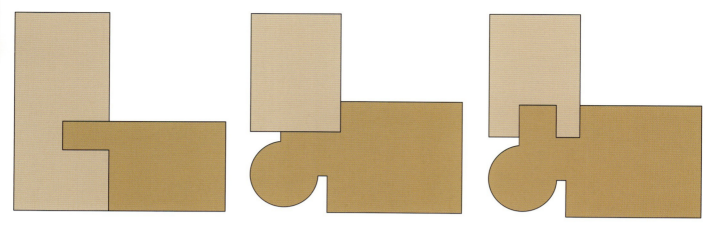

Angled joints

These joints are used for both edge and end jointing in frames and various other structures. They are very versatile and come in varying degrees of complexity.

The simple grooved and tongue joint can be used for both edge and end jointing. A bead can be applied on the edge to hide the joint.

The basic rebated joint can be masked, also with an applied bead. It should be used for edge jointing only and fixed with a nail.

Staff joint

Also called the return bead, the staff joint is used on framing. The nail fixing is driven down out of sight in the small trench.

Double-tongued and bead joint

The double-tongued and bead joint is superior to the staff bead joint and is used in better-quality cabinet work.

Simple miter joint

This joint can be used on edges or ends for framing. It is typically used for jointing internal and external angles when fixing baseboards or for architraves and picture frames. The easiest and most effective way to reinforce a miter joint is to drive nails through it after the glue has set.

Tongued miter

This is mainly employed when end grain jointing. The joint is strengthened by the use of a full-length cross-tongue or the popular flat dowels.

Stop miter joints

These joints are used when one component is thicker than the other, allowing the overlap to take place.

Lipped miter

Easily made and very strong, this joint is usually fixed with nails.

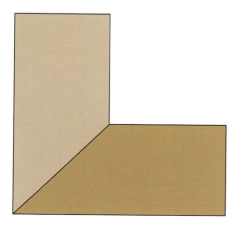

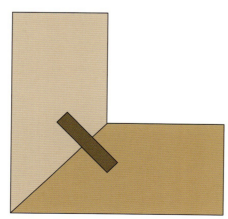

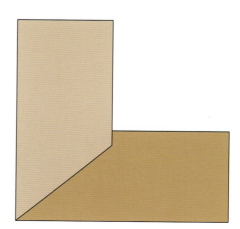

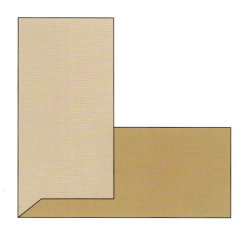 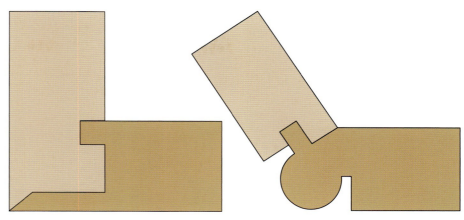

If you prefer not to nail, you can use the lipped and tongue miter joint. The adjoining surface areas are increased and this enables the adhesive to form a very strong joint.

The mitered double-tongued and beaded joint can be varied to suit other angles.

Other joints

Both the single-tongued and double-matched joints can be used in conjunction with round corner work. The double-matched joint is often left dry so that it can be taken apart easily. It must, therefore, be made as a tight fit.

The false rule joint is used in box work around windows and doors to match other molded work. The applied molding helps to mask the joint.

The simple corner locking or finger joint is the precursor to the dovetail joint. Glued only, never nailed, it is usually employed with box work in which the contrasting end and face grain appears quite attractive.

Dovetail and other joints

Made up from pins and tails, dovetail joints are strong and decorative when they are exposed. They are most commonly used for constructing boxes and cabinets from solid wood. They have also been an essential component of drawer-making for many centuries, as their inherent strength means that they can resist the pressures involved in the opening and closing of drawers.

Dovetail joints come in three types; through, lap, and secret. The through joint—which is the most basic form of the joint—shows both the end grain of the pin and tail and is visible on both sides of a corner, the lap joint shows only the end grain of the pin, and the secret joint, as the name suggests, shows nothing at all.

The through dovetail is widely used to create corner joints in box work. It is also this version of the joint that is most commonly used for the back joints in drawers and the use of contrasting timber creates an interesting feature.

Above left A lipped miter joint.

Above center A lipped and tongue miter joint.

Above A mitered double tongued and beaded joint.

Below left Single tongued and double matched joints.

Below center The false rule joint.

Below A simple corner locking or finger joint.

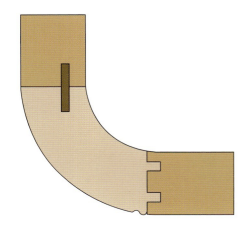 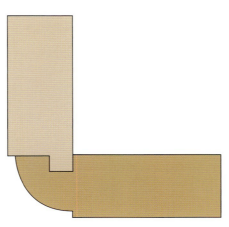 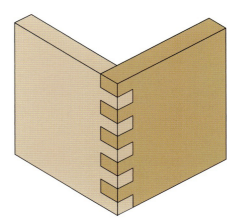

Above A through dovetail joint.

Above center A lap dovetail joint.

Above right A single dovetail framing joint.

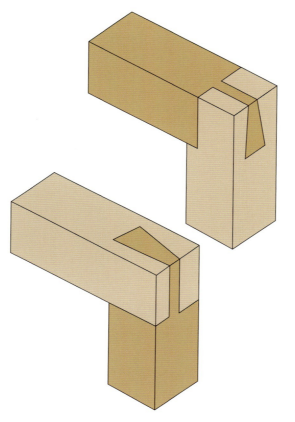

Right Two alternative versions of the single dovetail framing joint.

Below A dovetail sliding housing joint.

Below center A sliding housing joint.

Below right A lipped sliding housing joint.

The lap dovetail joint is also most commonly found in drawer work, securing the front to the two sides. The joint is designed so that it does not show on the face of the drawer.

The secret mitered dovetail looks complicated but is actually not too difficult to reproduce. It forms an extremely strong joint for quality work.

Simple through dovetails can be employed in framing work. They may be used to stop a rail lifting or a stile coming out.

A dovetail can also be used as a sliding housing joint when, for example, shelving is to be placed on a side. This forms a strong joint that holds the components tightly together.

Housing joint

This is the simple alternative to the sliding dovetail. This can be a through or stopped joint depending upon how it is being used.

Knowing which is the best joint to use for a given purpose takes time and experience. Inevitably you will develop preferences for certain types of joint—doubtless those which you manage to make the most successfully.

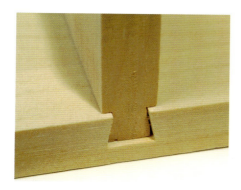

Wastage

Waste can mount up when working projects down from raw materials —especially when you are jointing. Yield is the amount of usable lumber cut from a log. When you are creating and jointing projects, the yield from lumber to planed component also needs to be calculated to ensure that enough material is available to produce the final product.

Above Sadly, whenever you cut wood, wastage is inevitable.

Preparing your cutting list

Unless you are aiming to use ready-prepared sections from your local timber yard you will need to design the project first and identify the size of each component. You can then compile a cutting list of lengths, widths, and thicknesses, including both nominal and finished sizes. The former is the size of the raw material you will need in order to produce the latter.

Briefing your supplier

You now have a number of options. Let's assume you don't have the materials in stock and therefore need to purchase them. You could simply ask your supplier to provide enough material "to cut" the nominal sizes on your cutting list. Under these circumstances you will need to saw and plane the material to its finished sizes yourself.

The second approach is to provide your supplier with the same list and ask for the material to be "sawn to size." They should cut the wood to the nominal size for you to plane up. The final method is to ask for the cutting list to be supplied ready-planed. This should be "PSE," planed square-edged and could be in lengths to cut or cut to length. This is by far the most expensive option of the three.

Below Cutting list sizes.

Finished size	Nominal size
1/8" (3mm)	ex 1/4" (6mm)
1/4" (6mm)	ex 3/8" (9mm)
3/8" (9mm)	ex 1/2" (12mm)
1/2" (12mm)	5/8" (15mm)
5/8" (15mm)	3/4" (18mm)
3/4" (18mm)	7/8" (22mm)
7/8" (22mm)	1" (25mm)
1" (25mm)	1 1/8" (28mm)
1 1/8" (28mm)	1 1/4" (32mm)
1 1/4" (32mm)	1 3/8" (34mm)
1 3/8" (34mm)	1 1/2" (38mm)
1 7/8" (47mm)	2" (51mm)
2 3/8" (60mm)	2 1/2" (63mm)
2 7/8" (72mm)	3" (76mm)
3 7/8" (98mm)	4" (102mm)

This chart is based on being able to reduce sawn stock to planed material with 3mm (1/8") wastage. You may find that this is not possible, depending on the machines you have and the wood you use. You may need to allow greater waste, nearer 6mm (1/4"). Note that the nominal sizes in bold text are those that are most commonly available in timber yards.

Below Wastage according to purchase method.

Form of purchase	Hardwoods	Softwoods	Sheet materials
Off the shelf	Maybe 5–10% from end waste		
PAR, cut to length	At cost, no waste unless you allow extra		
STS, cut to length	At cost, but you lose shavings		At cost
PAR or STS, lengths to cut	Probably 10%, or a little more		
Timber to cut, square edge	23–35%	15–20%	
Timber to cut, through cut	70% plus		
General sheet materials			About 20%

Finishing wood

A good finish can turn an ordinary piece of furniture into an outstanding one. Equally, a poor finish can ruin a well-made and constructed piece. One of the keys to successful finishing is therefore to test beforehand the materials that you intend to use. This could be on a separate, prepared piece of gash stock or on the underside of part of the workpiece. However you choose to do this, always make sure that you are happy with the result before proceeding to the final, finishing stage.

Preparation

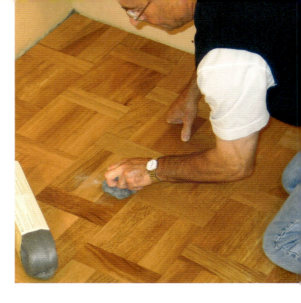

Unless you are aiming for a rustic effect finish, you will need to have fully worked down the surface of the workpiece. In any case, this will, very probably, follow on from the original planing through a full sequence of scraping, sanding, and filling. The item may then require staining before the final finish is applied.

Above right Wire-wooling a parquet floor prior to finishing.

Preparation tools and materials

Scrapers

Scrapers act as very fine planes, taking a thin shaving off the surface. Once the planing process is complete they are used to smooth the surface, and are particularly useful when working hardwoods with interlocking grain. To a large extent, the introduction of powered sanding tools has reduced the usefulness of the scraper, although there is still a place for them in fine cabinet work.

A successful scraper must have a good cutting edge, or burr. This should be carefully prepared before use, by removing old edges with a file or on a honing stone (see "Sharpening and setting," pages 122–5). Once these are straight or their shape is restored, the burr is applied using a burnishing tool.

Some scrapers are used by hand while others (called cabinet scrapers) are set in some form of stock or plane body. These are best used for large areas while the handheld types can finish off into corners and around shaped sections.

Right A standard cabinet scraper.

Using a scraper

Scrapers used in a stock will have setscrews designed to bow the blade slightly. If used by hand they should be grasped in both hands, placing the thumbs in the middle of the blade. When addressing the work, put pressure on the blade with your thumbs to create the bow. Hold the scraper slightly angled forward from yourself and push away parallel to the direction of the grain. With a straight stroke the scraper should produce a fine shaving, providing it has been prepared well and is being used correctly.

Abrasives

"Sanding" something down is a phrase used by many of us, but it is actually incorrect! Rather than sand, abrasives are actually made from several different materials: glass; garnet; aluminum oxide; and silicone carbide.

Glass paper is probably the oldest type of paper-bonded abrasive. It consists of crushed glass stuck onto a paper base and, today, is generally used for medium to fine finishing work. Crushed garnet stone has, in most cases, superseded the use of real sand. Garnet has better wearing qualities than glass and is mainly used for hand finishing. Aluminum oxide is the hardest wearing. It is tough and hard, retaining its properties and shape under duress, making it an ideal abrasive for use on power tools. Silicone carbide has similar properties to aluminum oxide, but is probably slightly harder. These last two examples are the abrasives that we find applied to both fabric and paper backs and are available in the full range of grits from very coarse to very fine.

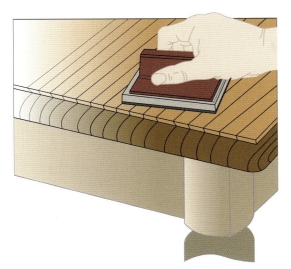

Above Using an abrasive pad prior to finishing.

When using a power sander or working by hand, it is likely that you will be sanding a planed surface ready for finishing. In this case, you will work down from a medium grit size to the final, fine grit size required for your finish. Something like an 80 grit gauge will take out all the slight ridges created when machine planing. Once this has been done, or if the workpiece was hand planed, move to a finer grit of, say, 120.

Final sanding can be finished off with 180 or finer grit sizes and should, in my opinion, be carried out by hand. It must be done with care and in the direction of the grain. At this stage you will be preparing the surface to take whatever finish you apply and you will need to remove the "arrises" (sharp corners). Slightly rounding the corners will allow the finishing coats to provide even coverage; a sharp corner will result in a thin layer of finish.

Steel wool

Another abrasive material is steel wool, or wire wool, as it is sometimes known. Steel is stripped into various sizes (grades) of sharp-edged wool-like material that can then be used as a fine abrasive. It is available in six or more grades, from the very fine double nought-double nought through to numbers four or five, the coarse grades. The fine steel wool can be used directly, with wax, to produce a luster-type finish. Medium grades are used for cutting back sealed

Below Sandpaper grit grades/sizes.

Grade	Silicon carbide, aluminum oxide	Garnet	Glass
Very Fine	600		
Very Fine	500		
Very Fine	400	400 (10/0)	
Very Fine	360		
Very Fine	362	320 (9/0)	
Very Fine	280	280 (8/0)	
Very Fine	240	240 (7/0)	00 flour
Very Fine	220	220 (6/0)	0
Fine	180	180 (5/0)	
Fine	150	150 (4/0)	1
Fine	120	120 (3/0)	2
Medium	100	100 (2/0)	F2
Medium	80	80 (0)	
Medium	60	60 (1/2)	
Coarse	50	50 (1)	
Coarse	40	40 (1½)	
Very Coarse	36	36 (2)	
Very Coarse	30	30 (2½)	
Very Coarse	24	24 (3)	
Very Coarse	20	20 (3½)	
Very Coarse	16	16 (4)	

surfaces, ready for the next coat of finish, and the coarse grades can do the stripping and heavy cleaning work.

Abrasives and French polishing

Other powdered abrasive materials are used when French polishing, the most common being pumice and rottenstone powders. Both provide a very fine finished surface and can be applied as a cream, paste, or powder.

Left Two different grades of steel wool.

After using abrasives

To get a really good base surface before applying your finish, try wiping over the workpiece with a slightly damp rag. This raises the grain of the wood as it dries, creating a slightly fluffy surface. However, be careful not to get the wood too wet when you are wiping it, and allow everything to dry off properly before moving to the next stage. When you are ready, rework the surface of the workpiece with your finest grit abrasive.

Stoppers and fillers

Stoppers can fill cavities such as small splits, worm holes, and knots while fillers are used to fill the grain so that a fine finish can be produced. You can buy a wide range of stoppers ready mixed in a variety of colors to suit the wood you are working with. You may need to experiment a little with these before using them on your project, though. If you are staining a piece, you may need to use what appears to be a slightly darker stopper than the natural wood. The absorption rate of the wood and stopper might vary, so try out the process on a piece of gash stock first, or on an underside of the workpiece which cannot be seen.

Compatible stoppers from the same supplier can be blended to produce a better match. The alternative is to make your own, mixing an adhesive with sawdust and sanding dust from the same wood that is being used (see the sequence of images on this page). Plaster of Paris mixed with a pva or animal glue should absorb water-based stains, but do test first.

Right and below The materials needed for mixing up a stopper (1) and how to make the stopper: Mix the sawdust into the adhesive (2); press the mixture into the fault in the wood (3); once dry, sand off the excess stopper (4); the finished result (5).

Beaumontage

Beaumontage, a mixture of beeswax, crushed rosin, and shellac, and colored wax sticks, are available for repairs and stopping up some blemishes. Pressed against a preheated file tang, or something similar, the wax stick is held over the area to be repaired and the stopper drips in (see above). Once set, this can be cleaned back level with the finished surface.

Filling and French polishing

Filling is a technique used during the French polishing process. The objective is to fill the grain of the subject wood so that a mirror finish can be achieved. Without filling, the wood will draw the polish in and will remain uneven. Some users fill prior to application and others during the first or second coats.

Stains

There are many reasons why staining wood might be your choice. You may wish to match existing pieces of furniture, create something that looks old, or perhaps you simply desire a colorful solution.

Types of stain

There are two basic types—dye and pigment stains—plus a few variations on the theme. Dye stains are transparent and penetrate deeply into the wood. These stains are designed to enhance the natural beauty of the wood. Most are soluble with water or alcohol (the latter being called a spirit stain). Dye stains are often referred to as "fugitive"; this is because they fade if they are exposed to sunlight over long periods of time.

Pigment stains are made up from finely ground minerals that are suspended in a varnish-type base. When applied to the wood they sit on the surface, filling and slightly obscuring the grain. Pigment stains provide a more solid color to the surface that does nothing to enhance the grain of the wood. They do, however, hold their colors well when exposed to sunlight. Out of choice, though, dye stains are probably more appropriate for the serious woodworker.

Chemical stains

Chemicals can be used to stain some woods, reacting with the natural chemicals contained within some woods. Oak, for example, contains tannic acid. When this is subjected to a fuming process with ammonia, it darkens wood. The depth of darkness depends on the strength of the ammonia solution and the length of time the wood is exposed to it. This type of fuming is normally carried out in a sealed chamber. Other chemicals produce different effects on different woods. Like most stains, they fade when exposed to sunlight over long periods of time. Always take care when using these stains, as they can cause skin damage and other side effects.

NGRs

NGRs are commercially prepared non-grain raising stains. They are made up with various mixes of the base colorant with tuluol, glycol, acetone, and possibly alcohol. Each manufacturer has its own special recipe. NGRs are usually sprayed on and are used more in commercial applications due to their quick-drying tendencies.

Above left Applying Beaumontage with a heated file tang.

Above Wipe off any excess stain from the workpiece.

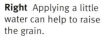

Right Applying a little water can help to raise the grain.

Far right Dampened, raised grain.

Below Staining an old piece of furniture can help to give it a lift.

Below right Applying wood stain with a paint brush.

Water versus spirit stains

Which to use is often the subject of debate. Both have pros and cons. Water-based dyes are easy to use and equipment can be quickly cleaned up afterwards. Unfortunately, though, they have a tendency to raise the grain, as they dry off after application. You can avoid this by applying the dampening of the surface technique described on page 188 and illustrated above. Failure to do so may alter the depth of color when the raised grain is resanded. Diluting the stain with water and applying several coats rather than just one can help overcome this problem. By following this process, any raised grain can be sanded down in between coats to remove it.

Spirit stains dry a lot quicker than water-based ones, so more care needs to be taken when applying them. What you need to avoid is "lapping," in which the stain has been overlapped during application, producing a darker color at that point. You need to work quickly and efficiently. Once applied, wipe the surface all over with a dry cloth to spread the dye evenly.

Applying stains

These stains can all be applied with a brush, sponge, or lint-free cloth. Pay particular care when close to end grain, because it will absorb more stain than the other faces. You may need to mask some sections off and deal with them after you have done most of the staining, testing it out first. Try not to apply too much stain on or near the end grain. Just lightly touch it in and wipe off any excess as quickly as you can. You could opt for a chemical stain to change fundamentally the color of the base wood, using a lighter stain afterwards to achieve the desired result.

Finishes and their application

The surface finish you choose for a piece of work depends on how much effort you are prepared to put into it, the associated wearing qualities, and the type of luster or shine you want. There are many different options to choose from, but you are bound to develop your own particular preferences over time.

Waxes

Waxes can provide good protective surfaces and are particularly resistant to moisture. If standing water is left on a surface, however, it will soon penetrate and mark it. If spotted quickly, this can be simply wiped off and another wax coat applied to restore the surface. Waxes are easy to apply and, after years of polishing, can produce some of the best patinas seen on older furniture.

Types of wax

Ranging in type from hard to soft, wax can be used in isolation or blended and colored to produce a product that may have universal use. The following waxes are the most commonly available:

- **Beeswax** Secreted by the honey bee as part of its eating and food storage process, beeswax is used to make honeycombs in which the honey is stored and prepared as a by-product after the honey has been harvested. Colors vary, depending upon which plants the pollen has come from, from a pale creamy "white wax," through to a darker "yellow wax." Because beeswax is not water soluble, it is probably the most water-resistant of all the waxes. It is easy to blend and can be mixed with all other waxes.
- **Carnauba** This comes from a palm tree in Brazil. It is one of the hardest waxes and, if used alone, produces a high luster. It is also compatible with other waxes. When mixed with beeswax, for example, it improves the latter's polishing qualities.
- **Paraffin** This wax is produced via the petroleum industry and is most easily

recognized in the form of a candle. Paraffin wax is water-resistant and inert, and does not react chemically with wood. On its own it has few qualities, but it can be blended effectively to bulk out other mixes and this can be an inexpensive way of getting the desired result.

Above Wax can create a beautiful, burnished finish on many woods. (See this project on pages 262–7.)

Below This solid wood carved seat has been waxed to a fine finish.

Above Waxing wood: applying the wax (top); removing the excess wax (center); polishing the wax to a fine finish (bottom).

Using wax

Without specialist knowledge you will probably find it difficult to use hard wax on furniture. It tends to be used in wood turning, in which higher surface temperatures can be generated to melt the wax onto the work and then buff it up. Soft waxes are usually blended and mixed with a solvent; each manufacturer has its own special recipe. It should be applied to a section at a time using a lint-free cloth. As soon as the wax has been worked in, remove the surplus with a fresh, clean cloth. You can leave this while you start another section, giving a final buff up to raise the luster.

Waxes can be used directly onto wood and, over time, will build up a quality finish. To speed the process up, you may consider giving the project a coat of sanding sealer, or light varnish. Afterwards, use steel wool to cut this back and follow the three-part waxing process. The wax buffs up more easily with the wood pores slightly filled with sealer. If you use plain wax, you will find that wood with open pores builds up a lighter deposit. Color-tinted waxes that complement stained wood are available to overcome this. When these are worked into the wood, the color remains within the pores.

Oils

Natural, plant-extracted finishing oils have been used for generations. They can penetrate the wood, providing it with a wear- and moisture-resistant surface, but it is difficult to raise a high luster using them. Oils that have been boiled, or that have additives to aid drying, are called drying oils. These will not penetrate as deeply and, with some effort, can be brought to a semi-gloss finish. A number of these products are readily available on the market. They are often blended and branded under a specific name. Some of the most common ones include:

- **Linseed** This is probably one of the most easily recognized oils and comes from the seeds of flax plants. As a finishing oil, it is probably best used in its boiled state. Some manufacturers add chemicals to speed up the drying process. Linseed oil tends to darken wood, so is not often used on light-colored woods. This oil is used as the base for a range of manufacturer-specific products that are often labeled as teak or Danish oils.

- **Tung** Tung oil comes from the nuts of a Chinese tree. Originally only available in China, these trees are now grown in plantations, especially in America. Tough and very water-resistant, it also darkens wood and is therefore unsuitable for a blonde finish. In its raw state, tung oil dries very slowly. Consequently, most manufacturers blend raw and boiled oils together, adding a little thinner (probably mineral spirits). The result is a drying oil that is much easier to use.
- **Walnut or "nut"** Produced from cold-pressed nuts of the walnut tree, this oil is very light and suitable for a light wood finish.

Other oils can also be extracted from poppy seeds, sunflower seeds, and so on.

How to use oils

Surface preparation is the key to getting a good finish when using oils. The surface should be as smooth as possible before you begin. Manufacturers usually recommend ways of applying oils which, in most cases, will involve building up a surface finish over time and with several coats. The first of these can be thinned down, allowing the oils to penetrate the wood deeply. Remove any excess with a lint-free cloth and leave to dry off for a day or so. Second and third coats follow, reducing the thinning ratio, until a final coat of the pure product is applied. Do leave each application to dry off thoroughly and then buff up with a dry cloth (changing this regularly to ensure the removal of captured excess oil). If the cloth drags on the workpiece, there is probably too much oil on it.

To maintain a surface it is often best to repeat the oiling process annually, at least. This helps to remove any light marking and builds up a protective surface. If the surface is badly marked or scratched, it can be worked down with sandpaper and the whole process repeated. Different oils can be blended together and mixed with special dyes to help color the base wood. Some blended products might also use beeswax to help produce a more easily polished surface.

French polishing

French polishing is one of the oldest forms of finishing still practiced today.

Where French polish comes from

The polish is made up from a natural resin, shellac, produced during the reproductive cycle of a lac bug, found in and around the Indian subcontinent. Once harvested, shellac is graded and refined. The least refined variant, seed-lac, is the base material from which all the other variations are produced. Button-lac used to be the next, more refined stage of the process, but more common today is flake shellac, produced by further refining of the base materials. Flake shellac comes in a number of different colors, ranging from the darker orange and garnet through to the blonde and white versions.

Above Applying tung oil to a workpiece. Wear rubber gloves and work the oil well into the workpiece with a soft, dry cloth.

Left Shellac flakes—otherwise known as French polish. These come in a variety of colors.

Producing the polish

Shellac is mixed with an alcohol solvent. This process can be carried out in the workshop using shellac flakes and the traditional solvent, ethyl alcohol, which has been modified to meet modern legislation. To make up the polish, dissolve around 12oz (340g) of flakes in three cups of solvent.

Once this has been done, the mixture can be filtered through layers of cloth and stored until needed. At that stage, some further thinning may be required and you will also need to add an oil lubricant—probably just a little linseed oil—to aid the application process.

Many different shades of shellac are available. You can either use these individually or blend them together to produce your own unique color or to match into an older finish.

The alternative to making your own shellac is to buy it ready mixed, which is probably the easiest way to get started if you have not done this before.

French polishing pads

The shellac is applied by hand throughout the process using a pad called a tampon or rubber. These pads are made up from linen with a core of wool or raw cotton. Note that wool feeds the shellac out slightly quicker than raw cotton. Before use, the core material should be prepared by soaking it in a diluted shellac solution, which is then squeezed out and allowed to dry.

There are several different shapes of pad, the most popular being the pear-shaped and the egg-shaped. The first gets into corners while the latter is useful for large pieces of work.

To make a pad you will need a piece of linen material measuring about 9in (225mm) square and some pretreated wool or raw cotton to make a ball of between 2–3in (50–75mm) in size. Follow the sequence of drawings on this page to make up your pad.

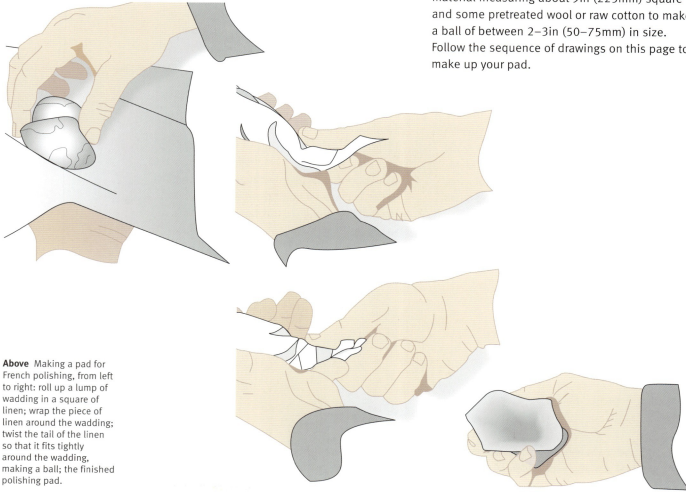

Above Making a pad for French polishing, from left to right: roll up a lump of wadding in a square of linen; wrap the piece of linen around the wadding; twist the tail of the linen so that it fits tightly around the wadding, making a ball; the finished polishing pad.

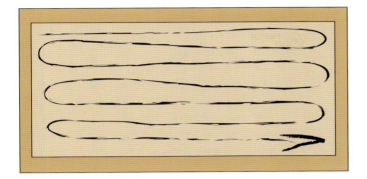

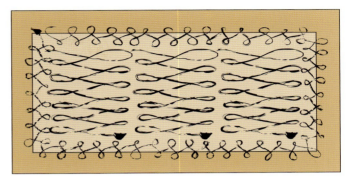

In use, the pad should be opened and the shellac applied directly to the core material. The key to French polishing is to release the shellac slowly from the pad by squeezing it as you work across the surface. If the shellac is poured onto the pad as a whole it will be too wet, contributing towards a poor surface finish.

There are some subtle variations between application techniques. In the early stages some polishers use a "fad" rather than a rubber. This is a wad of raw cotton, or alternatively, a soft, lint-free cloth. When shellac is applied with one of these it is referred to as fadding.

Once your pad has been used, store it in a sealed glass jar. This stops it drying out and it can then be reused many times.

If you are using a rubber, make sure you control the rubber by using all your fingers. This allows for an even pressure to be applied, releasing a steady flow of shellac and resulting in an even coverage.

Applying shellac

When you are ready to start, plan your application process surface to surface. Charge the rubber by putting the shellac onto the core material. The first coats must be applied in long, slightly overlapping strokes. Wait a few minutes between coats and apply, at this stage, up to three. This should now be left for fifteen minutes or so to harden before lightly cutting back with a fine grit abrasive or steel wool.

The next stages follow on continuously. Using small figure eights, cover the whole surface of the workpiece, working methodically. To ensure that the edges are also well covered, use smaller strokes all round. Do not go back over any areas

that have been missed, as this will break up your rhythm—you will have to catch up with these at the next stage.

Change the stroke pattern to larger figure eights and follow straight on with a second coat. If at any stage something goes wrong or some stray lint gets on the surface, you will need to stop applying the shellac, allow the work to dry, rub it down, and start again.

Finish the sequence off with straight strokes running along the grain and do not overlap. Work the rubber right through, end to end, one way, and then return the other way for the adjacent stroke.

This is the end of the first stage and the workpiece should be left to dry and harden overnight. This allows the shellac to settle and, probably, sink a little. This surface now needs to be cut back and leveled with a fine grit abrasive.

The final stages now take place. Start by applying the shellac in the same sequences as before, from the small figure eights through to the straight runs. This should be left to dry for fifteen minutes or so and then the whole process repeated. This process should be continued until a good, deep sheen has been created evenly across the workpiece as a whole.

To complete the surface, it will need to be spirited off—sometimes called stiffing—on the following day. The surface should first be very lightly cut back with a fine abrasive. Then, charge a rubber with a diluted solution of shellac, three parts to one denatured alcohol, and follow the three stage application process. Carry on for two or three times until you feel a slight pull on the rubber when it is in contact. At this point the process should be complete.

Above left Start by applying shellac in long, lengthways sweeps.

Above Progress to an even series of smaller figure eights.

Right To create a high-gloss mirror finish, sprinkle Vienna chalk from a pounce bag and burnish the workpiece.

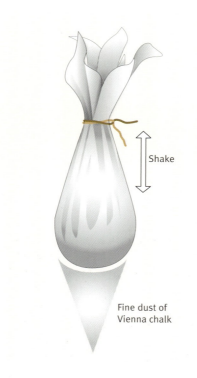

Shake

Fine dust of Vienna chalk

Below A magnificent mahogany chest of drawers with a high-gloss mirror finish.

Below right Applying varnish with a paint brush.

High-gloss finish

To create a high-gloss mirror finish, you could use a fine, premixed cutting paste, cream, or powders in a pounce bag, to cut the surface back once more. Dust the surface with the cutting powder or apply a thin coat of cream or paste. Using a little pressure, work along the grain.

Once the whole surface has been covered, wipe off the excess with a slightly damp chamois leather. This should, with practice, produce a fine mirrored finish.

Shellac polishes can produce high-gloss surfaces and enhance the natural beauty of the wood to which they are applied. Bear in mind, though, that they are not hardy and can easily be marked by water and other liquids.

Varnishes

To most of us a varnish is a preprepared oil- or water-based solution that is applied with a brush. Technically, the term also encompasses shellac polishes and any other resinous substance that can be applied to a surface, drying with a transparent finish. Which varnish you choose depends on how and where the finished product is to be used.

Types of varnish

Originally most varnishes were oil-based. The resinous substance was suspended in oil that evaporated, leaving a sealed surface. These have been mainly superseded by synthetic products such as polyurethane. Some of these are colored and others offer finishes ranging from satin through to gloss.

Most of these varnishes are designed for internal use. Those that can be used outside will not last indefinitely. You will need to clean the surface of the wood and apply a fresh coat of varnish every few years.

Before applying varnish, it is important to ensure that the wood is dry, otherwise any moisture may be trapped and could bubble up to the surface. One way to overcome this is to use a micro-porous product which has been formulated to enable moisture from the wood to pass through the surface while resisting any moisture coming through the other way. Such products are ideal for use outside and can also be applied to wood that is not thoroughly dry. Another alternative is to use acrylic products, which, despite being mainly solvent-based, are just as tough once they have dried and cured.

Yacht varnishes are based on alkyd resins and produce a tougher, thicker finished surface than polyurethane. With their natural resistance to the effects of chemical attack, they have traditionally been used extensively for marine work. However, this thick varnish tends to run, so do take care when applying it.

The development of solvent-free, acrylic varnishes has mushroomed in recent years. Their benefits—the fact that they are quick-drying and brushes are easy to clean—have made them popular. Bear in mind, though, that their shelf life is less than those of the alternatives and you should not buy a larger tin than required for the job in hand. If you do, you may find, on reopening the tin, that the varnish has been contaminated with rust from the container.

Above left A satin varnish finish.

Above center An eggshell varnish finish.

Above A high-gloss varnish finish.

Left Hanging pieces while varnishing them makes it easier to create an unblemished finish.

Woodworking projects

This chapter contains a selection of real woodworking projects. All 18 have been made especially for this book; what you see in the following pages is what you get. Each one has been selected prior to publication and personally crafted by the author. Collectively, these projects represent a wide range of skill sets that can be adapted to suit any keen woodworker's level of experience. We hope this section of the book will inspire you to take up your tools and begin, or continue, working with wood.

Introduction

The great satisfaction to be found in woodworking lies in its unparalleled versatility as a craft and the fact that you can make so many things out of wood. The following projects range from a set of spice drawers (right) to a baby's crib (below), with everything from a shelf unit and a garden bench in between (opposite). Enjoy them!

Above right The set of spice drawers that is featured in the project on pages 256–61.

Below The Shaker cradle that is featured in the project on pages 232–5.

Below right It may be useful to draw a full-size template for more complex projects.

Designs and plans

In most cases, if you choose to make one of the 18 items in this section, you will have the opportunity to increase or decrease the size of the project to suit your own specific needs. To help with proportions and accuracy, the text accompanying the projects will often suggest that full-size drawings are made of one, two, or more different elevations. This is good practice. It will help the maker to visualize the finished item, adjust any of the dimensions to suit their specific needs and ensure that the proposed construction will work. It also gives the maker an insight into the processes to follow, to ensure that the project can be assembled in an orderly and workable fashion. Full-size drawings will also allow the maker to take measurements, angles, and shapes directly from them and transfer these to the wood being worked.

Techniques and choice of tools

The techniques discussed in this section can also be applied to a wide range of other projects of your own devising.

Although a number of large and small powered tools have helped in the production of the projects, traditional hand tools will achieve exactly the same outcome, albeit over a longer period of time and with more effort involved.

The choice between cutting a joint by hand, or partly or entirely using a machine, is down to the maker and the tools that he or she has available. The key to success is not how the joint is made but its integrity and how good it is for the job in hand. Some joints can be both structural and decorative—the dovetail, for example. When cut for their appearance, then precision is necessary. In this case the old adage "measure twice cut once" is very appropriate. However, wood is very

forgiving: mistakes can be rectified and often will remain undetected if they are repaired with care.

Another good practice is to always try to have a "dry run" with the components before assembly. This gives the maker a chance to see if those joints do actually fit. There is nothing more annoying, or careless, than to start gluing up and find a tenon is too long or too tight. On a hot day with a number of joints to get up together and the glue starting to go off, panic will quickly set in!

Choosing the right wood

The timbers chosen are those that are either the most appropriate for the end use or those that should be readily available. In the text accompanying each of the projects you will find, in most cases, a description of why a particular wood was used. You will also find comments on alternatives. Some of the projects use more than one timber. In these cases, this is usually because the overall design of the project benefits from the use of more than one wood. However, availability, cost, and choice of finish also come into the equation.

Don't be afraid to change the type of wood used and experiment with the finishes applied. Careful use of stains can create dramatic effects when only one wood is used, if that is the desired result. It is the detail that counts. The small table in cherry with walnut inlay is a good example of this (see pages 278–83).

Outdoor projects really require timbers that have been treated with preservative or are naturally durable. To maintain the integrity of the preservative, all fresh cuts into treated wood should be recoated. Other timbers can have their useful life extended by applying preservatives or water-resistant finishes by hand.

Above left Have a "dry run" to check that components fit before starting to glue everything together.

Above The integrated garden bench and trellis that is featured in the project on pages 214–17.

Left The room divider/ shelving unit that is featured in the project on pages 246–9.

Cutting board

Materials	Sycamore, *Acer pseudoplatnus*; beech, *Fagus sylvatica*; iroko, *Milicia excelsa/regia*
Time to make	1 day
Skill level	Basic

This is an interesting project that is both decorative and practical. The size and shape can be varied to suit the wood available or the end use; smaller boards could act as trivets. Using end grain means that when something is cut, and the board is wiped clean, any cuts in the surface of the wood will close up.

Toolbox

Essential	Basic hand tools
Useful	Planing machine; powered saws

Making the cutting board

If the board or boards are not to be used for food preparation, then any contrasting woods will do. However, if, as with this one, the intention is to use the board for cutting food upon, then some thought needs to go into the woods selected. All three chosen here are often used for cutting boards. Naturally, anything that is used for food preparation should be kept spotlessly clean.

Making up the first stage of the end grain checkerboard is a bit like preparing rock candy; you start out with strips that are joined and then

Below The finished chopping board. It is suitable for cutting vegetables and so on, or alternatively could be used as a bread board.

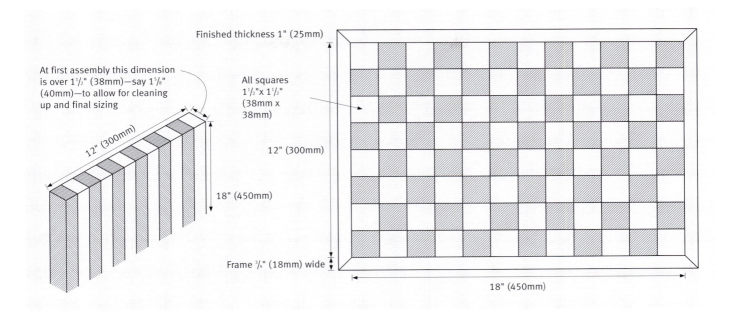

At first assembly this dimension is over 1½" (38mm)—say 1⅝" (40mm)—to allow for cleaning up and final sizing

12" (300mm)

Finished thickness 1" (25mm)

All squares 1½"x 1½" (38mm x 38mm)

12" (300mm)

18" (450mm)

Frame ¾" (18mm) wide

18" (450mm)

reduced in size. The first thing to do is to settle on the size of board. Then divide the length and width by whatever you feel will be an appropriate sized square. You should aim for an even number in width and length so that the squares can be alternated to contrast the colors. Here it is eight squares wide by 12 long. The frame would balance the squares by being half one of their widths. The actual size of the finished squares might be influenced by the dimensions of the raw material. Make sure they are a practical, pleasing size. Squares that are too large on a small board or too small on a large one might look odd.

Surprisingly, you don't need a lot of wood for this project. This board only needed four strips each of iroko and beech. The wood was

Cutting list

Component	Pieces	Length, nominal		Width, finished		Thickness, finished	
Dark blocks	4	18"	450mm	1½"	38mm	1⅝"	41mm
Light blocks	4	18"	450mm	1½"	38mm	1⅝"	41mm
Frame	2	24"	600mm	⅞"	22mm	1"	25mm

selected and sawn to nominal sizes so that it could then be square planed (**1**). A tip here is to plane the squares oversize on one parallel face to create a rectangular cross-section (**2**). If joined correctly, this then allows for cleaning up and

WARNING Please note that although many of these images show machines unguarded for clarity, you should ALWAYS ensure that when operating equipment the appropriate guards are in place.

1 The strips are sawn from the raw material.

2 Plane the wood "with the grain," face first then square edge.

3 Put plenty of glue on one or two adjoining faces.

4 Continue through to the last piece.

5 Once the glue has cured, sand it back level with the wood surface.

6 The strips are now turned into a series of block bands.

final thicknessing before the second stage of the board building takes place.

With the eight strips to hand, all square-planed, you can begin the first assembly process. Use food-friendly resin glue. The clamps should be laid out ready and the glue applied to the faces of the strips one at a time (**3**). As each one is matched, the adjoining faces of each strip should be rubbed together to make sure that the glue has worked well in (**4**). Process all eight like this before mounting in the clamps. Make sure

that the width of the board is now made up from the smaller dimension cross-sections. Set in the clamps; try to level the strips on the face surface and ends as best you can. Tighten off the clamps with some on both faces to balance the pressure. Leave well alone until the glue has gone off.

Once the glue has set hard, release this first stage assembly and clean off as much of the excess glue as you can (**5**). The joined strips now need to be sliced off to just above the desired finished thickness (**6**). They should be planed to

7 Put all the bands of blocks down and check they will be square.

8 Having applied the glue, make sure the block bands are lined up.

9 Trim any excess material off if necessary.

10 Work in plenty of glue, one face at a time.

the finished thickness along the edge grain. In most cases this will be just like planing with the grain, but some care should be taken to avoid the exit end breaking out. Lay the end grain blocks on the bench and alternate the bands so that the checkerboard effect is created (7, previous page). Check that the dry assembly is roughly square; this is not critical but will be helpful later. You should now be ready to make the final end block assembly. Get plenty of glue worked well in and set the bands in your clamps (8, previous page). It is more important to get the faces flush at this stage, so do not tighten off until you are satisfied that the ends are level and the surface flush. Clamp from both faces and leave the whole lot to set.

Later on, once the glue has hardened, release from the clamps and clean off all the excess. You may need to just trim the outside edges to get them flat for the frame. Combine this with checking that the board is square and make any fine adjustments as you clean up. If the outer end blocks are slightly smaller, nobody will notice. If the board is to be framed, sort out and plane up

the material for that now. Cut some simple miters for the corners. Check that these corner joints are a good, tight fit (9). With the frame and board ready to joint, set out your clamps and have a dry assembly run. Once you are satisfied that this will work, mix up the glue and put it all together (10). Clamp from both faces again and at the corners (11). Check that the frame sits flush with the board faces to avoid too much cleaning up afterwards. Leave the completed board clamped up while the glue dries.

The project is now nearing completion. Clean off any excess glue. Work the faces and edges flush and smooth down, using a 180-grit abrasive. Remove all the arrises with sandpaper. The surfaces need to be sealed. Use tung oil, because it is food-friendly, hard-wearing, and less odorous than linseed oil. The first coat can be thinned down, 50/50, with turpentine. Rub it well in (12), wipe off the excess and leave for a day or two. Apply the second coat full strength, rubbing well in and wiping off the excess again. Once this has dried off, the board is ready for use.

11 Position in the clamps and tighten up, but leave slack enough so that the corner cramps can be fitted.

12 Work the sealing oil well in to the wood to complete the project.

Dog house

Materials	Pressure preservative-treated softwood; exterior grade sheet material; strip of sanded roofing felt
Time to make	1–2 days
Skill level	Basic

Toolbox

Essential	Basic hand tools
Useful	Bandsaw; large sheet of paper

This project has been designed for a small to medium-sized dog. However, if required, it can be scaled up in a variety of sizes to suit even the largest of dogs. The finished dog house can be left to weather naturally or be painted with some exterior grade finish to a color of your choice.

Making the kennel

This is a simple project made up using halving and butt joints with the rigidity being provided by the "feather-edged" boarding applied to the frame. The easiest way to get the measurements right is to draw the entrance end of the kennel out full size (**1**, overleaf). This enables you to take measurements directly from the drawing to ensure the joints, angles, and sections are correct. With

this done, cut the end section components to length. The back of the kennel will need two fewer vertical pieces because it has no opening. Place one vertical piece on the drawing and mark the joint positions (**2**, overleaf). This one then acts as a pattern for the others to be marked out against. A simple try square and gauge are required for this process (**3**, overleaf). Each of the halving

Right The finished dog house. It can be painted or stained in any colors of your choice.

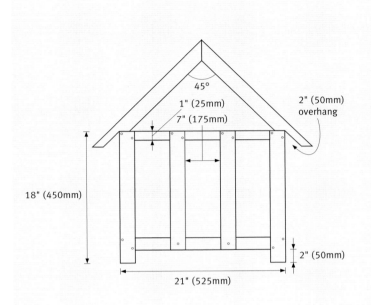

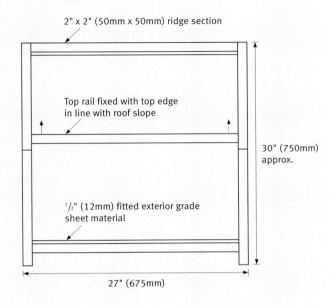

joints can be cut with a handsaw and, for the cross halving joints, cleaned out with a chisel (**4**, **5**, **6**, overleaf). If you have a bandsaw, ripsaw, or pull over cross-cut saw, some or all of this can be done by machine. Mark out and cut the horizontal pieces next. With the joints cut, check that they fit and the loose assembly is the right overall size.

The two ends will be joined with four side rails and a ridge between the rafters. These rafters are simply made by cutting to length with a 45-degree angle on each end (**7**, overleaf). They are then notched, on the lower section, to fit over the end frames. There should be a decent amount of overhang here to allow for water to run off (**8**, overleaf). The side rails and ridge can now all be cut to length. Four smaller sectioned corner battens are required to tidy off the ends of the feather-edged boarding once it is in place. These can also be cut to length with a 45-degree angle on the end. By this stage, all the joints and sections for the frame of the kennel should be prepared. The fresh cuts in the wood should all now be treated with a clear preservative and left to dry off.

Cutting list

Component	Pieces	Length, nominal		Width, finished		Thickness, finished	
Front frame	2	21"	525mm	2"	50mm	1½"	38mm
	2	18"	450mm	2"	50mm	1½"	38mm
	1	24"	600mm	2"	50mm	1½"	38mm
	1	24"	600mm	1½"	38mm	1"	25mm
Back frame	2	21"	525mm	2"	50mm	38mm	1½"
	1	24"	600mm	2"	50mm	38mm	1½"
	1	24"	600mm	1½"	38mm	25mm	1"
Side rails	4	27"	675mm	2"	50mm	1½"	38mm
Rafters	4	24"	600mm	2"	50mm	1½"	38mm
Ridge	1	27"	675mm	2"	50mm	2"	50mm
Corner battens	4	21"	525mm	1½"	38mm	1"	25mm

Enough feather-edged boarding to cover the frame when assembled
Piece of ½"/12mm exterior grade sheet material approximately
21"/525mm x 27"/675mm
4"/100mm or wider strip of sanded roofing felt

⚠️ **WARNING** Please note that although some of these images show machines unguarded for clarity, you should ALWAYS ensure that when operating equipment the appropriate guards are in place.

1 A large, plain sheet is used to draw out the front frame section full size.

2 Measurements are taken off the drawing and transferred to the components.

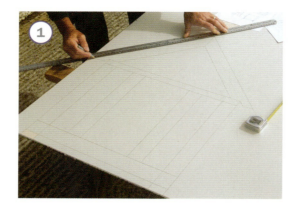

Construction begins by putting the end frames together. Predrill all leading screw holes. Put the first frame together on the ground or bench, check it is square, and screw up each joint. Repeat for the other end. Each rafter can be jointed at the top with two screws, one driven in from one side and another from the other side. They can then be positioned on the appropriate end frame and screwed on with a couple of longer screws (**9**, opposite). Prop the two completed ends up

and, with some sash clamps in place and loosely tightened up, position the lower side rails and the ridge. Once they are in the correct place, tighten up the sash clamps. The ridge needs to be turned so that it matches the angle of the rafters. Before starting to fix these rails, measure and notch out the floor board. This should be slipped into place before the top two side rails are put in place; you probably won't get it in if you don't do this (**10**, opposite). That done, slot in the last two rails and

3 Each joint is squared across the face and two edges.

4 The depth is marked with a gauge.

5 The end halving joints can be cut with a saw.

6 Cross halving joints need to have the waste trimmed out with a chisel or on a pull over saw.

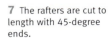

7 The rafters are cut to length with 45-degree ends.

8 Check that the rafters are set at the right pitch and fit.

9 The roof assembly is fixed to one end.

10 The floor is notched round the frame's sections and dropped into place.

tighten everything up. Following this, drill and fix down the floor board.

The whole frame should now be fairly firm and ready for the feather-edged boarding to be fitted. Start on the sides. Work out how many boards you will need. Allow an overlap of at least 1in (25mm), to allow for seasonal changes in dimensions. Having cut the right number of boards to length, fix the bottom one first (**11**). Overlap the next one and fix that down near the bottom edge, but not through the previously laid board.

Fit the corner battens to cover over the ends of the boards laid on the sides. Now follow the same procedure to construct the roof of the kennel. Once more, work out how many feather-edged boards are needed for each side of the roof. Cut them to length and fit, again allowing for overlap, in case of seasonal changes in dimensions. The ridge now needs to be sealed. The traditional method is to use a strip of ready-sanded shingle (**12**). Cut a piece to length and simply fix it in place with a heavy-duty stapler.

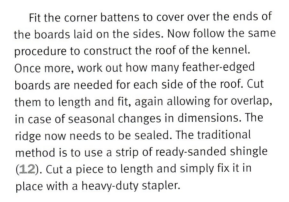

11 Fit the side feather-edged boarding first.

12 The ridge is sealed with a strip of shingle stapled into place.

Cold frame

Materials	Pressure preservative-treated softwood; exterior grade clear plastic sheeting
Time to make	1–2 days
Skill level	Basic

Toolbox

Essential	Basic hand tools
Useful	Bandsaw; large sheet of paper

The beauty of this project is that it can be scaled up or down to suit the space available. The only caveat is that you should try to work it around standard sizes of exterior grade plastic sheeting. These plastic sheets give you much more flexibility than the glass used traditionally and will withstand an impact better.

Making the cold frame

Draw out a full-size end section on a sheet of ply or paper. This provides you with all the sizes and angles to make up the two ends. All the joints are simple halving or butt joints. There is no need to build the frame with anything else—the cladding will hold it all rigid and firm. Select the four pieces for each end and mark the positions of the joints from the drawing. Use a sliding bevel to mark the angles and a gauge to mark the depth of the halving joints. Trim the ends of the components to length and cut the joints. This can be done with a hand saw or, if you have one

available, a powered band or pull over saw (**1**, **2**, overleaf). If cutting by hand, the shoulders of the cross halving joints should be sawn down to the required depth and then cleaned out with a chisel. On a pull over saw, set the depth and simply chop away the waste, a saw blade's width at a time. Once all the joints are made, treat the freshly cut wood with a clear preservative to ensure the integrity of the treatment is maintained. Leave overnight to dry off. Repeat this process with any other cuts you make to the treated wood.

Assembly of the cold frame now begins. Predrill the screw holes, two per joint. Set out each end frame's square and drive in the appropriate length screws. Once the two end frames are made, position the width rails and hold them firmly in place with sash clamps (**3**, overleaf). Predrill the screw holes once more (**4**, overleaf). One long screw per rail is required, driven right into the center of the piece.

Below The finished cold frame. This is a practical, hard-wearing piece of garden equipment which should last many years.

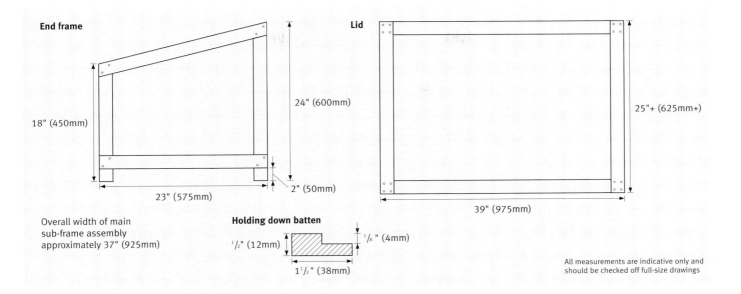

End frame

24" (600mm)

18" (450mm)

23" (575mm)

2" (50mm)

Overall width of main
sub-frame assembly
approximately 37" (925mm)

Holding down batten

$^1/_2$" (12mm)

$^1/_8$" (4mm)

$1^1/_2$" (38mm)

Lid

25"+ (625mm+)

39" (975mm)

All measurements are indicative only and
should be checked off full-size drawings

"Feather-edged" boarding has been used for the exterior cladding. This is a traditional exterior cladding or siding. Rectangular, cross-section boards are cut diagonally to produce two triangular pieces. This is both more economical and effective as a cladding. However, simple, thin boarding can be used instead. Start by fixing the straight front and back. Work out how many pieces you need. The minimum overlap should be 1in (25mm). Cut the required number of boards to length, flush with the overall width of the frame. Fix the first one in place with screws, predrilling the holes, along the bottom edge. Make sure you drive a screw into each end frame and one or two in the width rail. Set the overlap for the next piece and fix in place with a screw through the bottom edge (5, overleaf). Make sure you don't screw through the previously fixed board. The whole idea is to get one fixing only, so that the wood can expand and shrink with seasonal changes and not split. Work your way to the top. The last piece should be lined up carefully with the top edge. Use a loose piece of flat boarding projecting over the edge and bring this last one tight up to it to ensure there will be no gaps at the top. Fix the last piece in place.

Cut four corner battens to length and fix them so that they overlap the feather-edged boarding laid to front and rear. Two or three screws will hold these in place. Make sure they are parallel. Cut to length

Cutting list

Component	Pieces	Length, nominal		Width, finished		Thickness, finished	
Frame							
Backs	2	27"	680mm	2"	50mm	2"	50mm
Fronts	2	21"	530mm	2"	50mm	2"	50mm
Top rails	2	27"	680mm	2"	50mm	2"	50mm
Bottom rails	2	27"	680mm	2"	50mm	2"	50mm
Width rails	4	36"	900mm	2"	50mm	2"	50mm
Corner battens	2	27"	680mm	$1^1/_2$"	38mm	1"	25mm
	2	21"	530mm	$1^1/_2$"	38mm	1"	25mm
Top frame	4	42"	1055mm	3"	75mm	1"	25mm
and lid	4	27"	680mm	3"	75mm	1"	25mm
Rabbeted battens	2	27"	680mm	$1^1/_2$"	38mm	$^1/_2$"	12mm
Interior, spaced shelf	10	27"	680mm	3"	75mm	1"	25mm

Enough feather-edged boarding to cover the frame when assembled
24"/600mm x 36"/900mm sheet of $^1/_4$"/6mm thick exterior grade
   clear plastic
Pair of $2^1/_2$"/63mm butt hinges, aluminum or chrome plated
Pair of 12"/300mm window stays
Screws, glue, clear preservative

1 Cut down the shoulder to the required depth.

2 Rip down to remove the waste.

3 Making up the carcass with the four width pieces.

4 Drill right through the middle of each corner.

the required number of boards for each end. Attach the boards, starting at the bottom once more. Now the top frame can be made. Measure the overall width and length and cut the boards with butt mitered joints. Lay them on and fix the back one in place first with a couple of screws (**6**). Check that the others are square before fixing them all down permanently. To ensure that the cold frame is frost-free, a raised shelf has been built into the design. Battens are cut to length and fixed in place with one screw each per end.

Next, make the lid frame. This frame should be made to fit the width of the box assembly. To make it easy to open, the depth can be made slightly oversize to overhang the front edge. Corner halving joints are used this time. Fix the halving joints with glue and four screws each (**7**, opposite). The lid frame should be left for a bit while the glue cures. You will need two small battens which are rebated to accommodate the plastic. Make sure the width of the rebate is at least ½in (12mm). Measure and cut the clear sheeting to width.

5 The screw is driven into the overlap gap to ensure the boards can move.

6 The top frame is mitered and screwed in place.

7 The lid joints have glue applied and are then screwed together square.

8 Hinges are fixed to the lid frame and then this assembly is fixed to the main body.

A pair of butt hinges should now be fitted to the lid frame and then the frame to the lower box assembly with one screw per hinge only (**8**). Check that the lid swings into place, lined up as you want it, and make any slight adjustments as necessary; then drive in the rest of the screws. With the cut plastic sheeting to hand, drill one hole in the center at the top (**9**). You need to allow the plastic room to move. This one hole accommodates a round-headed screw, with washers if required, that should not be tightened down (**10**). The two battens hold the whole thing in place by overlapping the edges. Fix with the one screw first, then bring the battens up in line with the edges (**11**). Ease them back slightly, to give room for expansion, and fix them in place with two or three screws each. Finally, make up a couple of lid stays with strips of hardwood predrilled incrementally or fit two window stays to each side of the lid and box assembly (**12**).

9 The plastic sheeting is trimmed to size if required.

10 This one screw holds the sheet in place.

11 The rabbeted side battens hold the sheet at the sides.

12 Stays are fitted to enable the top lid to open and ventilate the plants.

Integrated bench and trellis

Materials	Main construction: preservative-treated softwood Seat slats: hardwood
Time to make	2–3 days
Skill level	Basic

Toolbox

Essential	Basic hand tools
Useful	Bandsaw; router; over and under planer

Although this integrated, decorative backyard bench and trellis is a stand-alone unit, ideally it needs to be set in the ground for stability. It is not a difficult project to construct, and once it is placed in a sunny spot, with some scented roses growing up the trellis, it will soon repay the effort involved.

Making the bench and trellis

Make up the back frame first. Use slot mortise and plain tenon joints to fix the top rail to the two posts (**1**, overleaf). Mark and cut by hand or on a band saw if you have one (**2**, overleaf). There are two more, thinner, rails to joint to the back posts. A middle rail supports the back of the seat and the lower rail is used to fix the curved seat bases at the back. The position of these rails should be marked and the halving joints cut (**3**, overleaf). The waste will need to be chopped out with a chisel (**4**, overleaf). There is

a matching rail to joint into the two front legs. Make sure it is positioned level with the one in the back, or you may get an unwanted slope on the seat. Cut the curves on the seat bases as per the drawing or adjust to suit your preference. Use a thin strip of waste wood to mark out the main curve; you may need some help to hold or mark round this (**5**, overleaf). Keep one of the longer bits of waste for the two arm support blocks needed later on (**6**, overleaf). Once all these new cuts have been treated, the back frame can be assembled.

Below The finished bench and trellis. Plant up this project effectively and in time the trellis will become a beautiful backyard feature.

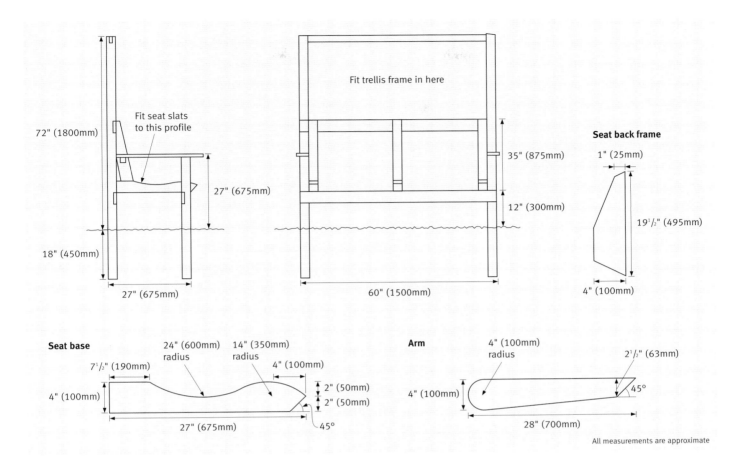

Fit trellis frame in here

72" (1800mm)

Fit seat slats to this profile

27" (675mm)

18" (450mm)

27" (675mm)

35" (875mm)

12" (300mm)

60" (1500mm)

Seat back frame

1" (25mm)

19¹/₂" (495mm)

4" (100mm)

Seat base

24" (600mm) radius

14" (350mm) radius

4" (100mm)

7¹/₂" (190mm)

4" (100mm)

2" (50mm)

2" (50mm)

27" (675mm)

45°

Arm

4" (100mm) radius

2¹/₂" (63mm)

4" (100mm)

45°

28" (700mm)

All measurements are approximate

Start by fitting the plain tenons into the slot mortises at the top of the frame. Drop the bottom rail into the halving joints and square the frame up freehand. Screw these joints in place. The top joints need to be screwed from both sides for added strength. Fix the rail onto the front legs and, to hold it square, screw on a strip of spare wood across the front of the legs a little lower down. A couple of saw horses or stands are now required. On level ground, prop up and cramp the main, back frame to the supports and check that it is vertical with a spirit level. Position the front leg frame and cramp on the two end seat bases. Now check and adjust everything so that it is vertical and square. Fix the front of the two seat bases to the front legs and the rail with long screws. Fix the backs as well and then position the middle one and fix that in place. The whole frame should now be free standing. Position the middle, back rail and fix that on. If your joints are all good and tight, you should now be able to move the main frame around if you wish.

Cutting list

Component	Pieces	Length, nominal		Width, finished		Thickness, finished	
Back posts/ legs	2	90"	2280mm	3"	75mm	3"	75mm
Front legs	2	36"	900mm	3"	75mm	3"	75mm
Top rail	1	66"	1675mm	4"	100mm	2"	50mm
Seat, back frames	3	24"	600mm	4"	100mm	2"	50mm
Seat bases	3	30"	750mm	4"	100mm	2"	50mm
Back middle and lower rails	2	66"	1675mm	4"	100mm	1"	25mm
Front rail	1	66"	1675mm	4"	100mm	1"	25mm
Arms	2	30"	750mm	4"	100mm	1"	25mm
Trellis frame	4	66"	1675mm	2"	50mm	1"	25mm
Trellis laths	about 16	72"	1800mm	2"	50mm	½"	12mm
Seat slats	about 18	60"	1500mm	1½"	38mm	⅞"	22mm

1 Use a gauge to mark out the edges of the slot mortises.

2 Check for fit and adjust as necessary.

The seat backs have to be individually shaped to fit. Line up a blank and, using a sliding bevel, mark one of the angles and cut it. Position the blank on the frame, mark and cut the other angle. Check that the slope and position are correct before using this first back rail as a pattern to cut the other two (**7**, opposite). All these and subsequent cuts must be treated with preservative before fixing (**8**, opposite). The arms need small blocks on the back posts to support them. Some of the waste from the seat bases should be saved and cut for this job. With a spirit level, mark their positions off the top of the front legs and fix in place. Measure, mark out, and cut to shape the two arms. These can be fixed on with long screws down into the front legs and the support blocks and back posts (**9**, opposite). The main frame assembly is now complete.

For the trellis, a simple corner halving joint frame is made to fit into the space

3 Cut to the depth on the shoulders and odd spaces in between.

4 Chop out the waste with a chisel or on a pull over cross-cut saw.

5 Getting the curve on the seat bases might require a bit of innovation.

6 The curves can be cut by hand or on a bandsaw.

7 Once one of the blanks has been cut to shape, mark round it and cut the other two.

8 Screw the three vertical seat back rails into place.

9 Fix the bench arms on, front and back.

10 Use a spare board to provide regular spaces between the slats. Trim off once fixed in place.

behind the seat of the main frame. Check the measurements, cut the joints, and joint up this frame, making sure it fits snugly in place. The trellis slats can now be fixed to it. Having fixed the slats on one side, they were trimmed off and some of the waste ends retained for the other side (**10**). The process was followed on the reverse until the trellis was completed.

Next, fit the hardwood seat slats. The slats need to be sawn to size and square-planed first. For greater comfort, apply a small bevel to each top corner using an appropriate cutter on a router table (**11**), or by hand.

If the framework is to be painted with a backyard color, now is the time to do it, before everything is put together.

Position the trellis frame. This should only need half a dozen screws to hold it in place. The seat slats can now be fitted (**12**). Start with the one at the front. Fix it flush with the front of the seat bases. Use a spare slat as a spacer and work backward. Even up any odd spaces, and the job is done.

11 Apply bevels to the slats on a router, or by hand.

12 Finally, fix on the hardwood seat slats.

217

Corner cupboard restoration

Materials	Various woods to match and replace originals
Time to make	5–6 days
Skill level	Basic/intermediate

Salvaged from an old farmhouse in Wales, this piece of country-style furniture had been subjected to abuse for many years. Thought of as functional and of little value, the corner cupboard had stood for a long time in the damp, and had been attacked by woodworm and rot. It really was in a very poor state.

Restoring the cupboard

Somewhere, underneath all the old dirt and wallpaper, was what would have originally been a simply made corner cupboard (**1**, **2**, opposite). Back at the workshop, the worst of the dry dirt was brushed and vacuumed off so that it could be seen what was salvageable. With a hammer, saw, and angle grinder the back was taken off and half the shelves removed (**3**, opposite). The doors had to be cut off, because the screws had rusted

in solid. Eventually, all that remained was the front facade, the two doors, part of the top, and a couple of front sections of shelves.

Woodworm attack was severe and had to be stopped from getting much worse. *Anobium punctatum*, the common furniture beetle,

Below The restoration is complete. The cupboard probably looks different from its original state, but the wood is beautiful again now it has been fully renovated.

woodworm, has a three-year lifecycle. With woodworm infestations one of the main problems to contend with, it had to be stopped. High temperature is one method, but not the best with a quality antique. Freezing is another—and probably the best method if you are restoring an expensive piece—or a liberal dose of wood preserver should do the trick over time. All surfaces must be soaked with an insecticide. Apply at least two coats; let the first dry off before applying the second. The idea is that no new grubs will bore into the wood after hatching, because they will die as they chew into the treated timber. The same applies to the adults as they emerge. Therefore, in theory, over three years the infestation should be completely eradicated. Once the cupboard had been liberally soaked, attention was turned to other jobs while it dried off.

Interestingly, the bulk of the cupboard was made from elm, probably *Ulmus procera*, with a few bits of oak, *Quercus robur*, in the shelves. The exterior looked as if it had been treated with a red stain, brick dust, and something else—perhaps lead. It was only after soap and water had been used to remove the wallpaper and dirt that it became obvious which wood the cupboard had been made from. Following discussions with the owner, it was decided to carry out the main repairs and rebuild in elm again. The proportions of the piece were also closely looked at. It was concluded that it was the top half of a two-piece corner unit; the missing, bottom piece would have been shorter and slightly wider. After further discussions as to the best way to proceed, it was decided to restore the cupboard as a one-piece floor standing unit.

1 Here you can see the condition of the interior, with the doors removed; the back was falling out and had been patched with hardboard.

2 The infestation is clearly visible in this close-up of a corner.

3 Brutal but necessary: all the bits that were too badly damaged had to be removed.

4 One elm plank is chopped in half at a suitable point.

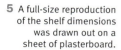

5 A full-size reproduction of the shelf dimensions was drawn out on a sheet of plasterboard.

6 One prepared piece of elm was marked out judiciously.

7 Two complete replacement shelves were required. These were jointed using flat dowels.

8 One complete shelf cramped up using a variety of clamps in odd positions to stop them from slipping.

After preparing a rough cutting list, a trip to the local sawmill secured two large planks of elm cut through and through. As with all projects like this, several things need to happen at the same time; the trick is to try and coordinate everything so that all the processes involved finish together. The rough elm planks were cut to economical lengths, square-edged on the band- and ripsaws then planed square to size (**4**, previous page). Needless to say, the original shelves were not all exactly the same dimension. A judgment had to be made and an average size/angle taken. A full-size reproduction was drawn out on a large, plain board and this was used as a template (**5**). Three shelf extensions were then cut, plus the two replacement shelves (**6**). The latter were jointed with biscuits and clamped up (**7**, **8**). Later, these and the extensions were cleaned up, ready for fitting. One middle shelf had a full round, stopped both ends, applied with the router.

There was a huge amount of small repair work to do. The bottoms of part of the outer frame

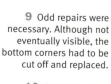

9 Odd repairs were necessary. Although not eventually visible, the bottom corners had to be cut off and replaced.

10 Something had gnawed at the front of this oak shelf, so a section was cut out and a new bit fixed in.

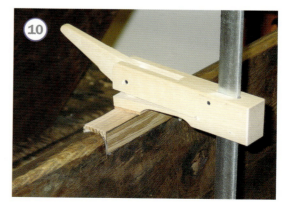

had rotted away. These were cut off and new bits scarf-jointed and biscuit-jointed in place (**9**). A couple of other parts looked as though they had been gnawed by something. These were cut out and replacements inserted (**10**). A large hole in one door, originally blocked and masked with filler, had to be cut out, cleaned up, and a solid piece inserted with the grain matched as best as possible (**11**, **12**). The actual woodworm attack had created a mass of holes all over the piece. Although this was useful for preservative

penetration, it looked like a mess. All the holes were slightly enlarged to make a sound base for the stopper and then filled up. This took several attempts. Each consecutive sanding, although light, exposed more holes or loosened some of the stopper. Eventually it was decided that any others would disappear when they were waxed later. With all the main repairs carried out, the rebuild could commence (**13**).

Originally the carcass had been made from a simple mortise and tenon frame, with the rest

11 The soft wood had to be cut back and a symmetrical cavity created.

12 The replacement piece was grain-matched, as best as possible, and knocked into place with its own scrap piece.

nailed on. Where possible, glue, glue blocks, and screws would be used. The bottom shelf was fitted in place slightly higher than the original (**14**). This allowed for some stub feet to be fixed underneath it. The shelf extensions were glued and screwed on after trimming to line the back edges up. The last new shelf was then fitted. Some screws into this through the face were plugged with new elm. A long batten was then screwed, temporarily, down the back to hold each shelf in place. Three short feet were cut

from some handy square-planed ash, *Fraxinus excelsior*. These would protrude slightly beyond the shaped, face-mounted bracket feet. Each was glued and twice screwed in place down through the bottom shelf (**15**, overleaf).

New elm was planed square to size and then molded on the router table for the cornice and baseboard (**16**, overleaf) The cornice was made up of two pieces built up to give it depth. Another smaller, strip molding was made to run down each back edge of the frame to tidy

13 Rebuilding commences. The top rail of the outer frame had dropped off; therefore, a support piece had to be fixed in behind.

14 Glue blocks and screws were used to fix the bottom shelf in place—not nails, as in the original piece.

things up. Although the joint angles for both cornice and skirting should be 22½ degrees, they varied from side to side. A bit of care and judicious cutting eventually got the fit right without loss. The bracket feet shape was cut into the baseboard (**17**) and they, along with all the other molded pieces, were cleaned up ready for staining. The new wood had an extra coat to try and bring it to the same as the old. A "Georgian Oak" spirit stain was used for this first coat, making sure that not too much was applied near

the end grain to darken the joints. With one coat applied, these were then left to dry off.

The doors were cleaned and sanded up and filling done as necessary. The hinges were then fitted (**18**). Using longer screws than in the original, each recess was extended to avoid hitting the old, broken-off screws. The doors were fitted to the frame and some adjustments made (**19**, opposite). With the doors off, everything now received a coat of the final stain (**20**, opposite). For this an "Indian Rosewood" stain was used,

15 Three stub feet are fixed through the bottom shelf with glue and screws. Note the batten holding the shelves in their spaced positions.

16 Molding the profile for the cornice and baseboard.

liberally applied, and wiped off with a rag. Everything was left to dry off for a couple of days, while work started on the back of the cupboard.

Some thin boards of sweet chestnut, *Castanea sativa*, were an ideal choice for the cupboard back. These through and through planks had to be straight-edged, cross-cut to length and then planed square all round. They were then treated with preservative. Sweet chestnut is a softwood and, no doubt, if left without treatment any hatching grubs would chew straight into it. When

the back was fitted later on (**21**, opposite), the edges were simply mitered to overlap and the sections nailed on with some "cut" nails (**22**, opposite). This was an attempt to maintain some of the original integrity of the piece.

Back onto the main rebuild. The first pieces of cornice were screwed down through the front into place, making sure that these screws would be covered by the second pieces. The second, smaller pieces were then pinned in place, with the brads popped into the back of a small groove. These

17 The "bracket" feet shape was cut out on the bandsaw.

18 Slightly larger hinges were used to avoid the broken off screws from the originals.

19 The doors are fitted before the back is put on or the staining done.

20 The shelves were masked off before the staining commenced, to avoid getting splashes on them.

were then punched below the surface and filled. Both lots were also glued. The baseboard/bracket feet were fixed in place with glue and screwed from the back so that nothing showed. Now the two back edge moldings could be trimmed to length and fitted as well. Glue and brads, punched in and filled, did the job. Once all the filler had dried, it was lightly sanded back and, with a fine brush, a small amount of stain was applied and wiped off to blend them in. The whole lot was then

sealed with one coat. Every showing face was then waxed with a rich mahogany wax.

The main carcass was flipped over onto its face on a well-padded bench. The back was fixed on. Next, hinges were refitted to the doors, along with the lock (**23**). A nice old mahogany knob was found that was just the right color to match. The original hole was bored out and this glued in place (**24**). The doors and internal cranked bolt were refitted and the restoration was complete.

21 Lying on its face, the back is nailed onto the unit.

22 A simple overlap joint and cut nails were used for the back.

23 A steel lock was all that could be found that was large enough.

24 An old mahogany knob was just right for the right-hand door.

Turned and painted lamp

Materials	Beech, *Fagus sylvatica*, or any wood that turns well
	A lampshade, holder, and cable
Time to make	2 days
Skill level	Intermediate

The beauty of this project is that you can finish the lamp off to match the decor of wherever it will be used, or alternatively, as you choose. The project combines both faceplate work and turning between centers. Each needs a slightly different technique to start with, but they soon come together.

Toolbox

Essential	A lathe
Useful	Bandsaw; long-hole boring kit

Making the lamp

The blanks for the base and stem need to be cut out first. Allow a little on the length for the stem to accommodate the round tenon joint and a small section of waste at the top end. Start by planing a flat face on the base. On the prepared face, find the middle by marking across the diagonals, corner to corner. With a compass, mark the exact size of the base's diameter. This should then be cut close to the line on a bandsaw if you have one (**1**, overleaf). If not, saw off as much of the waste evenly all round with a hand saw.

Measure the diameter of the electric cable. The first cable hole in from the side of the base to the center should now be drilled. Choose a side grain face, rather than end grain; this will turn easily without any tear out around the hole. Choose a central spot on what will be the first level surface and drill an angled hole through to the center of the base. Now set the base blank down on the bench with the flattened face up ready to fix the faceplate. Mark the screw positions with a bradawl and drill some pilot holes. Screw the faceplate to the blank (**2**, overleaf). Mount the blank in the lathe and set the tool rest up as close as you can to the rough, outer surface.

With the base blank mounted in the lathe, select a speed that gives enough peripheral pace to make cutting easy. With a large gouge, carefully bring the rough blank down to a true disc (**3**, overleaf). Adjust the tool's rest for the face side and trim this back, level and parallel with the faceplate, to the desired thickness. The stem is to be jointed to this base with a central, round tenon. A central, round mortise hole needs

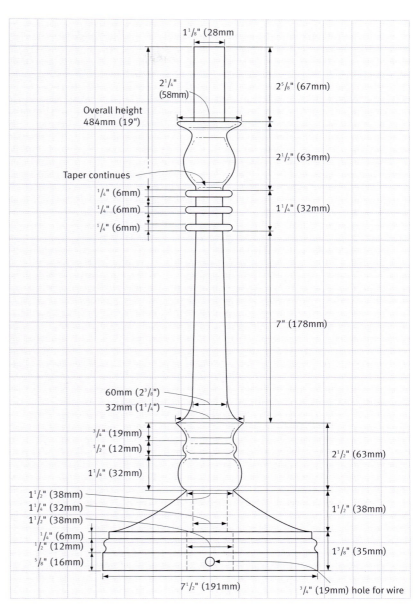

1⅛" (28mm)

2¼" (58mm)

2⅝" (67mm)

Overall height 484mm (19")

2½" (63mm)

Taper continues

¼" (6mm)

¼" (6mm)

1¼" (32mm)

¼" (6mm)

7" (178mm)

60mm (2⅜")

32mm (1¼")

¾" (19mm)

½" (12mm)

2½" (63mm)

1¼" (32mm)

1½" (38mm)

1¼" (32mm)

1½" (38mm)

1½" (38mm)

¼" (6mm)

½" (12mm)

1⅜" (35mm)

⅝" (16mm)

7½" (191mm)

¾" (19mm) hole for wire

to be cut in the disc. With this job done, some real lathe work can be started. Using the large gouge, rough down the shape and finish off with the smaller tools (**4**, overleaf).

The blank stem needs to have its centers found and marked (**5**, overleaf). Mount this blank between centers and turn it down to a rough cylinder (**6**, overleaf). Mark out and turn down the round tenon that will go into the base. Check it for size and fit. It does not have to be too tight, but should slide in and out with a little pressure. Take the stem off the lathe and remount the base attached to the faceplate. The tenon should now be sliced down both sides about ⅛in (3–4mm) in. This is to accommodate the secret "fox-wedges" that will help to hold it in place. Cut a couple of slim wedges just larger than the saw cut widths in the tenon. Put them in place and insert the tenon into the mortise. Push it home until some resistance is felt. There should still be a little gap between the shoulders of the tenon and the mortise in the base. Some adjustments may have to be made to trim the lengths of the wedges. The idea is that as the wedges are forced into the saw cuts, they expand the tenon to fit

Cutting list

Component	Pieces	Length, nominal		Width, nominal		Thickness, nominal	
Stem	1	18"	450mm	2½"	62mm	2½"	62mm
Base	1	9"	225mm	9"	225mm	3"	75mm

A lamp fitting; 10'/3m of three core cable; grain fillers; primer; finishing paints

1 Cut the disc on a bandsaw or take the corners off by hand.

2 Fix on the faceplate and mount in the lathe.

3 Turn the base to the required diameter.

4 Turn down the finished shape on the base.

tightly in the mortise hole. It has to be just right, or the shoulders will not fit down flush with the base. When you are happy that everything is ready, mix up some glue and spread it liberally on both the tenon and wedges and into the mortise. Now push the two together and use a mallet, if necessary, to knock them tightly together. Bring up the tail stock and remount the protruding end of the stem in this. It should fit back into the original center point. Leave the assembled components in the lathe while the glue goes off.

Retrim the stem cylinder if necessary and start to shape it. It is a fairly simple shape, but care needs to be taken. The three beads are probably the hardest parts to shape. Use a small beading gouge or a smaller skew chisel to shape them (**7**, opposite). Start to part the top of the candlestick from the waste but don't go right through yet. Now you need the long-hole boring kit. Set the guide up in the tail stock end and start to feed the borer into the end. Take small chunks out only and clear the waste regularly. To

5 Mark the centers with a bradawl and mount on the lathe.

6 Turn the stem to a cylinder.

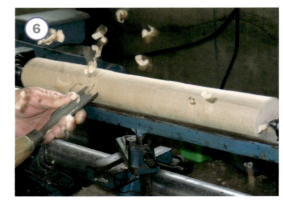

7 Cutting the beads with a small gouge.

8 If any blemishes need filling, they should be taken care of before the paint is applied.

finish off this stage, sand down through different sandpaper grit sizes, finishing on 180 or finer. If the wood used is open-grained, or perhaps you have had a slight dig in, use a lightweight filler before you go too far (**8**). Sand this back as well.

You should now be ready to put the first primer coat of paint on. Use cans of automobile spray paint, because they are easy to apply, there is a large range of colors and they produce a good, smooth surface. A gray primer is best to start with (**9**). Make sure it is shaken well. Set the lathe at a lower speed and start it up. Spray along the lamp as it revolves, following the manufacturer's directions. Change the angle of the nozzle to make sure you get into the corners. Once one coat is applied, leave it to dry for the period stated on the spray can. Apply another. Any small blemishes will now show up; fill these if necessary and cut back. If you have been too enthusiastic and there are some runs in the paint, don't worry—just cut them back and put another layer on. A couple more coats should suffice to finish off. Cut back in-between with very

fine steel wool. Leave this to dry and harden off. Take the lamp off the lathe and drill the large, central cable access hole in the bottom of the base before the final coats of paint are applied.

The main top coat colors can now be sprayed on. Start with an off-white color for the candle. Once you have sprayed on three or four coats, you should have enough depth of color. It is important to leave this to dry and harden off before you start to mask it, otherwise the tape will mark the paint. Decide on your color scheme and mask and spray until you are satisfied with the finish. Once all the finished paint surfaces have hardened off, you can fit the threaded lamp spigot to the top of the candle section with small brass screws. Thread the cable up the middle of the stem and wire in the lamp holder (**10**). If you are not sure about this part of the job, get a qualified electrician to do it for you. The other end of the cable should now be fed through the side hole and the plug fitted. A disc of baize on the bottom finishes the job. All you need now is a suitable, stylish lampshade.

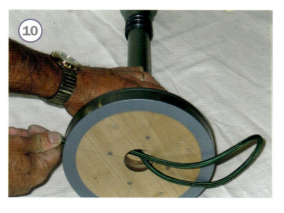

9 With the lathe running, spray on the gray primer.

10 Having connected the lamp holder, thread the rest of the cable out of the side hole.

Antiqued, painted wall unit

Materials	Laminated softwood
Time to make	2–3 days
Skill level	Intermediate

This project has been deliberately selected because it can be made from materials that are readily available at hardware stores. Using basic, laminated softwood board, the components can be cut out to create a stylish wall unit. By distressing the surfaces, the quality of the underlying wood becomes less important.

Toolbox

Essential	Basic hand tools
Useful	Band-, rip- and cross-cut saws; over and under planer; mortise machine; disc and bobbin sanders

Making the wall unit

The cutting list identifies the individual component sizes. However, the original pieces were both 2ft 9in (850mm) long. One was 1ft 11in (585mm) wide, and the other was 1ft 7in (495mm) wide (**1**, opposite). Any manmade sheet material could be substituted for the softwood, but if this course is followed a little care might need to be taken not to expose core materials when distressing edges.

Most of the preformed sheets of laminated softwood appear to have rounded edges from the factory (**2**, opposite). These must be removed before the individual components can be sliced out. Plane them off, set the ripsaw to width and cut the first piece. Then plane the edge and cut the next. The sawn edges can be used at the back or planed up if showing. To joint the front section, use a recessed cross-halving joint. This is much stronger than a simple cross-halving joint. If made correctly, the edges of the joint, next to the cutaway sections, are held firmly in place in the recess/trench.

Unlike a simple cross halving joint each half of this one is slightly different. Start by marking the positions of the trenches that will be the full thickness of the board. In this case about ¾in (18mm). A trench this wide needs to be cut both sides of the joint, about ⅛in (3–4mm) deep. The depth of this trench determines the width of the trench on the other jointing piece. For example, at ⅛in (3mm) deep times ¹⁄₁₀in (2mm), for both sides, this is taken off the thickness—¾in (18mm)—to result in a trench ½in (12mm) wide on the second part of the joint. This information

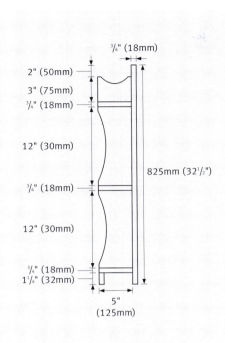

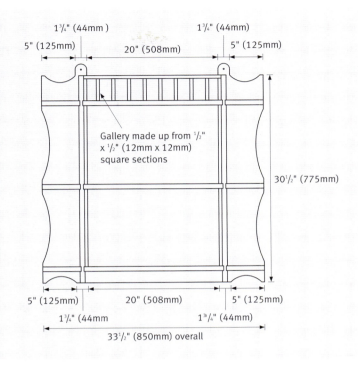

Gallery made up from ¹/₂"
x ¹/₂" (12mm x 12mm)
square sections

is required now so that the cut out in this first
part of the joint can be marked (**3**, overleaf),
and made halfway across the width of the piece.
Having marked the position of the second part of
the joint, this is trenched on both sides and the
entire remaining, middle bit, cut away halfway
across the width of this piece (**4**, overleaf).
When the joint is assembled, it should slot
tightly together.

Once the half dozen joints have all been made,
dry-assemble them to check that all is square.
At this stage a small mortise hole needs to be
cut into each inner face at the top of the vertical

Cutting list

Component	Pieces	Length, nominal		Width, finished		Thickness, finished	
Back sections	2	36"	900mm	6³/₄"	170mm	³/₄"	18mm
Shelves	3	36"	900mm	5"	125mm	³/₄"	18mm
Vertical supports	2	36"	900mm	5"	125mm	³/₄"	18mm
Infill strips	3	24"	600mm	³/₄"	18mm	³/₄"	18mm
Lower front filler	1	24"	600mm	1¹/₄"	32mm	³/₄"	18mm
Gallery top rail	1	24"	600mm	³/₄"	18mm	³/₄"	18mm
Gallery pieces	8	3"	75mm	¹/₂"	12mm	¹/₂"	12mm

⚠️ **WARNING** Please note
that although many
of these images show
machines unguarded for
clarity, you should ALWAYS
ensure that when operating
equipment the appropriate
guards are in place.

1 Unwrapping the
two prefinished pieces
of laminated softwood.

2 The boards are
supplied with a
rounded edge.

3 The position of the first slot for the halving joint is marked out.

4 This is what a joint should look like before assembly.

supports to take the gallery top rail. With this fitted, the positions of the gallery pieces can be marked. A series of small mortise holes have to be cut to accommodate the gallery pieces. Plane these square at ½in (12mm), and cut the holes to match; there is no need for shoulders. A dry run at assembly should be made once the pieces are cut to check that they all fit together easily (**5**). The main joints are all cut, so the shaping of the profile can begin. Use a circular object to mark around that will give the desired result. Sometimes an old paint tin will do or, say, the lid of a large container (**6**). Having marked out the shapes, cut the profiles on a bandsaw, and finish off with a disc and bobbin sander. The whole of the front section can now be glued up. With plenty of glue applied, slot the joints and gallery into place. You may need to adjust the tenon on the gallery top rail to make it fit. Working off a flat surface, check that everything is square (**7**, opposite). If you have got it right, there should be no need for clamps or cramps! The back sections are screwed onto the front assembly from behind.

Lay the now fixed complete front section on the back pieces and mark around the profile. By doing this you can then mark out where you want the screw holes to go. Each of the holes should be bored out and countersunk (**8**, opposite).

At this stage, add a bit of detail to the lower front filler. Mark out a series of squares on this piece. Center the holes. Cut down one side first, creating half the holes. Then turn the piece around and cut down the other side (**9**, opposite). Be sure to position a waste backing piece behind if cutting straight through. An easy option might be to cut some round holes with a flat disc; it is only a piece of decorative detail, so not really important. When it is finished, drill, glue, and screw the front filler into place (**10**, opposite).

The back of the unit is now ready to be attached. Apply plenty of glue to the adjoining edges of the front section first. Position the two back pieces and screw them on. Wipe away any excess glue with a damp rag. Three more fillers are now needed to go on the backs of the shelves. Some glue and a few brads or oval nails

5 Testing the gallery assembly for fit.

6 Any suitable round or curved object can be used to mark out the profiles.

7 Checking for square. There should be no need for cramps or clamps.

8 The holes are drilled and countersunk, ready for final assembly.

9 On the machine, the piece is turned around to create the square cut out.

10 Plenty of glue and some screws hold the front filler section in place.

will do the job nicely. The wall unit is now fully assembled and fixed. A light rub down, to take the arrises off the edges, finishes this stage off.

If you are working with laminated softwood there will, no doubt, be some knots. These should be treated with a proprietary knotting solution to stop resin "bleeding" through to the top surface (**11**). Next, a couple of coats of primer/undercoat need to be applied; sand down in between each coat to ensure a smooth finish. Finally, some decisions need to be made on the desired finish.

In this case, a dark base coat of paint was applied and then the unit was finished off with three top coats of a pastel blue matt emulsion paint. Once this had been left to harden off for a few days, the top coats were lightly sanded through to create the effect of wear (**12**). Once the results were satisfactory, the whole thing was coated with one layer of satin finish sealer. This was lightly cut back with a very fine steel wool. A clear wax was then applied and buffed up to finish off, and the job was done.

11 Treating the exposed surfaces with knotting.

12 Lightly sand through the paint layers to create the distressed look.

Shaker cradle

Materials	Yellow Pine, *Pinus strobus*
Time to make	3 days
Skill level	Intermediate

Traditional Shaker cradles can make attractive pieces of furniture as well as being functional. Get the rocker curve right and they will rock from side to side with little effort. Most are made from pine. In this case Yellow Pine was used—one of the harder varieties. Any lighter-weight hardwood would be suitable as well.

Toolbox

Essential	Basic hand and power tools
Useful	Bandsaw; router; disc and bobbin sanders

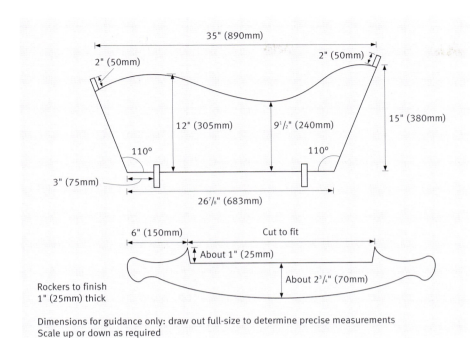

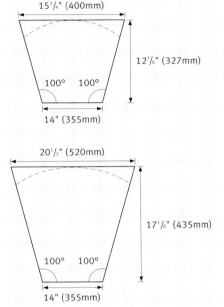

35" (890mm)

2" (50mm)

2" (50mm)

12" (305mm)

9½" (240mm)

15" (380mm)

110°

110°

3" (75mm)

26⅞" (683mm)

15¾" (400mm)

12⅞" (327mm)

100°   100°

14" (355mm)

20½" (520mm)

17⅛" (435mm)

100°   100°

14" (355mm)

6" (150mm)

Cut to fit

About 1" (25mm)

About 2¾" (70mm)

Rockers to finish
1" (25mm) thick

Dimensions for guidance only: draw out full-size to determine precise measurements
Scale up or down as required

Making the cradle

The sizes given for this cradle are for guidance only. On that basis, it is a good idea to draw it out full-size so that the dimensions can be taken and checked off the drawing (**1**).

For this project, the components were cut out of some old, discolored 2in- (50mm-) thick boards at a local sawmill (**2**). Although dirty and showing some signs of blue staining, the centers of these pieces were bright and clean when cut. These were the faces that were intended for the outer faces of the cradle. Because of the widths involved, it is both necessary and best to joint them from two or

Cutting list

Component	Pieces	Length, nominal		Width, finished		Thickness, finished	
Sides	2	39"	990mm	15"	380mm	¾"	18mm
Head end	1	24"	600mm	17⅛"	435mm	⅞"	21mm
Tail end	1	18"	450mm	12⅞"	327mm	⅞"	21mm
Bottom	1	30"	750mm	12¾"	318mm	⅝"	16mm
Rockers	2	30"	750mm	3¾"	95mm	1"	25mm

Dimensions for guidance only
Wide widths to be made up from two or three pieces

⚠ WARNING Please note that although many of these images show machines unguarded for clarity, you should ALWAYS ensure that when operating equipment the appropriate guards are in place.

1 Drawing out, full-size, both side and end profiles.

2 Checking out the raw materials.

three pieces. If distortion is to be avoided, the widths should be made up by alternating the direction of grain as the boards are jointed.

Having left the cut pieces for a few days, to allow any residual tension to relax, they need to be planed up. Surface and edge them first (**3**), then plane them to finished thickness. To get a good, strong joint, use one shot resin glue with two or three flat dowels down each adjoining face. Make sure that any of the dowels are well away from areas that may be shaped or cut later

on. With plenty of glue applied, and the flat dowels in place, rub the joints together to make a good bond (**4**). Clamp up each series of pieces to make the full width board, check that they are flat and leave for the glue to cure. Sand any excess off flush with the surface. Now edge plane each piece again to bring it to its finished size.

Apart from making sure that the corners all match and fit, you can interpret the top of the sides and end shapes as you wish. Sticking to the basic, overall dimensions, find round or curved

3 The pieces need to be face planed flat, then square-edged.

4 The edges are rubbed together to make a good joint.

objects that produce the shapes you want (**5**). Cut the end angles on the sides first and then these can be shot by hand or on a planer to straighten them up. Any break-out that occurs can then be cleaned off when the profiles are cut. Shape and finish one side only (**6**). This piece can then be used as the template from which to cut the matching side. Follow the same process for the ends but, obviously, make the head end taller than the tail end. The simple arc on these pieces can be cleaned up by hand or on a disc sander.

Use a marking gauge to set the depth of the tails and pins on both sides and ends. Mark out and cut the tails first and then mark round these to form the sockets and pins. Set an end in a vice so that a side can be laid on it level. Clamp the side in place and, taking care, use an awl or marking knife to go round the outline of the tails. Now take away the side and confirm the outline with the matching dovetail square. You will then need to square down each face to show the cut line (**7**, opposite). Cut each of the pins and

5 The profiles are drawn using any appropriate tools.

6 This first side is cleaned up to the finished size.

7 Square the markings for the sockets and pins down the faces.

8 Fit the ends to one side first.

sockets down these lines to the depth required. Chisel out any waste. Clean up as required. Test the joint and, if you have got it right, there should only be a little easing to make it a good fit.

Make all four corner joints, clean them up and fit ready for final assembly. Sand up the internal faces. Once ready to start, set up your clamps and get them close to hand. A lighter-weight glue will do with this number of dovetails. Apply plenty of glue to all jointing surfaces. Fit the two ends to one side first (8). Then apply more glue and fit the second side on. Clamp up, and before leaving the glue to set, check the whole thing out for square and adjust if necessary. Once the glue has dried and hardened, clean the excess off both inside and out.

Next, fit the bottom panel. The edges need to be beveled to match the slope of the sides and ends. Trim the panel to size. Take care not to cut the panel too small at this stage. Oversize is best; you can always trim it back later on. The bevels can be shot by hand or on a planer. Adjust the fence to match the required angle.

Shot the ends first and trim off any break-out when the sides are done. Check it for fit and trim if required (9). Clean up the panel and fix it in place with some glue. A weight on the center, top side, will hold it steady while the glue sets.

Make a template for the rockers out of an old bit of fiber board (10). This will help check the fit and how the proportions work in relationship to the rock. Once you are happy with this, plane up some stock to the finished thickness and draw out the profiles. Cut the profiles on a bandsaw and clean them up using a variety of shaves and sanders. Fix each rocker in place with a couple of screws driven down through the bottom panel.

After a final, light sanding, the cradle is ready for its first coat of sealer. Once this has dried and hardened, cut back with a coarse steel wool and recoat. Two coats are probably sufficient. A third could be applied with a further, light cut back in between. You could use a satin finish and leave it at that. The alternatives are to wax or oil the bare wood and work up a luster over time. Whatever you choose to do, ensure you use a child-friendly finish.

9 Checking out the bottom panel for fit.

10 The rocker template is made up and checked for fit and rock.

Shaker mirror

Materials	Kiln-dried elm, *Ulnus spp.*, or similar
Time to make	3–4 days
Skill level	Intermediate

Traditionally, simple Shaker furniture has been constructed from temperate hardwoods such as ash, maple, the oaks, cherry, and elm, which is used for this project. Pick your framing wood from those you have available, or buy to suit the decor of the room in which the mirror will hang.

Toolbox

Essential	Basic hand tools
Useful	Router; lathe; dowel jointer; powered saws and planes

Making the mirror frame

Plain mirrors are available from many hardware stores. Vary the size of the frame to suit. In this case, a couple of leftover pieces of elm with waney edges were used (**1**, opposite). Having matched the cutting list from these pieces, the nominal sizes were cut ready for planing. As with all planing jobs, by hand or machine, start by preparing one face first (**2**, opposite). Square and edge from this and square to width and thickness from these two.

There are a number of ways in which the mirror can be secured into the frame. Corner, metal clips can be used. With these, a wider deeper rabbet is required. A solid sheet of thin ply, or something similar, can be set into a rabbet behind the mirror as another alternative. Otherwise, you could choose to use thin strips of wood set at 45 degrees across each corner, as in this case. This requires one rabbet for the mirror and one rabbet for the retaining strips. The first one is quite deep and, when cut with a

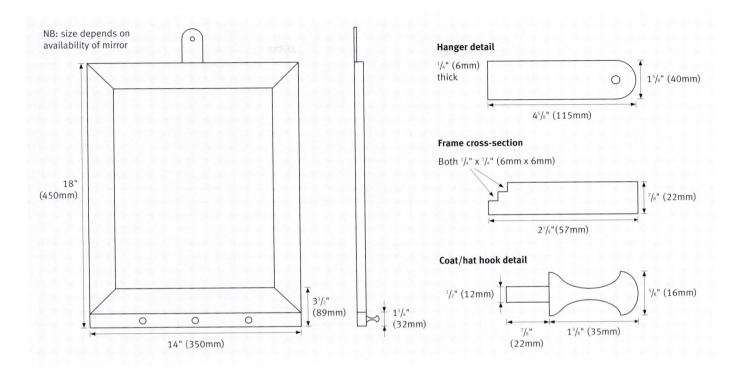

NB: size depends on availability of mirror

18" (450mm)

3¹/₂" (89mm)

14" (350mm)

1¹/₄" (32mm)

Hanger detail

¹/₄" (6mm) thick

4⁵/₈" (115mm)

1⁵/₈" (40mm)

Frame cross-section

Both ¹/₄" x ¹/₄" (6mm x 6mm)

2¹/₄" (57mm)

⁷/₈" (22mm)

Coat/hat hook detail

¹/₂" (12mm)

⁵/₈" (16mm)

⁷/₈" (22mm)

1³/₈" (35mm)

router, needs a couple of goes at it to make sure the cutter does not overwork or break. It should be possible to cut the second rabbet in one go, however (3, overleaf).

Once the rabbets are set, the actual size of the frame needs to be determined. The height and width of the mirror should be noted. Two widths of frame are added to each of these and two widths of rabbet taken off. This should provide the overall size of frame. Add a small amount back on to allow for the mirror to fit into the finished frame easily. Before cutting the miters, check and check again that the measurements

Cutting list

Component	Pieces	Length, nominal		Width, finished		Thickness, finished	
Frame							
Top rail	1	18"	450mm	⁷/₈"	22mm	2¹/₄"	57mm
Sides	2	24"	600mm	⁷/₈"	22mm	2¹/₄"	57mm
Bottom	1	18"	450mm	⁷/₈"	22mm	3¹/₂"	89mm
Coat/hat hooks	3	3"	75mm	⁵/₈"	16mm	⁵/₈"	16mm
Hanger	1	5"	125mm	1⁵/₈"	20mm	¹/₄"	6mm

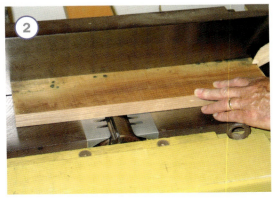

WARNING Please note that although many of these images show machines unguarded for clarity, you should ALWAYS ensure that when operating equipment the appropriate guards are in place.

1 Cutting the uneven edge off.

2 Plane the faces first, then the edges.

3 Here are the frame components, ready rabbeted.

4 A special miter saw can be used to cut the frame joints.

are correct. If the frame is too big, you can make it smaller, but you won't be able to make it larger!

The bottom rail is wider to accommodate the hangers. The miters on this piece will be cut on the side adjacent to the rabbets at the same width as the rest of the frame. With the overall lengths marked and the miters scribed, they can be cut by hand or machine (**4**). Once this has been done, check the frame for size and mirror fit. Any slight adjustments can be made now. For jointing, use a flat dowel joint for the top corners and a slot, Domino dowel joint for the bottom corners. This latter dowel is cut to fit at rightangles to the face of the joint and should help to stop the lower ones slipping out of place (**5**). The positions of each dowel, in the center of the joints, should be marked and the appropriate slots cut. Once more, check for fit.

Rather than leave the bottom rail as a wide, flat section, delineate between the frame and the hook section with a groove (**6**). Using a small, round end cutter, run the groove across the piece so that the top edge finishes exactly at the point of the

miters. This then leaves the lower portion into which the hooks can be fitted. Mark three ½in (12mm) diameter holes and cut them into this lower portion, ready for the hooks when they are turned. You also need to cut the groove for the hanger in the top rail of the frame. Mark the shoulders and cut. Remove any waste. To fit flush with the back, the hanger and the retaining strips, finish about ¼in (6mm) thick. Plane these to width and thickness from some of the smaller scraps. Mark a round edge and cut it out on the top of the hanger (**7**, opposite). A fairly large hole needs to be drilled in this, from which the mirror will be suspended by a cord.

The simple frame can now be finally assembled. Use powdered resin glue that will set solid with no slippage. Mix the adhesive to a thick, creamy consistency and apply it to the dowel recesses and faces of each joint. With the dowels inserted, assemble the frame and clamp it tightly.

While the frame is setting, prepare the three small hooks. Ideally these should be turned, but hand-carved ones will be fine if you don't have a lathe. Set the scraps in the lathe between centers

5 Marking the positions of the dowels in the joints.

6 The round bottom groove being routed on the wide, bottom rail.

7 Rounding the top of the hanger on a bandsaw.

8 On the lathe, the round tenon is turned to fit the hole first.

9 Once shaped and finished, the hooks can be given a coat of sealer.

10 The hanger is fixed in place.

to start each of the round tenons (**8**). The shape is not critical. Just make sure that the end is slightly larger, to stop anything hanging on the hook from dropping off. When each of the hooks has been turned, give them a coat of clear sealer (**9**).

When the glue has set on the frame, it is ready for cleaning up and finishing. Next, predrill the hanger with three holes for retaining screws. Apply plenty of glue to the hanger face and fix the screws in place (**10**). Then, give each hook a covering of glue on the end and work it into

its appropriate hole. Turn the frame over and apply glue to little wedges; then knock them in to retain the hooks in place (**11**). Later, when the glue has set, trim the hook wedges back, flush with the back of the mirror frame.

Traditionally, Shaker furniture is simply waxed or oiled. The choice is yours. Finally, the four corner strips should be predrilled and positioned across the mirror, but not too tightly, so as not to crack it (**12**). After a final buff-up, the mirror will be ready for hanging.

11 Some more glue applied to the wedges ensures they stay in place.

12 Finally, the mirror is secured in place.

Carved seats

Materials	Well-seasoned oak, *Quercus spp.*
Time to make	3–4 days
Skill level	Intermediate

This project may appear to be fairly simple, but it does actually contain some interesting and testing detail. The stools have been designed to look hand carved and in fact can be so constructed. However, in this case a number of powered tools have been used, such as the chainsaw, to speed this process up.

Toolbox

Essential	Basic hand tools, carving chisels
Useful	Bandsaw; chainsaw; mortise machine; powered carving tool

Above and left The finished carved seats, and a couple of close-up photographs of detailing in the project.

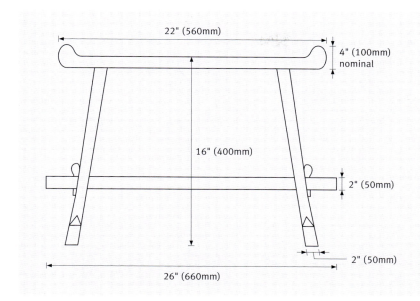

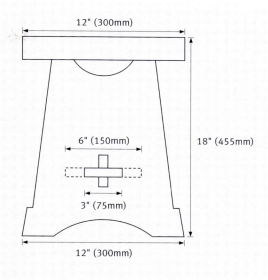

Making the carved seats

The raw material of choice is oak, but any reasonably durable hardwood will suit. 2in (50mm) and 4in (100mm) thick pieces form the basic sizes. These can, no doubt, be purchased ready cut to size. You could buy in waney-edged boards and make those cuts yourself, as economically as possible (**1**, **2**). A very useful technique, when dealing with angles in a project, is to make a full- or part-size drawing of the piece so that dimensions can be taken directly from it. Once this is done, the individual components, in their nominal sizes, can be sawn out and prepared.

The construction work starts by marking out the positions of the mortise holes on the underside of each seat. These will be cut about two thirds of the way through the thickness.

Cutting list (for one seat)

Component (per unit)	Pieces	Length, nominal		Width, finished		Thickness, finished	
Seat	1	24"	600mm	12"	300mm	3¾"	95mm
Ends	2	21"	530mm	12"	300mm	2"	50mm
Brace	1	27"	685mm	6"	150mm	2"	50mm
Wedges (to fit)	2	6"	150mm	2"	50mm	1"	25mm

Once the waste has been removed from the top surface, to shape the scrolled ends, the holes will be exposed. The seats are rather large blanks; therefore, there will be few mortise machines big enough to take them. Consequently, it is

WARNING Please note that although many of these images show machines unguarded for clarity, you should ALWAYS ensure that when operating equipment the appropriate guards are in place.

1 Marking out the most economical cuts from the waney-edged material.

2 Putting a straight edge on the thinner stock.

most likely that the holes will have to be cut by hand. Start by using a large auger or flat bit in a powered drill to remove the bulk of the waste. Avoid getting too near to the outer edges of the holes. Trim to size, removing the waste with a large mortise chisel and mallet. Once this is done, you will have some mortise holes into which the end section tenons can be fitted.

It is a good idea to cut all the joints on the ends and fit them before cutting out the final shapes. If a mistake is made, this will save having to redo everything. Working off the drawing, mark the shoulder positions onto one end. Having done this, mark the face lines (**3**) and then the edge lines. Depending upon the number of stools in production, these dimensions need to be then transferred to all the other ends. The one, long shoulder, on the inside of each end, needs to be set in about ½in (12mm) from the face. The easiest way to make this cut is with a portable circular saw set at the appropriate angle. This is about 15 degrees, but do check it off the drawing.

3 First stage of marking the tenons on the ends.

4 A hand-held circular saw, set at an angle, can be used to cut the shoulders.

Use a batten to run the saw up against and make a smooth cut from side to side (**4**).

The next stage is to cut out and shape the tenons. A bandsaw will help with some of this work, but it is not absolutely necessary. Cut down the side edges of the tenons first, making sure that the angle is cut to both lines on each face. The outer shoulders can now be cut (**5**). The inner shoulder is more difficult; a bandsaw definitely helps here (**6**). If you don't have one, the cuts can be made by hand with saw and chisel. Now the tenons need to

be marked and trimmed to length. A small template replicating the width of the tenon and set at right-angles to the shoulders will enable the final shapes to be marked. A simple saw-cut down one face removes this waste (**7**, opposite); however, on the other face, a large chisel assisted by a mallet will be needed to remove the rest (**8**, opposite). Check now that each pair of tenons fit the matching mortise holes and make any necessary adjustments.

The center brace position should next be marked on the ends and the mortise holes cut.

5 The outer shoulders are cut by hand.

6 The inner shoulders can be cut by hand or on the bandsaw.

7 The easy, outer angle is cut by hand with a saw.

8 The inner angle needs to be trimmed to shape with a chisel.

A simple way to start this process is by loosely assembling one seat and a pair of ends on a flat surface. With a parallel board of the right size, on edge, the one shoulder line can be marked on the sides of the two ends (**9**). The holes need to be marked and cut out in a similar fashion to those in the seats (**10**, **11**). Take care when working through each end; the mortise holes are at angles. It is best to start from each side and meet in the middle. Now the braces can be marked out.

Take the shoulder measurement positions from the working piece or from the full-size drawing. There is also the mortise hole in each end for the securing wedge. Mark and chop this out first, by hand or machine (**12**). Finish off by cutting the shoulders and sides of the tenons by hand or on a bandsaw. Check each brace for fit and trim the end corners off at an angle to tidy them up.

The ends can be shaped at last. Start by marking the sloping angle to the outside of the

9 The position of the brace can be marked on the partly assembled seats from a flat surface.

10 The mortise holes for the braces need to be marked out on the ends.

11 The holes are then cleaned out and shaped with a chisel.

12 The mortise holes in the braces can be cut on a mortise machine or by hand.

13 The first splay on the ends needs to be marked.

14 A template is used to mark the detail.

detail measurement (**13**). Slice these off by hand or machine. A small template, with a 45-degree end, can be used to mark the side detail. The depth of this is about ½in (12mm) (**14**). Another sloping line needs to be marked, parallel to the first cut, to make sure this detail stands out. This, and the curved bottom and top, can be marked and cut out now. The side detail needs to be cut by hand because of the angles involved (**15**). To finish the ends off, trim the feet at the rightangle

so that the stools sit level (**16**). Both ends and braces can be cleaned up at this stage. This is not meant to be a highly smooth finish; therefore, a light rub down will be more than sufficient.

The final shaping of the seats is now undertaken. Hand carving tools can be used for all of this process, but some mechanical aids will speed things along. The shapes need to be marked out on both edges (**17**). This enables you to keep track of the waste removal and make

15 The side detail is cut by hand.

16 Trimming the feet off to length at an angle.

17 The shape of the seat ends can be marked using a suitable round object.

18 Cuts are sliced across the seat to provide a depth guide for the chisel to work to.

19 The bulk of the waste is cut out with a mallet and chisel.

20 More waste can be removed with a powered chisel.

sure that the finished seat is evenly shaped and not sloped. Trim the rounds on the seat ends first. Secure the seat in a firm position and cut as much of the bulk waste out from the central section as quickly and easily as you can (**18**, **19**, **20**). Work the shape down to just full of the final size and put each seat to one side. Mark out and cut however many wedges you require to fit into the ends of the braces (**21**). These can be cleaned up ready for the final assembly.

Make a saw cut down each of the tenon's ends on the inner face; this is to take a wedge to secure them in place. You will need to cut at least eight wedges per stool. Make them from some of the waste stock you have cut away while shaping the ends and so on. Now try a dummy run at assembling each stool. Once satisfied that they all fit together, disassemble them and prepare all the components. Mix or prepare a waterproof adhesive; these stools are for use

21 The wedges can be cut out on a bandsaw.

22 The wedges are driven in using a hammer and a piece of gash stock.

outside. With the brace in place, apply plenty of glue to the end tenons. Drop the seat on and drive the shaped wedges home in the ends of the brace. Now load all the cuts and gaps on the ends of the tenons with plenty of glue. Make sure the seat is right down on the shoulders of the tenons and drive the wedges home, leaving them proud of the surface (**22**). A small, copper pin in the lower section of the brace wedges will secure them in place; there should be no need for these to be removed. Place each seat on

one side and leave for a day or so to allow the adhesive to cure and harden.

Trim off the protruding wedges flush with the current surface of the seats and remove any excess glue from the underside. With a large, straight carving gouge, cut all the surfaces back to their final shape and size. To finish off, lightly sand all those surfaces on the seat as required. Finally, think through the type of treatment the finished seats might benefit from. Clear preservative or oil will help prolong their lives.

Room divider/shelving unit

Materials	Black walnut, *Junglans nigra*; hard maple, *Acer saccharum/nigrum*
Time to make	3–4 days
Skill level	Intermediate

This simple room divider/shelving unit is made stylish through the use of contrasting timbers. It features black walnut and hard maple, but there are alternatives: the vertical uprights could be made from oak and stained or fumed darker, with the shelves in, say, ash, or the piece could be made entirely out of one species.

Toolbox

Essential	Basic hand tools
Useful	Over and under planer; rip-, cross-cut and bandsaws; mortiser; pillar drill; plug cutter

Making the room divider

Once you have selected the lumber, it needs to be prepared for jointing. In this case, the vertical supports/legs came out of a couple of wide pieces of 1¼in (32mm) thick black walnut stock (**1**, opposite). The shelves were made from two pieces of 10in (250mm) wide hard maple. Once the nominal sized components are ready, they need to be square-planed. When planing by hand, or machine, always start by flattening one face (**2**, opposite). The edges should follow. Because they were so wide, the shelves for this unit were ripped slightly over-width once the first face and edge had been squared. The sawn edge was then lightly planed to remove the cut marks before being planed to the finished thickness. The legs were simply faced and edged, then finished off by passing them under the planer.

Right and below The finished unit, and a close-up detail showing the contrasting use of timbers that gives this project a decorative boost.

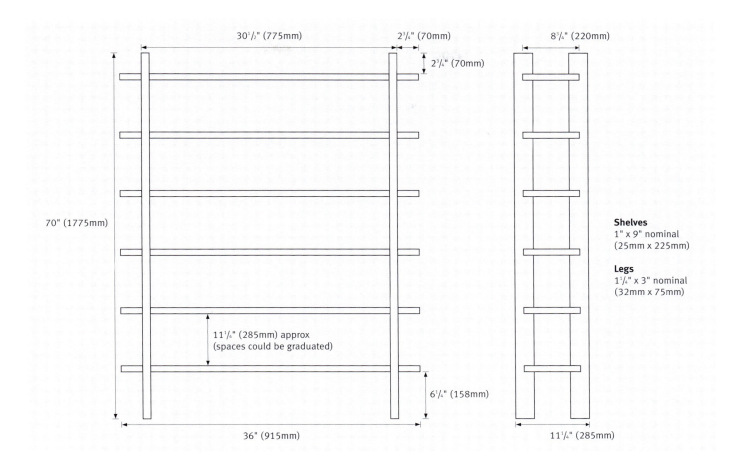

30¹/₂" (775mm) 2³/₄" (70mm) 8³/₄" (220mm)

2³/₄" (70mm)

70" (1775mm)

Shelves
1" x 9" nominal
(25mm x 225mm)

Legs
1¹/₄" x 3" nominal
(32mm x 75mm)

11¹/₄" (285mm) approx
(spaces could be graduated)

6¹/₄" (158mm)

36" (915mm) 11¹/₄" (285mm)

Although this project is designed to be made up from straight, clean lines, there are some tricky bits involved in construction. The key to the project is the integrity and positioning of the joints. The best way to sort out how the joints will work is to make up a dummy one first. Work with a leg scrap and a suitable piece of softwood to represent the shelves. Mark out the sample trench and roughly cut out

Cutting list

Component	Pieces	Length, nominal		Width, finished		Thickness, finished	
Legs	4	72"	1800mm	2³/₄"	70mm	1"	25mm
Shelves	6	39"	990mm	8⁵/₈"	220mm	⁷/₈"	22mm

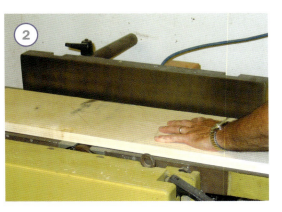

1 The legs are ripped out of wider stock.

2 Each shelf needs to be planed flat on the face.

3 This is how the final joint should look before assembly.

4 When the joint is closed up, all the detail disappears.

the bulk of the joint, which will be on the legs, on a mortise machine. Trim and clean this up before working out the size of the cutout on the shelf section of the joint. The slot for the shelves can be simply cut by hand or on a bandsaw. Once the sample joint has been made, you can then move forward onto the main project itself (**3**, **4**).

Ensure that the shelf overhang will be the same as the face measurement of the legs. Then fair-end all six together and make the edge marks. Each individual piece should then be face-marked with a square from the edges. You will need a calculator to work out the spacing of these shelves on the legs. A similar process then follows with the legs. Mark the edges in a group and square the faces from these. Use a marking gauge to clearly mark the depth on each one (**5**). Starting with the leg part of the joint, the shelves can now be made to fit. Use a mortise machine to cut part of the trenches on both sides. Follow this by cutting the rest of the waste out on a pull over cross-cut saw (**6**). Using stops, you will be able to position the joint exactly on each leg so that the whole unit will

square up nicely later on. On the bandsaw, set the fence up to cut the outer shoulder of the slots in the shelves. Use a stop, so that the depth of each cut will be the same every time.

Each leg and shelf should now be individually tested for fit and adjusted as necessary. Number the shelves from the top down so that they go back in the right order. Although the recessed cross-halving joint is quite strong in itself, one screw in each shelf will add a bit of insurance. Mark out the legs for plugs. The plug holes will accommodate the screws and can be filled with maple to contrast decoratively with the walnut. Center-punch each of the plug hole positions and bore them out on a pillar drill using a ½in (12mm) single winged multispeed bit. Each plug hole should then have a smaller pilot hole drilled through its center. This latter hole should be slightly larger than the shank of the screws you are going to use. The plugs themselves are cut from a piece of gash maple stock (**7**, opposite). After using a suitable plug cutter to bore as many as you will need, slice them out on a bandsaw (**8**, opposite).

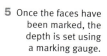

5 Once the faces have been marked, the depth is set using a marking gauge.

6 Part of the leg joint is made on the mortise machine, and this bit on a cross-cut saw.

7 The plugs are cut into some spare gash stock.

8 They are then sliced out on the bandsaw.

9 Each shelf is coated one side, turned over, and finished off on the top surface.

10 Two legs are laid out and assembly starts from both ends.

At this stage, all the wood used in the unit should be carefully sealed. Apply one coat of sealer to all parts (**9**), and when the sealer has dried, cut it back with a very fine steel wool.

Final assembly commences by laying two legs out on the bench and applying a small dollop of glue to the center of each joint. The numbered shelves are then inserted (**10**). When they are all in place, apply some glue to the joints of the other two legs and ease them both carefully into position on the other side of the shelves (**11**). Check for square, and then drop some screws into each plug hole. These screws should be 1¾in (45mm) long. They will bite for a little over a third of their length into each shelf. Drive all the screws in on one side of the unit, then turn it over and repeat the process on the other. Next, glue and hammer all the maple plugs carefully in place. Leave for a day for the glue to set and then trim and sand back the plugs until they are level with the surface of the unit's legs (**12**). Wax the unit and buff it up to a nice luster finish, and the job is done.

11 The other legs are then placed into position.

12 Later the excess plug is trimmed back, prior to final finishing.

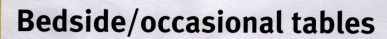

Bedside/occasional tables

Materials	"Olive" ash, *Fraxinus excelsior*
Time to make	3–4 days
Skill level	Intermediate

This is an interesting project. The sub-frame structure is what is called a skeleton frame; the drawer is not enclosed, so the joints can be seen, and therefore care needs to be taken with the dovetails. The table can be scaled up or down, and one or two tables could be used in an occasional setting or as bedside units.

Toolbox

Essential	Basic hand tools
Useful	Bandsaw; ripsaw; over and under planer

Making the tables

The choice of wood, in this case, was "olive" ash. This comes from ash boards that contain some darker streaks. Particular use of this has been made in the tops of the tables. Obviously any timber of your choice could be used, but ideally select something that shows off the grain.

It is a good idea to begin by starting with the top of the table. Once this is jointed up, it can be set to one side while other preparatory work is carried out. With most timbers, wide tops should be jointed out of several pieces to avoid distortion. Roughly cut to size each piece and plane it flat on the face and square on the edges. Once this is done, it is easier to select and match the boards so that both tops would be of a similar grain configuration once jointed. Remember to alternate the growth ring direction; this is crucial, to avoid the completed top from cupping one way or the other. Although not absolutely necessary, add biscuits to the edge joints. Ensure that the end ones are well in, so that when the top is trimmed to size they are not exposed (**1**,

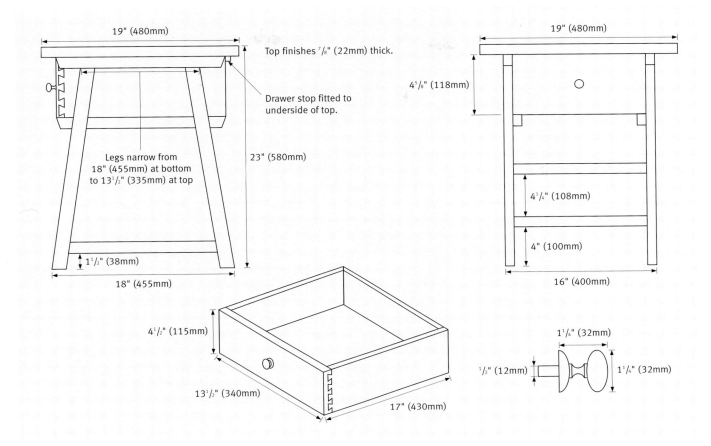

Top finishes ⁷/₈" (22mm) thick.

Drawer stop fitted to underside of top.

Legs narrow from 18" (455mm) at bottom to 13¹/₂" (335mm) at top

23" (580mm)

1¹/₂" (38mm)

18" (455mm)

19" (480mm)

19" (480mm)

4⁵/₈" (118mm)

4¹/₄" (108mm)

4" (100mm)

16" (400mm)

4¹/₂" (115mm)

13¹/₂" (340mm)

17" (430mm)

1¹/₄" (32mm)

¹/₂" (12mm)

1¹/₄" (32mm)

overleaf). With each one ready to assemble, mix up some powdered resin glue with water, to provide a rigid joint. Spread plenty of glue into the edges and the biscuit sockets. As each piece is added, rub the joint back and forth to ensure that the glue is worked into the grain. This provides the key and improves strength. Once in the clamps, make sure that each top is flat and that the edges of the joints are flush on the surface (**2**, overleaf). The tops can be put aside to allow the glue to set and harden. Later, the excess can be cleaned off and the faces finished.

When constructing a project with angles or difficult joints, it is extremely useful to draw out full-size sketches showing the exact position of the components and joints. For this project, draw out the side elevation only; this is the one with all the angles. This working drawing will then help with the production of each of the individual pieces and how they fit together. With this done, the stock needs to be selected, sawn, and planed to size. Occasionally,

Cutting list (for one table)

Component (for one unit)	Pieces	Length, nominal		Width, finished		Thickness, finished	
Legs	4	30"	750mm	1⁵/₈"	41mm	1¹/₄"	32mm
Side rails	2	18"	450mm	1⁵/₈"	41mm	1¹/₄"	32mm
Top rails	2	21"	525mm	1⁵/₈"	41mm	1¹/₄"	32mm
Drawer runners	2	21"	525mm	1¹/₄"	32mm	⁷/₈"	21mm
Front and back rails	4	18"	450mm	1¹/₄"	32mm	1¹/₄"	32mm
Top, to make	1	19" finish	480mm	19" finish	480mm	⁷/₈"	21mm
Drawer							
Front	1	30"	750mm	12³/₄"	318mm	⁵/₈"	16mm
Sides	2	24"	600mm	17¹/₈"	435mm	¹/₂"	12mm
Back	1	18"	450mm	12⁷/₈"	327mm	³/₈"	10mm
Knob	1	30"	750mm	12³/₄"	318mm	1¹/₄"	32mm

1 Cutting the joints.

2 Make sure that the three pieces are clamped up flat and with the edges of the joints flush.

3 Mark out the bad section with a miter square.

4 Fit the patch piece and cramp it in place. A small block was also made for the opposite side both to help the cramp grip and to protect the face of the component.

defects will appear at this stage. Rather than waste a piece of wood, see if it can be salvaged with a patch, plug, or repair (**3**, **4**).

With all the planed components to hand, mark one off the drawing and transfer the dimensions to its matching pieces. End-trimming the top rails with their angles is probably the best place to start (**5**). The positions of the mortises can then be taken off the drawing. They can be batched up again for marking out (**6**) and separated when the marking gauge is used to set the position of the holes in the

width. Once marked out, the mortise holes can be cut in the top rails and the legs to make each side. Marking out and cutting the other mortise holes for the front and back rails should follow. With the legs trimmed to length, the tenons are marked out. Shoulders can be cut on the bench and the bulk of the waste removed on a band- or cross-cut saw (**7**, opposite). The tenon on the top of each leg is at right-angles to the shoulders. A strip of waste, squared off on one end, placed in position on the face of the tenon, can be used to mark it out. The

5 The top rails are trimmed to length with 45-degree ends.

6 The others are all batched up and the positions of the tenons marked.

7 The bulk of the waste can then be removed with a pull over, cross-cut or bandsaw.

8 The tenons being trimmed off on the bandsaw.

remaining shoulders and waste removal can then be done by hand or on a bandsaw (**8**).

Now is a good time to fit the tenons into the mortises and dry-assemble each end. Place the made up ends on the full-size drawing to see how close it is to the original concept. If you have got it right, it should fit! The top is going to be fixed to the sub-frame, through the top rails, with some brass screws. The holes through these rails need to be slotted to allow for movement in the top itself. Having marked their positions out, use a pillar drill, if possible, to bore a pair of holes about $^5/_8$in (16mm) apart. With the drill bit rotating, you should be able to apply some side pressure and joint these two holes up to form the slot. If not, chisel out the central waste.

Once all the components have had all their joints fitted, tested, and each piece has been cleaned up, the sides are ready for fixing. Use resin glue mixed with water to ensure strong joints. The bottom rail goes into the sides of the two legs first and then the top rail is fitted. Because of the angles involved, only two clamps should

be required (**9**). Lift the end assembly onto the full-size drawing and tweak the clamps until the profile is an exact match. Once the glue has set, and any excess has been cleaned off, the drawer runners can be fixed on (**10**). These are the same length as the top rails and are fixed directly below them on the inside of the legs. They can be simply screwed and glued on. Use a piece of waste cut to the depth of the drawer and squared at one end to help position the runners. A little PVA glue around the back side of the screw hole will ensure that they stay in place. Cramp the one end down while driving the screw in at the other end.

Final assembly of the sub-frame can now take place. First, apply plenty of glue in and on all the joints. A couple of sash clamps should be sufficient. Stand the assembled sub-frame on a flat, level surface to ensure it sits correctly when released. At this stage, the top can be finished off by trimming the sides and ends to the required size. When the glue has set on the sub-frames, clean off any excess and tidy up ready for sealing. It is much easier to apply one coat

9 Due to the angles and joint configuration, only two clamps are needed. It is important to check that each assembled section is as per the drawing.

10 Later the four side assemblies are laid out ready to fix the drawer runners on.

of sealer at this stage than when everything has been put together (**11**).

At this stage you will know what the exact sizes of the drawers are going to be, so work can start on these. Once the pieces have been planed-up square and to size, trim off the fronts to length just slightly narrower than the width of the recess. Start by marking each front with the depth of lap; leave about ^{1}/8in (4mm). The thickness of the sides now needs to be marked on the inside (**12**). The marking gauge can be used to set the spaces of the sockets and pins, or simply use a tape measure. First cuts down the marks should be made with a fine dovetail or tenon saw (**13**). The bulk of the waste can be removed from the sockets with a router or on the bench with chisels. The trimming of the pins and sockets should be done in the vise (**14**). Mark the tails and cut by hand or on a bandsaw. No doubt there will be some trimming off required before a good fit is made. As each joint is completed, mark the front and sides appropriately so that you will get the right ones back up together.

11 All the prepared bits and pieces are treated with one coat of sealer.

12 The lap dovetails are marked out across the face of the drawer.

Do this in the joint itself or, lightly, with pencil on the outside faces. Next, run a groove for the drawer bottom around the inside face of the fronts and sides. The width of the back can now be measured and cut from the top side of this groove. If you wish, joint the back to the sides with dovetails, or you could choose to use a simple groove and tongue joint, as here. Clean up all the inside faces and the drawers are ready to glue up and fix. Don't forget to check that they are both square and flat (**15**, opposite). Once the glue has set, measure for the exact dimensions of the drawer bottom. This should simply slide in from the back and can then be pinned in place (**16**, opposite). Clean up the assembled drawers and make any fine adjustments to the fit in the sub-frame.

The last stage is to turn the knobs from some of the waste. Having found the centers, mount them between the head and tail stocks (**17**, opposite). Turn down to a cylinder first and then cut the round tenon on the tail stock end (**18**, opposite). If you have already drilled the sockets

13 Once squared down the inside face, a fine-toothed dovetail saw is used to cut down the marks.

14 The sockets and pins are cleaned up in the vise.

15 With the drawers clamped up, they need to be checked for square and adjusted if necessary.

16 Once cut to size, slide the bottom in and fix with brads into the back.

in the drawer fronts, test for fit off the lathe. Now mount a chuck into the head stock end and, turning the blank round, push the tenon into the chuck and tighten up. The tail stock can still be used at this stage while the shape is cut (**19**). It is best to pull this back when the last, small bit is removed. Sand-up each knob in the lathe. Fit the knobs now if you wish, or wait until they and the drawers have been sealed (**20**). Cut back the completed drawers and knobs ready for waxing.

Before fixing the top to the sub-frame, wax and buff up all the made pieces. Place the finished top on the bench, with some protection underneath, face down. Invert the sub-frame and fix it in place with the screws of your choice. Now slide the drawer into place. A small bit of planed all-round waste is used as a stop. A couple of brads and a touch of glue will do the job. Take the drawer out, turn the whole unit over, and give it all a final buff up. Slide the drawers in and the job is done.

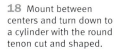

17 The knobs are made from rail offcuts. Find the centers and drill a short pilot hole in each end.

18 Mount between centers and turn down to a cylinder with the round tenon cut and shaped.

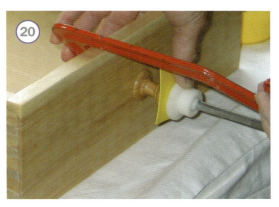

19 Remount in a chuck; the tail stock can be used until the last waste is removed.

20 Once sealed and polished, the knobs can be glued and fitted to the drawers.

Spice cabinet

Materials	Elm, *Ulnus spp.*
Time to make	4–5 days
Skill level	Intermediate

This project calls for some skill in the setting out and cutting of the joints for the drawer gaps, but once you get the idea it will all fall into place. This one has sixteen drawers, graduated in size from the bottom up. Larger, smaller, more or fewer drawers are all options open to the maker. A matched pair would look very attractive.

Toolbox

Essential	Basic hand tools
Useful	Lathe; router; biscuit jointer; powered saws and planes

Making the spice cabinet

The first job was to convert the odd piece of elm into square-edged components to be planed up. The wane was cut off on the saw bench, freehand, and then the individual pieces sawn and square-planed to finished size. The spacer pieces were then prepared, using some $^5/_{16}$in (8mm) fiber board. Slightly oversize strips were sliced off the main board and then a straight edge planed on

Below The finished spice cabinet. Note the interesting mix of different colors and textures in the woods used, selected for maximum variety.

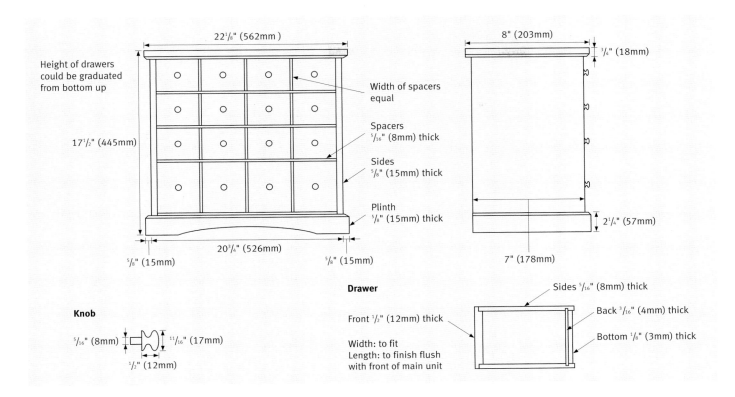

Height of drawers could be graduated from bottom up

22⅛" (562mm)

17½" (445mm)

Width of spacers equal

Spacers ⁵⁄₁₆" (8mm) thick

Sides ⁵⁄₈" (15mm) thick

Plinth ⁵⁄₈" (15mm) thick

20¾" (526mm)

⁵⁄₈" (15mm)

⁵⁄₈" (15mm)

8" (203mm)

¾" (18mm)

2¼" (57mm)

7" (178mm)

Knob

⁵⁄₁₆" (8mm)   ¹¹⁄₁₆" (17mm)

½" (12mm)

Drawer

Front ½" (12mm) thick

Width: to fit
Length: to finish flush
with front of main unit

Sides ⁵⁄₁₆" (8mm) thick

Back ³⁄₁₆" (4mm) thick

Bottom ⅛" (3mm) thick

one side. The edging strips came from a short plank of cherry (**1**, overleaf). These were cut and square-planed to ⁵⁄₁₆in (8mm) to match the fiber board. No special joints were required to fix the edging strips to the fiber board. Once a liberal amount of glue had been applied, they were simply rubbed back and forth to make a good bond (**2**, overleaf). The half dozen spacer pieces were then left for the glue to set. Later on, the excess was cleaned off, the ends trimmed and each one was finished to the required width.

The main carcass of the cabinet is biscuit-jointed together. Each joint position should be marked and then chopped out in the matched pairs as required. When they are cut, dry-assemble the carcass and check that the joints are correctly positioned and that the whole thing comes up square. The positions of the stopped grooves for the spacer pieces need to be marked out. Across the width these will be set out to produce equal gaps between the spacers and sides. In height, they can be graduated from a slightly larger size at the bottom through to a smaller one at the top. If this seems complicated, then set the whole thing up with gaps/drawers

Cutting list

Component	Pieces	Length, nominal		Width, finished		Thickness, finished	
Main unit							
Top	1	24"	600mm	1⅝"	41mm	1¼"	32mm
Sides	2	18"	450mm	1⅝"	41mm	1¼"	32mm
Plinth, front	1	27"	675mm	1⅝"	41mm	1¼"	32mm
Plinths, side	2	9"	225mm	1¼"	32mm	⅞"	21mm
Spacers, horizontal	3	24"	600mm	1¼"	32mm	1¼"	32mm
Spacers, vertical	3	18"	450mm	1¼"	32mm	1¼"	32mm
Packing	1	24"	600mm	19"	480mm	⅞"	21mm
Back (ply/ hardboard)	1	24"	600mm	19"	480mm	⅞"	21mm
Drawers							
Fronts	16					½"	12mm
Sides	32	6⅝"	170mm	To match fronts		⁵⁄₁₆"	8mm
Backs	16	To match fronts		To match fronts		³⁄₁₆"	4mm
Bottoms	16	6⅜"	162mm	To match fronts		⅛"	3mm
Knobs	16	2"	50mm	¹¹⁄₁₆"	17mm	¹¹⁄₁₆"	17mm

1 The edging strips are in cherry and are cut from a short length.

2 The strips are rubbed along the glued edge to help form a key.

of exactly the same size. Use a straight, $^5/16$in (8mm) cutter set in a router to cut the grooves. A simple jig can be made for the router base to slide against. The edge of the jig should be cut with the router and this then set exactly along the line of the groove. The jig is fixed in place for each cut with a couple of screws. Cut each set of grooves in pairs so that they are matched (**3**). Remember to drop the router in and avoid running out to create the stopped grooves.

The back edge of the sides and top have a rabbet cut in them for the back panel. The bottom piece of the carcass should be cut to the internal width so that the back panel can overshoot this when fixed in place. The rebate can be cut with the same router cutter, on a saw bench or by hand (**4**). Now the rest of the spacer fitting needs to take place. Small notches, to match the stopped grooves, are cut on their front edges. $^5/16$in (8mm) slots are cut in from the back on

3 The router runs along the jig edge to cut each stopped groove.

4 A stopped rabbet is cut and cleaned up along the rear edges of the sides and top to take the back panel.

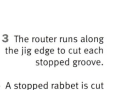

5 The slots are cut on a bandsaw or by hand.

6 The spacers are dry-assembled to see how they fit.

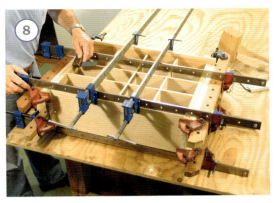

7 The small bevel on the underside of the top is cut using a bearing-guided router cutter.

8 The spacers and main carcass are glued, clamped up, and checked for square.

the horizontal spacer pieces to match the vertical positions already cut in the top and bottom pieces of carcass. Mark these out in a batch on the back edge and then square across the faces halfway. Cut each slot by hand or on a bandsaw (5, opposite). Then repeat the process for the vertical spacing pieces. This time, mark to match the sides and cut the slots from the front. Take care with both the setting out and cutting of these slots. Double-check your measurements to make sure they all line up.

If anything is slightly out, it will show when the cabinet is assembled. Have a dry run once the slots have been cut (6, opposite). If it is not right, you may have to start again or, if you can get away with it, make some fine adjustments.

Finally, at this stage, apply a small bevel to the underside of the top piece (7). This will help to lift and lighten the unit and will also match the bevel you will apply to the plinth. Before finally gluing up the main structure, have a dry

9 The plinth is mitered on the corners.

10 Fit the front piece first with plenty of glue, then drive the screws in from the backside.

run at it. Because there are so many joints, use a slightly slower-setting adhesive like PVA. This will give you a chance to make sure everything is lined up before you clamp up (8). Check that everything is square before leaving the piece to one side until the glue has gone off. Now prepare the plinth. Plane square to size and apply the bevel. The corners are to be mitered. Cut the front piece on one end first. Match one side to it and mark the position of the joint on the other end (9). Cut this second joint and the associated

side piece. Always cut miters longer rather than shorter. You can trim them to fit, but filling a gap will stand out. Cut a shallow curve into the front piece of plinth (10). It is a good idea to fix a piece of softwood across the front, behind the plinth, so that you can fix through it. When you finally position the front piece of plinth, make sure that about $5/16$in (8mm) of the bottom panel is showing to match the spacer pieces. Apply plenty of glue behind the plinth pieces before you fix them. Position the front piece first and

11 Apply some glue in the rabbet on the back panel to add to the rigidity of the cabinet.

12 Small brads fix the back panel in place.

clamp it in place. Drill some pilot holes in from the back and drive the securing screws home. Finish off by fixing the two side pieces in a similar fashion. Now cut the back panel to fit. To add a bit of rigidity, you can bed this onto some glue (11). A few brads, equally spaced, will finish the job off at this stage (12).

You need to make the drawers to fit the gaps you have created. If you follow my example, there will be four identical drawers per row graduated in size (13).

Cut and plane all the drawer components to size except for the backs and bottoms. The fronts are simply trenched to take the thickness of the sides. Grooves are cut along the lower, inside faces of the fronts and sides to take the bottoms (14). The width from the top of this groove to the top of the side determines the width of the back. They can now be finished off to size. Another slot is cut down the inside, vertical face of each side to take the backs. Once this is cut, the bottoms can be measured from the depth of each groove for the width and from the front groove over

the back for the length. When you know these dimensions, the bottoms can be cut to size. Pilot holes are required for the retaining pins for the sides. Mark their positions on the inside, with a gauge (15, opposite), and then drill through from the inside at a slight angle.

Set up an assembly line to put all the drawers together (16, opposite). Make sure you have plenty of glue and brads to hand. The easy way to make them up is by applying glue to one of the front trenches first and popping this piece into a vise vertically. Drop the first side on, with brads inserted, hold it in place and drive the brads home. Turn everything over. Apply some glue to the other trench and the back slot. Put some glue into the other back slot and position the second side. Drive the pins home and extract the assembled drawer frame from the vise. Wrap a rubber band round the whole thing and check it is square. You might need to jiggle the drawer frame around until it is square. Make up all the other drawers. Later on, clean any excess glue out of the grooves along the inner, bottom faces. Apply

13 The drawers start out as a multitude of strips.

14 A groove for each of the bottoms is cut into the drawer sides.

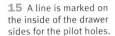

15 A line is marked on the inside of the drawer sides for the pilot holes.

16 An assembly line for making the drawers up is prepared.

17 Once the main drawer frame has dried, the bottoms are glued and slotted into place.

18 The first try at fitting the drawers shows that about half fitted exactly.

some fresh glue into these grooves and slide the bottom in (**17**). Finish off the rest of the drawers and leave them to cure. Finally, clean them up and make any final adjustments to fit (**18**).

The knobs of this piece were made from several different woods, for variety in the design. Turning them takes place in two parts. First, between centers, from the square to a cylinder with a double-length round tenon to fit an $^5/_{16}$in (8mm) hole in the center. These pieces should be removed and cut through the middle. The

shorter lengths are then remounted in a chuck and the final profile turned (**19**). Seal and wax to bring them up to a luster finish.

Clean up the carcass and drawers and apply one coat of sealer. Cut back lightly with steel wool. Drill the drawer fronts with a $^5/_{16}$in (8mm) hole in the center of each. Cut a single slot into the round tenon of the knobs. A small bit of glue on both knob tenon and drawer socket is all that is needed to fix them in place (**20**). Wax and buff the drawers and the job is done.

19 Each knob is turned and finished in the lathe.

20 A little glue in the socket and on the round tenon secures the knobs.

Stylish stools

Materials	Hard maple, *Acer saccharum/ nigrum*; cherry, *Prunus avium/serotina*
Time to make	5–6 days
Skill level	Intermediate

To add a bit of interest to this project, the species of timber used were mixed up together to make the finished product more striking. Any reasonably strong wood will do as an alternative to those used here, but if you decide to steam-bend the seat back, choose something that is not too brittle, such as ash or beech.

Toolbox

Essential	Basic hand tools
Very useful	Steaming chamber; bandsaw
Useful	Powered saws and planes; mortiser; router

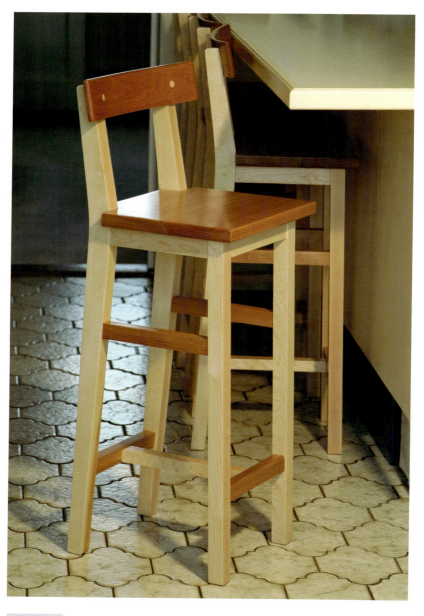

Making the stools

What is always useful, when working with angles, is to draw a full-size front and side elevation of the project. Any flat, clean surface will do, providing you are able to see and take the measurements off it. Before getting into making the main structure of the stools, you might decide to steam-bend the backs and make up the seat widths. In this case, the backs were cut from some thicker material, planed all round, cut to length and the rounded moldings applied. The alternative to steam-bending is to cut each back, from a thicker piece of stock, with the curve in place. Some additional cleaning and shaping up is required to make sure they are all the same.

If you decide to steam-bend, once you have prepared the seat back blanks, leave them in a tank of water to soak thoroughly for a day before the first bending session. The mold into which

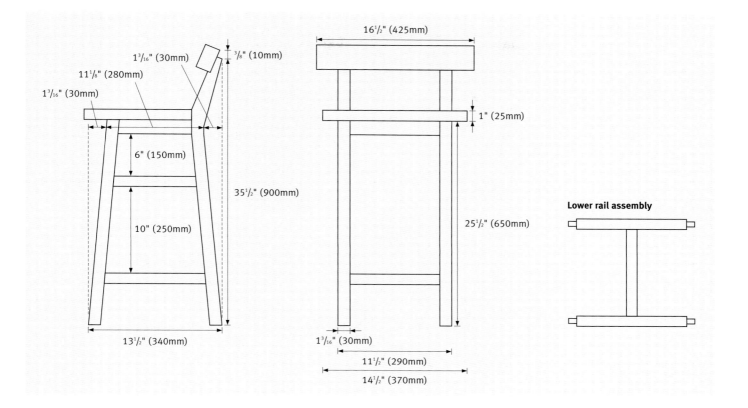

each back would go was carefully cut from a solid piece of oak (**1**, **2**, overleaf). To ensure a smooth finish, the adjoining faces were then cleaned and sanded to remove any saw marks. Once prepared, the mold could be used repeatedly. In this case, an improvized water boiler was used as a steamer. The backs were to be bent one at a time over a four-day period. With the boiler up to temperature, the first one was put in (**3**, overleaf). Every quarter of an hour it was turned round to make sure that steam was evenly applied. While this was going on, a mold was set up in a vise. After an hour of steaming, the seat back was taken out and quickly placed in the mold. The vise was tightened and the mold closed right up (**4**, overleaf). The seat back was left in the mold until the next morning.

Over the next few days the rest of the backs were bent. When each was taken out of the mold, it was set into a sash clamp with some slight pressure on. Each clamped set was then placed in a warm place to ensure that the excess moisture had dissipated and that the bend had truly set. One did crack, but not too badly (**5**,

Cutting list (for one stool)

Component	Pieces	Length, nominal		Width, finished		Thickness, finished	
Front legs	2	30"	750mm	1³⁄₁₆"	30mm	1³⁄₁₆"	30mm
Back legs	2	39"	975mm	2³⁄₄"	Ex 70mm	1³⁄₁₆"	30mm
Top rails	4	12"	300mm	1⁹⁄₁₆"	40mm	1³⁄₁₆"	30mm
Intermediate rails	2	12"	300mm	1³⁄₁₆"	30mm	1"	25mm
Lower rails	3	15"	375mm	1³⁄₁₆"	30mm	1"	25mm
Seat back	1	18"	450mm	⅝"	16mm	2³⁄₄"	70mm
Seat, to make	1	15"	375mm	13"	330mm	1"	25mm

overleaf). A little remedial work soon sorted it out (**6**, overleaf). Once dried and set, the backs were cleaned up and sanded ready for fixing later on.

Each seat is made up from two pieces (**7**, overleaf). This is for reasons of both economy and stability. Cherry, the choice of wood for the seats in this case, is not a large tree, so using two pieces was easier than trying to find a wide

WARNING Please note that although many of these images show machines unguarded for clarity, you should ALWAYS ensure that when operating equipment the appropriate guards are in place.

1 The steaming mold is marked out from an old chair back.

2 Carefully cutting the mold curve on the bandsaw.

3 Steaming in process.

4 The third stool back going into the mold.

piece. Additionally, wide pieces of temperate hardwoods tend to cup. Making the width from two or three pieces is a much better way to proceed. The seat parts were surface-planed on one face only to start and the edges squared off this face. A simple, rubbed joint would be more than adequate in this case (**8**, opposite). Use a powdered resin glue to secure the joints and set the joined up seats in clamps while the glue cures. Later on, clean off any excess glue and finish all the pieces to size.

Now, work on the sub-frame assemblies can begin. All the components should be square-planed, ready for cutting and jointing. The back legs must be made wide enough to accommodate the angles at both the top and bottom. Keeping these in their original widths, the first right-angle mortise holes, for the top rails, are now marked out (**9**, opposite). Each of these can be cut on the bench or in a machine (**10**, opposite). With these holes cut, the back legs are shaped (**11**, **12**, opposite). The finished

5 Sometimes cracks or splits are unavoidable.

6 This one can be cured by planing off the affected area and fixing a patch in place.

7 The seats, made of cherry, are also cut from thicker stock.

8 Apply lots of glue and rub the joints together.

legs are then marked out directly from the full-size drawing. If you are chopping out mechanically, keep some of the falling bits of waste, with their angles cut, to use as a base from which to cut the mortise holes. Once the first set of mortise holes, for the top and intermediate rails, have been cut in the back legs, they are "handed" to take the other top and lower rails (13, overleaf). Work on the front legs starts by establishing the angles off the drawings. The mortise holes can all

be cut. Once more, keeping some of the waste for packing might be a good idea.

Each of the rails needs to be marked out ready for cutting the tenons (14, overleaf). Concentrate on the top and intermediate rails first. The angles on the lower rails can follow later on. The seats are to be fixed in place with buttons. Therefore, a groove needs to be cut around the inside of each of the top rails. Once this is done, the side frame assemblies should be ready for a dry run.

9 The position of the first mortise in the back legs is taken directly off the drawing, then the measurements are transferred to the other back legs, and marked on all the edges.

10 The mortises can be cut by hand or on a machine.

11 The bulk of the waste is cut on a bandsaw.

12 The faces are then planed-up square.

13 The side mortises are cut, making sure the faces are square on.

14 The same two angles, for front and back, are marked on the rails.

Clean everything up prior to gluing the sides. With plenty of glue and clamps ready, assemble each side (**15**). Place each frame on the full-size drawing to check the positions and angles, once tightened in the clamps. If necessary, make any slight adjustments before the glue sets.

The lower rails are made up in an "H" pattern. After preparing the straight-shouldered tenons for the front and back lower rails, the central mortise holes in each must be marked out and cut (**16**).

The front rails can be beveled at this stage; this will reduce wear and tear from sitters' shoes. The central part of the rail assembly has two different shoulder angles. The one sliding bevel used to mark the angles on the front legs should match the front, but another sliding bevel needs to be set for the back. It is easiest to cut the shoulders and tenons of these rails by hand (**17**). All the components should now be ready to assemble the rest of the sub-frame. Clean everything up and have a dry run

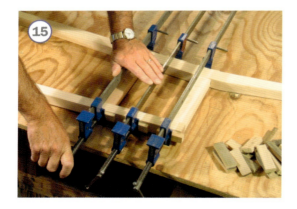

15 Apply plenty of glue and three clamps per side.

16 The mortise holes for the lower, central rails are marked out.

17 The tenons are finished off in the vise.

18 Apply lots of glue and clamps and join up each stool.

19 Each recess is cut out by hand with the leg fixed in the vise.

20 Some glue applied in the recesses helps hold the back in place.

to make sure everything goes up together. Due to the number of joints, you might find it useful to tape the packing pieces in place before you start. With clamps and glue to hand, get started. Each frame should be assembled and then checked for square (**18**, opposite). Make any adjustments as necessary and leave the frames clamped up while the glue cures. Later on, clean off the excess glue and give each frame a final clean up.

In this case, the square seats were given a bit of a lift by applying a bevel to the lower edges. The arrises were also taken off the top edges. Each seat was then marked out with the notches that allowed them to pass the back legs. The notches were subsequently carefully cut on the bandsaw. The buttons are made up from one strip of presized wood. It is easier to mark and cut out all the trenches and holes like this before chopping off to their final length. Now the seat backs were fitted to the top of the back legs. In order for them to sit proud of the legs, the lower, shoulder position was marked first. Using one of the curved backs, the depth of recess was then

marked out and these lines matched down to the shoulders. With care, and with each leg held firmly in the vise, the cuts were made (**19**).

Returning to your own stools, it is now time to apply the first coat of sealer, prior to final assembly. Once the sealer has dried and hardened, cut back the sub-frames with steel wool. Now fix the seat backs onto the frames. A plug of maple, to contrast with the cherry, can be used to mask the screws holding the backs in place (**20**). A little glue on the face of the recesses also helps. Once the holes are plugged, leave the glue to set (**21**). Later on, the plugs must be cut and cleaned back level with the surface. A second coat of sealer should then be applied to all the seats and seat backs.

When the second coat of sealer has dried and hardened, cut this back with steel wool and wax and polish everything to a luster finish. With the seat inverted, mount the sub-frame on top and carefully position the four retaining buttons (**22**). Fix the one at the back first, followed by the other three. Check that each stool is level, and make any final adjustments as necessary.

21 A plug fills the hole.

22 Fixing the seat to the frame with four buttons.

Garden table and benches

Materials	Oak, *Quercus robur/petraea*
Time to make	5–7 days
Skill level	Intermediate

This is not a project for the faint-hearted! Although it is not particularly complex in design or construction, you will need to be physically strong to make this one. This is because the oak used in the project is so dense and heavy. However, this is a beautiful set of garden furniture, which is hugely rewarding to make.

Toolbox

Essential	Basic hand tools
Useful	Chain-, rip- and cross-cut saws; over and under planer; mortise machine

Making the table and benches

The oak used in this project was well air dried. Because the sections are so large, they were set out to cut them down to more manageable sizes as quickly as possible (**1**, overleaf). Some were cut to length with a chainsaw and, where there was not one already, a straight edge was made from which to work (**2**, overleaf). The nominal sized components were then ripped off these blanks on a ripsaw bench (**3**, **4**, overleaf). This was followed with the planing process. As with hand-planing, one face first and an edge squared off this; the

Below and right The finished table and benches. If these are to be kept outdoors, they will need a suitable preservative to protect them and ideally a cover when not in use.

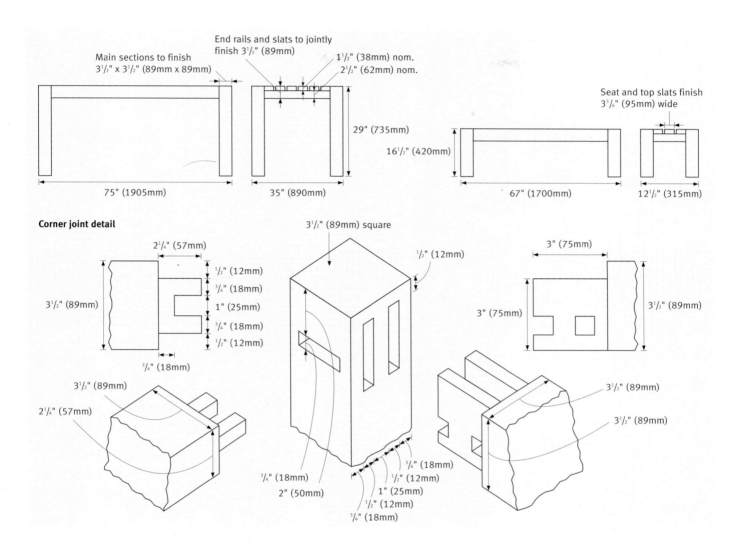

Main sections to finish
3½" x 3½" (89mm x 89mm)

End rails and slats to jointly
finish 3½" (89mm)

1½" (38mm) nom.
2½" (62mm) nom.

29" (735mm)

16½" (420mm)

Seat and top slats finish
3¾" (95mm) wide

75" (1905mm)

35" (890mm)

67" (1700mm)

12½" (315mm)

Corner joint detail

2¼" (57mm)

½" (12mm)
¾" (18mm)
1" (25mm)
¾" (18mm)
½" (12mm)

3½" (89mm)

¾" (18mm)

3½" (89mm) square

½" (12mm)

3" (75mm)

3" (75mm)

3½" (89mm)

3½" (89mm)

2¼" (57mm)

¾" (18mm)
2" (50mm)

¾" (18mm)
½" (12mm)
1" (25mm)
½" (12mm)
¾" (18mm)

3½" (89mm)

3½" (89mm)

other face and edge were then planed square to the finished sizes. Next, the legs were cut to length.

Because the legs are positioned in the very corners of the table and benches, use twin tenon joints. Large, flat ones for the side rails would make a good, solid joint. To lock these in place, drive through them at least one of the other, flatter twin tenons from the end rails.

Mark the larger, side rail mortise holes on the legs first. Use a mortise machine to cut these deep joints, although they can be done by hand. The top and bottom lines for the joints are marked on each leg. Only one leg needs the width positions, because the machine would be set to these to cut all the joints. With this in hand, each piece should be mounted in the mortiser and the joints cut out (**5**, overleaf).

Cutting list

Component	Pieces	Length, nominal		Width, finished		Thickness, finished	
Table							
Legs	4	36"	900mm	3½"	88mm	3½"	88mm
End rails	2	36"	900mm	3½"	88mm	2¼"	57mm
Side rails	2	78"	1950mm	3½"	88mm	3½"	88mm
Top slats	6	78"	1950mm	3¾"	94mm	1¼"	31mm
Benches							
Legs	8	18"	450mm	3½"	88mm	3½"	88mm
End rails	4	15"	375mm	3½"	88mm	2¼"	57mm
Side rails	4	72"	1800mm	3½"	88mm	3½"	88mm
Seat slats	2	72"	1800mm	3¾"	94mm	1¼"	31mm

1 A chain saw comes in handy for cutting through the thick, large sections.

2 Heart splits need to be broken right through.

Start one end and cut a little deeper as you move down the joint. Once full depth has been reached, return to the start, cutting the remaining waste out here and in the rest of the joint. Make sure that the drill bit clears the waste before cutting the next section. The position of the next pair of twin tenons has to be marked on each leg because the cut will be across the grain rather than with it. Once these are all marked out, cut the two deeper holes first and then join them up with the haunch section in the middle. Once all the mortises have been cut on the machine, clean them out by hand and put them to one side.

Trim the rails to length and mark the first sets of twin tenons on the side rails. Cut the outer and inner cheeks of the tenons first, on a bandsaw. The two external shoulders and flush haunch should then be cut, up to a stop, on the pull over cross-cut saw. Go back on the bandsaw and finish off the flush haunch (**6**, opposite). Cut out the middle waste on the mortiser by working in from both sides (**7**, opposite). Clean up the tenon

joints and check them for fit in the mortise holes. The end rail, flatter twin tenons are cut following a very similar process. These should be cleaned up and checked for fit (**8**, opposite). The sockets into the other twin tenons are not cut at this stage; do that after the first joints have been made.

Begin the assembly of the furniture. As it is intended for outdoors use, apply a waterproof resin adhesive to the joints. Sort out the clamps before you mix the glue. Apply plenty of adhesive to fit the joints together and clamp the sections up tight and square. Leave all joints overnight for the adhesive to harden and cure. Once the side frames are assembled, cut the rest of the waste out of the mortise joints to take the other pair of twin tenons on the end rails (**9**, **10**, opposite). Again, with plenty of glue to hand, these joints need to be made and clamped up. Put the assembled frames to one side to allow the adhesive to cure.

With the frames made, the seat and top slats can be cut dead to length. Clean them all up and drill the pilot holes and countersinks. To fix the

3 Thicker stock needs an initial, part-way through cut first.

4 The second cut completes the process.

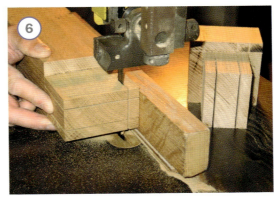

5 The first of the twin mortises are chopped out.

6 The haunches can be cut on a bandsaw.

7 Finally, the waste is cut out on the mortiser.

8 This is how the second joint should look.

second twin tenons permanently, drive a long screw right through them from the side. Because oak contains tannic acid, brass or stainless steel screws are best used, to avoid staining.

On the outer edges of the frames and across the ends of the slats, cut a small bevel to take the edge off, using a router. With this done, give everything a final rub down before fitting all the slats and completing the assembly.

Furniture that stands outside will last longer if it is regularly treated with an appropriate preservative. If you do not want to color the wood, it is best to select a clear preservative. At the very least, try to make sure that the bottoms of the table and bench legs are protected. A quick and easy way to do this is by placing a flowerpot saucer under each leg and filling it with preservative. The wood will naturally absorb the preservative and, if this is done annually, it will last a lot longer. Tung or teak oil will provide a good protective surface. Avoid varnishes, as they will break down over time.

9 A chisel is used to square and clean it out.

10 This is how the joint should look when it is finished.

Wood flooring

Materials	Any hard-wearing timber
Time to make	Variable
Skill level	Intermediate

As a flooring material, wood is one of the warmest and most comfortable available, and can give a distinct feeling of quality. Timber flooring does go in and out of fashion, and wall-to-wall carpeting hides many a classic wooden floor. However, a wide range of types and styles have seen a revival over recent years.

Toolbox

Essential	Basic hand tools; powered planes and saws
Useful	Sanders; router; builder's square

Selecting and laying wood flooring

Wood flooring can have a timeless quality; it can also look a mess. Today there is so much to choose from. There is the solid stuff, simple tongued and grooved softwood or hardwood flooring; old-fashioned random width floor boards; strip or block flooring. A recent newcomer is end grain solid wood flooring, in which the trunk is cut across and a pattern created from the circular grain. The latter is mostly seen laminated into a square similar to a carpet tile size for ease of laying. More complicated strip wood flooring will have been "end matched." This is where each strip of wood is not only tongued on one edge and grooved on the other but the ends are jointed also. The theory is that this enables each of the adjoining pieces to help hold each other flat. Premade parquet and small block flooring comes ready laid out in squares on a string, mesh, or paper base. The idea is to bed the wood face down, square by square, and then remove the backing to expose the finished surface.

Probably the easiest wood flooring to choose, use, and lay is the modern composite, engineered wood flooring. This is often still referred to and promoted as solid wood flooring (technically it is because it is made up from

Below A simple, dark wood strip flooring.

Below right The oak flooring featured in this project.

layers of wood). In this case, a board of single or multiple widths is made up with a face wood of choice and a base of two or more with alternating grain, lower-cost alternatives. The engineered board is more stable and less likely to move in service, it is usually prefinished and often comes with a unique locking system which can avoid the need for fixings. The best engineered flooring often requires no glue. It is simply laid straight onto a prepared surface. Poor quality stuff is terrible; it is too thin and crackles as you walk on it. The thicker, more solid engineered boards result in what appears to be an expanse of highly expensive timber flooring that is much more satisfying to both look at and walk on.

There are a few points to consider when choosing the timber for your floor. Color, of course, is one of the key issues. Remember that most wood, when laid and exposed to light, will slightly darken over time. Quality of finish and resistance to wear also have a bearing. You

Above left A variation on the herringbone theme.

Above Flooring that emphasizes the contrast between heart and sap woods.

Below The six most common and popular decorative wood flooring patterns.

1 The wood for this project came from a variety of different-sized planks.

2 All the boards had to be cut roughly to width.

may want to consider how much and what sort of foot traffic might go on, over, or through your floor. Will the floor be laid in a lounge or living area where casual use with light foot coverings occur? Is it going to be laid in an entrance hall, lobby, or kitchen, where all kinds of things could get spilled or walked onto it? Will it be in a moist setting such as a wash- or bathroom? Under-floor heating has an impact and care should be taken when choosing your flooring. Some suppliers will have their own systems. Always seek specialist advice in these circumstances. Floors laid in new builds also need care. Any new flooring screeds need to have been well finished off and the building thoroughly dried out before laying a wood floor should be contemplated.

For this project we have decided to keep it simple! We are going to show you how to produce, lay, and finish your own parquet flooring. This is not a speedy process and it needs to be done in several stages. Here goes.

Firstly the raw materials. Let's assume your room is established and has some sort of

heating associated with the building within which it is situated. The wood of choice should be as near as possible to the same moisture content enjoyed, seasonally, in its final location. Using "air dried" stock will mean that it will shrink in service, resulting in large gaps appearing and the blocks coming loose. If the wood is too dry it might pick up moisture, swell and distort, and become uneven. It is probably best to go for some artificially dried stuff that has a moisture content of around ten percent or so. If you start with something like this, we can bring it into equilibrium later on.

For this project we have settled on oak as the base material. It is probably a good idea to have a mix of plain and quarter-sawn material. Wear around the medullary rays—the "flower" figure—can be higher, giving a flaky appearance. Our blocks came from a variety of different thicknesses, all originally kiln dried (**1**). The first job was to rip all the odd sizes to width (**2**). After this, they could be deep-cut to the nominal thickness (**3**). If the project is not under any time

3 The boards had to be cut to a full thickness.

4 The blanks are face-planed first.

5 Each blank is then ripped slightly over width...

6 ...and then planed to the finished thickness.

7 A few pieces are cross-cut to check that the length is right.

8 Once certain the stop length is correct, the bulk of the blocks can be cut dead to length.

pressure constraints, then it is recommended that the nominally cut sections are brought into and stacked in the room in which they will be located. This will help them come into equilibrium with the actual room in which they are eventually laid.

Assuming that all the boards are now ready for planing, start by surfacing one face and an edge (**4**). The finished sizes have to be exact, so try and make all the blocks in one batch rather than having several goes at it. Rip all the blanks to just over the finished width and then plane them to the finished size (**5**). Follow up by planing to the finished thickness (**6**). For this "Dutch" pattern, each block's length is cut exactly to the combined width of three blocks. Try a few test pieces until you are certain that the length matches the combined widths (**7**). Once you are happy with this, chop all the blocks to length (**8**). You will know how many you need by working out the coverage of a set of four versus the area of the room. Keep a few odd lengths

9 It is important to check out if the room is square.

10 Find the middle and transfer this measurement right across the room.

11 Fitting a straight batten on the middle line makes things easier.

12 Lay the first blocks carefully; the others will all follow these.

back for the short blocks and any to go into alcoves and so on. There may also be a need to trim some of the blocks if the room is not square. To help the adhesive bond with the blocks, random trenches can be cut across the backs with a saw. To make sure each block fits snugly against its neighbor, cut a small bevel, up to half the block's thickness, all round the underside edge. Now remove any odd bits of spelshing, sawdust, or shavings from each of the blocks. A light sand on the underside edges will sort most of this out. Each block needs to be clean and ready to lay. Stack them in a convenient place, or on a small trolley, if you have one.

Time to check out the room. If the existing floor is not flat and level, you may have to seek professional help to sort this out. There are a number of self-leveling products on the market, but time has to be allowed for these to be applied. You need to know if the room is square. A large builder's square will help (**9**, previous page). Work out the middle distance down one wall and transfer this line to the center of the room (**10**,

previous page). Fixing a straight, lightweight batten to this mark helps ensure that the first row is straight (**11**). To make sure the pattern is balanced, start laying from the middle of the room outward. If the room is not square, an odd shape or elongated, you will have to decide where this center point is. The objective is to cut, if necessary, any edge blocks so that the margins are equal. In addition, you need to leave a gap between the outer edges of the blocks and the wall. This allows for any expansion and will also be covered by the baseboard you fix on afterwards.

Use a proprietary adhesive to lay the blocks. Talk to your local flooring specialist and ask their advice. You will not want a water-based adhesive, which will only make the blocks swell. Starting at the middle, apply a small patch of adhesive. Now set into this patch the first series of blocks (**12**). Make sure they are all snugly up together. Too much adhesive might hinder this process. Work in straight runs from the middle out (**13**). At the edges, unless it is an easy job, leave all the smaller trimming bits until later.

13 Lay the blocks in rows from the middle outward.

14 Corners can be a bit tricky; just make sure all the blocks are tightly up together.

15 Finishing off the sanding with an orbital disc sander. Without the baseboard in place, you can get right to the edge.

16 Start sealing in the corner farthest away from a door.

Work in quarters laying into one corner first (**14**). Carry on until you have laid the whole floor. It is a good idea to aim to exit from a door near the last quarter area.

Before starting the finishing process, cut and fit, but do not fix, all the baseboard sections. This enables you to clean off the floor any brick or block dust that may have been created while you do this. When you are ready, sand off the floor so that it has an even, flat surface (**15**).

The absence of the baseboard enables you to get right up to the edges. Work down through various abrasive grit sizes to around 120 or so. When the whole floor has been sanded and finished, vacuum off all the dust. Now the sealer can be applied. Look out for a hard-wearing floor sealer to use. If the floor has a high level of foot traffic, several coats will be required. If the floor is for occasional use only, two will probably be enough. Start in the corner farthest away from

17 A light rub down with steel wool before...

18 ...working up a sweat and giving the floor a final wax and buff up to finish off.

where you are planning to exit the room (**16**). Work with even, regular strokes in line with the majority of the grain. Once the first coat has been applied, leave it for a day or so to harden, unless the sealer manufacturer recommends otherwise.

In the workshop, or in another room, also apply the first coat of sealer to all the baseboard. Lightly sand or steel wool this first coat off both the floor and the baseboard when it is hard (**17**). Now fix the baseboard in place. Plugs and screws

are the best fixing options. Recess the faces for a filler plug once the baseboard has been fixed. Glue these in place and trim back flush once the adhesive has cured (**18**). Vacuum the dust off again and apply the second coat to both floor and baseboard. This may now be sufficient. If more coats are required, follow a similar process until complete. A waxed floor finish can also be achieved. Lightly steel wool the final coat and then wax and buff up the floor. Now it is time to stand back and admire your handiwork.

Inlaid hall/side table

Materials	Cherry, *Prunus serotina/avium*, with walnut (*Junglans nigra/ regia*) detail
Time to make	2–3 days
Skill level	Intermediate plus

Cherry is a lovely warm, pinkish wood that is ideal for this fairly challenging project. The use of walnut to highlight some of the detail makes the whole thing more interesting and decorative. You can of course vary the size, style, and woods used to suit your own particular needs and preferences.

Toolbox

Essential	Basic hand tools
Useful	Powered saws and planes; router; biscuit jointer; lathe

Making the table

Most table or worktops over 9–10in (225–250mm) wide will need to be jointed from narrower stock. There are some benefits to this. Wider boards tend to move more, even after planing flat. Ideally, an odd number of narrow pieces should be used to make up the desired width. The potential direction of "cup" can then be alternated (see the section on shrinkage on page 19). Check this out by looking at the end grain. In this case the top has been made from three pieces—a slightly wider one in the middle and two narrow ones up the edges. Not only will this help to avoid any major movement, it also balances up the top surface grain.

Each of the three pieces for the top was face-planed first. The center board had both edges square-planed and the two outer pieces one edge only. The reasoning behind this was that the top would finish 12in (300mm) wide. This is not too wide to go through an over and under planer. After the top was made, it would then be replaned to the finished sizes. Because of this, it was important to make sure that the direction of slope on the grain was aligned on all three pieces while also alternating the adjacent growth patterns. Failure to align the grain will probably result in some areas of the top surface plucking out when planed.

Begin by cutting out some biscuit dowels to help strengthen the edge joints (**1**, opposite). Keep the end ones in a little so that when the top is trimmed off to length they are not

Below The finished table. The inlaid walnut detailing and waxed, luster finish of this piece make it elegant enough to grace any hall or living room.

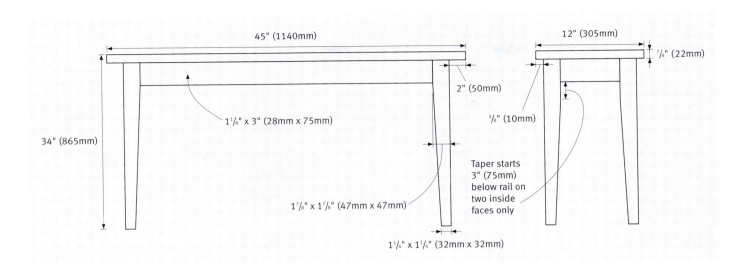

45" (1140mm)

12" (305mm)

⁷⁄₈" (22mm)

2" (50mm)

1¹⁄₈" x 3" (28mm x 75mm)

³⁄₈" (10mm)

34" (865mm)

Taper starts
3" (75mm)
below rail on
two inside
faces only

1⁷⁄₈" x 1⁷⁄₈" (47mm x 47mm)

1¹⁄₄" x 1¹⁄₄" (32mm x 32mm)

accidentally exposed. Work plenty of glue into the edges and biscuit slots on both pieces. Once the joint is made, rub the two pieces back and forth slightly to work the glue into the pores; this is what makes a really good, strong joint. Before clamping up, tight-check that the surface of the boards are somewhere near flush; the biscuits should help with this. Use as many clamps as necessary to close the joint and keep it flat (**2**). If the joint and consistency of glue are right, you should get an even, exuded bead of excess adhesive all along the made joint.

Return to the top when the glue has set and hardened. The excess can now be trimmed or sanded off (**3**, overleaf). Once that is done, replane the jointed board to the final dimensions required for the top and trim it off dead to length (**4**, overleaf). The rest of the components can now be prepared. The legs are ripped out of

Cutting list

Component	Pieces	Length, nominal		Width, finished		Thickness, finished	
Top, to make	1	48"	1210mm	12"	305mm	⁷⁄₈"	22mm
Legs	4	36"	910mm	1⁷⁄₈"	47mm	1⁷⁄₈"	47mm
Rails, side	2	12"	305mm	3"	75mm	1¹⁄₈"	28mm
Rails, front/back	2	42"	1065mm	3"	75mm	1¹⁄₈"	28mm
Buttons, to make	10	1½"	38mm	1¹⁄₄"	32mm	⁷⁄₈"	22mm

some 2in (50mm) stock (**5**, overleaf). Face, edge, and plane each of the leg and rail components to their finished dimensions (**6**, overleaf).

As mentioned earlier, the table is to be enhanced with some walnut detailing. Select the straightest grain piece of walnut lumber you

⚠ **WARNING** Please note that although many of these images show machines unguarded for clarity, you should ALWAYS ensure that when operating equipment the appropriate guards are in place.

1 Cutting the biscuit joints.

2 When clamping, tighten up evenly to avoid distortion.

3 Once hard, the excess glue can be sanded off.

4 Now the top can be finished to size as one piece.

can find and cut some thin strips off the edge (**7**, opposite). Then use a router to set a single flue, straight cut in it. Plane down the strips of walnut to fit. Use some odd pieces of softwood to test the final thickness in the trench before finishing off the walnut. It needs to be a nice snug fit, not too tight.

When you are satisfied that the walnut is ready, move on to marking out the top (**8**, opposite). The inlay is to be simply set about

1½in (38mm) in from the edge and joined in squared corners. The depth of cut is not desperately important; around ⅛in (3mm), is more than sufficient. Set the side fence of the router accordingly and begin cutting the trench to the corner marks. Some care needs to be taken to ensure there is no wobble as the trench is cut and that, in the corners, you don't overshoot (**9**, opposite). The edges of the corners can be squared off with a marking knife or chisel

5 Cutting the legs from a piece of lumber.

6 The rails and legs are planed smooth.

(**10**, opposite). The waste should be removed so that this section of the trench is the same depth as the rest (**11**, opposite).

Thin strips, that would sit slightly proud of the trench depth, must then be sliced off the ready prepared walnut blanks. Trim off the four pieces for the top inlay to length with miters on their ends. Fit each one into the trenches until they are filled continuously and have good corner joints (**12**, opposite). Work plenty of glue into each trench to make sure that the inlay stays

in place. Lay some waste pieces of softwood over each of the inlays and cramp them down tight (**13**, overleaf). Later on, once the glue has set and hardened, both this and the protruding inlay strips must be cut back flush with the top's surface and the whole piece cleaned up and finished, ready for sealing.

Now commence the sub-frame assembly. Mark mortise holes on the tops of each leg first. Chop out the mortises, allowing for haunches if you wish (**14**, overleaf). Trim the legs to length

7 A thin strip of walnut is sliced off the plank for the inlays.

8 Marking out the top for the inlay.

9 The routed trench should look like this in the corners.

10 Use a marking knife to trim out the edges of the trenches.

and then make up a jig to cut the taper for the legs on the ripsaw bench. This can be done by hand. Use a piece of flat, planed gash stock for this. Decide how much taper is required on each leg. The jig now needs to be marked out to the dimensions you decide upon along one edge and the waste cut out to accommodate each leg (**15**, overleaf). Slice off one, inner face edge first. Turn the leg to the other inner face in the jig and then make the second cut. Both these faces can now be planed up (**16**, overleaf).

The tenons are now made to fit the mortises. Cut the shoulders on a pull over cross-cut saw using a stop to ensure that they are all squared accurately around each piece. The depth of cut needs to be varied to allow for the final tenon dimensions. The rest of the waste should then be sliced off on the bandsaw (**17**, overleaf). Use a bit of waste first to make sure the fit is right. Around the inner face of each rail, cut a small groove to take some buttons to hold the top on. The use of this traditional fixing method allows

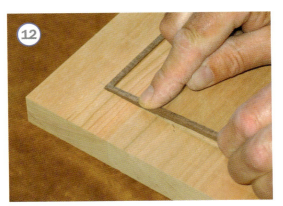

11 Chisel out the waste.

12 Check for fit.

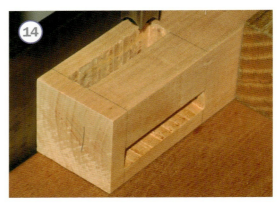

13 Strips of a softer wood hold the inlays in place while the glue cures.

14 The mortises are chopped out.

any future width movement of the top, one way or another, to take place without fear of splitting. Prepare the buttons themselves in a strip. Once the strip has been trenched out, check with a piece of waste that the tongue fits the groove, each being predrilled and countersunk. Chop the individual buttons out of the strip in two goes and tidy them up ready for use.

Next, make twin cuts into each outer face of the rails at about the same depth as that on

the top. With the strips of inlay ready, liberally coat these trenches with glue and insert each strip of inlay. A piece of waste and as many cramps as possible will hold everything in place until the glue has set. The rails and legs can be finished off subsequently before final assembly. Start this process by fixing the two short ends together (**18**, opposite). Check that the two sub-assemblies are square and that the legs are the same distance apart at the top and bottom. Set to one side for the adhesive to cure.

A pair of dowel pegs driven into each tenon will provide some extra strength and could be a decorative feature as well, to complement the walnut inlay strips. Select some mild-grained walnut and cut a number of short, square sections. The center of each of these should be found, marked, and a small hole drilled. Each, in turn, is then mounted in the lathe and roughly rounded down (**19**, opposite). Try to make your dowels around ¼in (5mm) in diameter. This will be about the smallest size you will be able to turn and otherwise prepare. With care, and quite

15 The jig for the taper is made from a bit of gash stock.

16 The sawn faces are then planed up.

17 The cheeks on a bandsaw.

18 The first stage of the leg assembly. Checking that they are square.

19 The peg dowels are turned from a small, square strip on the lathe.

possibly some breakages along the way, you should end up with more than enough material turned down to the right size. Just to make sure, bore a hole through one end of a clamp with a drill bit to match the one you would use on the tenons. Each length of dowel can then be knocked through this to finish it off exactly to size.

The first two pairs of leg sub-assemblies should now be marked out with the peg holes in line with the inlay strips. Each of these holes must be bored out to a depth that goes through the tenon into the other side of the mortise hole. Apply a dollop of glue in each hole, drive the pegs home, and trim them off just proud of the surface (**20**). Later, once the glue has set, they can be cleaned up flush with the leg surface. The final assembly of the sub-frame follows. Apply lots of glue in the mortises and on the tenons. Position the rails and cramp up the frame flat and square (**21**). Leave everything to set properly, and the following day release the cramp pressure and repeat the pegging and cleaning up process.

A waxed, luster finish will look good on this piece. Apply one coat of sealer all round. Once dry, cut this back on the sub-frame assembly with a fine steel wool. Give the underside of the top the same treatment. Sand the upper surface and edges hard with 180 grit abrasive paper and apply another coat of sealer. Cut this back with fine steel wool and then wax everything up. Finally, invert the top on a non-scratch surface and fix the sub-frame to it with the buttons.

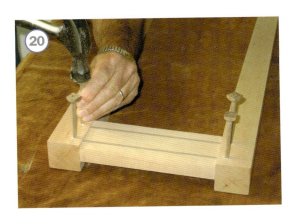

20 The pegs are driven home with plenty of glue.

21 Once the legs and rails are clamped up, check that the frame is square.

Table and wine rack

Materials White ash, *Fraxinus americana*
Time to make 7–8 days
Skill level Intermediate plus

This table and wine rack unit has been designed to be as versatile as possible. The drawer can be accessed from both sides and, if you choose to fit them, castors will make the piece highly mobile for those tight spaces. You can also scale the unit up or down to suit your particular requirements and preferences.

Toolbox

Essential Basic hand and powered tools
Useful Lathe; band, rip- and cross-cut saws; mortiser; pillar drill

Making the table and wine rack

The wood used in this project is white ash. It has been specifically selected to be as light as possible. It is most likely that a lot of this lighter wood is in fact sapwood; there is often no discernible difference between this and the heartwood. In this case, any included sapwood will be both strong and durable enough for its intended purpose. In addition to this selection process, we have used an acrylic finish. This tends to produce a lighter surface tone than if a standard oil or polyurethane sealer is used.

In every parcel of white ash there will be some boards with darker patches or streaks. This is the nature of timber. In this wood, when it occurs, it is often referred to as "olive ash"; we have used some of this in at least one other project in this book. Naturally, you should consider which wood to make this project from and match it to the final location in which it will sit, or choose a timber of particular interest to you.

Having sorted out the lumber for the job, the first step is to get the top underway. This one

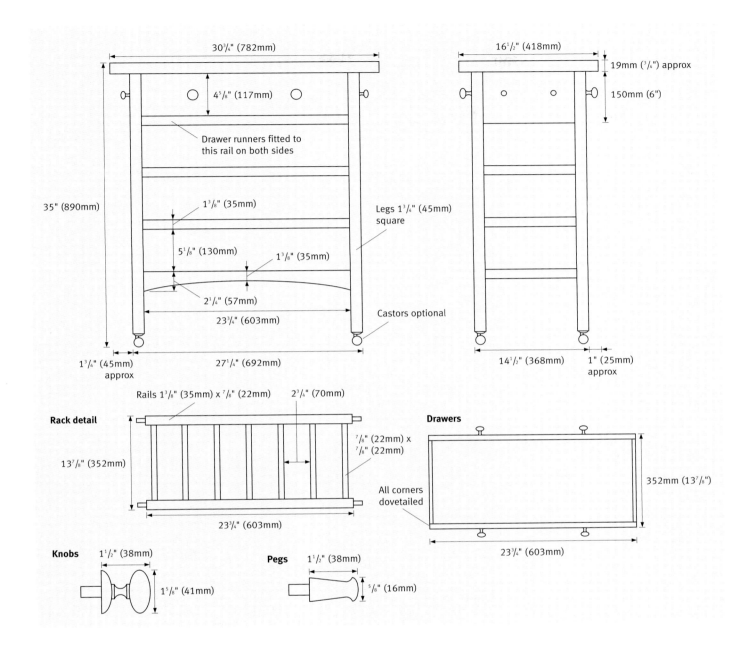

30³/₄" (782mm)

4⁵/₈" (117mm)

Drawer runners fitted to this rail on both sides

35" (890mm)

1³/₈" (35mm)

5¹/₈" (130mm)

1³/₈" (35mm)

2¹/₄" (57mm)

23³/₄" (603mm)

Legs 1³/₄" (45mm) square

Castors optional

1³/₄" (45mm) approx

27¹/₄" (692mm)

16¹/₂" (418mm)

19mm (³/₄") approx

150mm (6")

14¹/₂" (368mm)

1" (25mm) approx

Rack detail

Rails 1³/₈" (35mm) x ⁷/₈" (22mm)

2³/₄" (70mm)

⁷/₈" (22mm) x ⁷/₈" (22mm)

13⁷/₈" (352mm)

23³/₄" (603mm)

Drawers

All corners dovetailed

352mm (13⁷/₈")

23³/₄" (603mm)

Knobs 1¹/₂" (38mm)

1⁵/₈" (41mm)

Pegs 1¹/₂" (38mm)

⁵/₈" (16mm)

was jointed from three pieces (**1**, overleaf). For stability, it is often much better to use several pieces rather than fewer. Ash in particular can distort in wide widths. Whenever jointing from several pieces, make sure that the end grain configuration is alternated. This will help to hold the final piece as flat as possible. Plane each of the three pieces flat and square (**2**, overleaf). Mark and cut out the positions of the biscuit joints with the end ones well in; you don't want to trim the top to length and cut through a dowel

later! (**3**, **4**, overleaf). Once ready, liberally apply glue to each edge and joint socket (**5**, overleaf). Use a powdered resin mixed with water to ensure a firm, rigid joint. Once the glue is on and the biscuits are positioned, rub the edges together to ensure the adhesive works well into the pores of the wood. This provides the real strength of the joint. Three clamps are needed to hold the boards together while the glue sets (**6**, overleaf). Make sure, at this stage, that the top sits flat in the clamps. Once this is done, put the piece to

Opposite The finished table and wine rack. This elegant, practical piece will hold as many as 18 bottles of wine.

Cutting list

Component (for one unit)	Pieces	Length, nominal		Width, finished		Thickness, finished	
Top, to make	1	36"	900mm	16¾"	420mm	¾"	19mm
Legs	4	36"	900mm	1¾"	45mm	1¾"	45mm
Front and back rails	6	30"	750mm	1⅜"	35mm	⅞"	22mm
Bottom rails	2	30"	750mm	2¼"	57mm	⅞"	22mm
Top, side rails	2	15"	375mm	6"	150mm	⅞"	22mm
Rack rails	21	15"	375mm	⅞"	22mm	⅞"	22mm
Drawer runners	2	15"	375mm	1⅜"	35mm	⅞"	22mm
Drawer fronts	2	30"	750mm	4⅝"	117mm	¾"	19mm
Drawer sides	2	15"	375mm	4⅝"	117mm	½"	12mm
Drawer bottom, ply or similar	1 1	30"	750mm	15" nom	375mm	3⁄16"	4mm
Drawer knobs	4	3"	75mm	1⅝"	41mm	1⅝"	41mm
Side pegs	4	3"	75mm	⅝"	16mm	⅝"	16mm
Castors (optional)							
Braked	2	3"/75mm high, 2"/50mm wheel diameter					
Free-wheeling	2	3"/75mm high, 2"/50mm wheel diameter					

one side. It can be trimmed to size and cleaned up later on.

The rest of the components should then be cut from the rough lumber to their nominal sizes (**7**, opposite). Each of these must be faced, edged, and planed to its finished size. The next stage is to mark out the side rail mortise holes on the legs. The best way to mark the legs out is to batch them together, square-ended, and clamp them while you mark out (**8**, opposite). Cut them dead to the overall height of the unit. Because the top, side rail is wide, a pair of mortise and tenons would be best. Two mortise holes with a lower, central recess should be chopped out. Technically, there should also be an allowance for a haunch, but this is not absolutely necessary.

With the mortise holes cut, the rail lengths can be calculated and these cut to length with an allowance for the tenons. The rail tenons can be cut in a variety of ways; by hand or machine, but mark and cut the shoulders first. The cheeks of the tenons can be sliced off; use a pull over

⚠ **WARNING** Please note that although many of these images show machines unguarded for clarity, you should ALWAYS ensure that when operating equipment the appropriate guards are in place.

1 Three lengths are needed to make the top.

2 They are faced first, then edged and finished to size.

3 The positions of the biscuit joints are marked.

4 The sockets for the biscuits are cut.

5 Plenty of glue in the sockets.

6 Clamp up from both sides to make sure the assembled top stays flat.

cross-cut saw. Any further waste removal can then be cut away with a coping saw or on a bandsaw (**9**, overleaf). Each twin tenon should be trimmed to fit its mortise mate and marked so that you know which matches which. The top is to be buttoned on, which allows room for movement; therefore, a groove needs to be cut on the outside of the top rail. Without the drawer, the buttons would be on the inside, out of sight. A straight bit in a router will cut this,

or, set a ripsaw slightly proud of the table and slice out the groove. Think ahead at this stage and mark out and drill the pairs of ½in (12mm) holes for the side pegs in the top, side rails (**10**, overleaf). It is easier to do this before the unit is finally assembled.

Back to the legs. The front and back rail mortise holes need to be marked and cut out (**11**, overleaf). A similar process follows, making sure that each mortise is directly

7 Having selected the rest of the stock, it is cut into the individual components.

8 The positions of the double mortise holes in the legs are marked out.

opposite all the others on the same level to ensure that the unit is perfectly square when it is assembled. Once both mortise and tenons for these have been cut, thought needs to go into the spacing of the rack rails. Get some empty bottles and decide how far apart each rail will need to be to support a bottle (**12**, overleaf). This unit is designed for storing wine, so a gap of 2¾in (70mm) should be about right, but do please check it out yourself. With this information to hand, all the rails

can be batched up and marked out together. Allowance for the two drawer runner rails at the top also needs to be made. Cut a simple ½in (12mm) mortise for each joint. Now is a good time to have a dry run at putting the unit together. This will show you how it looks, whether it works, and, at this stage, what the shoulder lengths of the rack rails and drawer runners will be (**13**, overleaf). With the shoulder measurement calculated, cut all the tenons to fit the appropriate mortise holes.

Before the rail, rack, and drawer runner assemblies can be put together, the bottom rail needs to be shaped. You don't need to get too technical. A thin strip of waste wood can be bent to mark round. Just mark each rail with the starting point at the sides and the apex of the arc in the middle and bend the strip to match. You will probably need some help with this. Cut the curve by hand or on a bandsaw. It can be cleaned up with a spokeshave and finished with a light sanding (**14**, opposite). Now part of the assembly can take place. Once all the front and back rails, rack rails, and the pair of drawer runners are cleaned up, these four sections of the unit can be fixed up. Get all your clamps and packing ready and apply plenty of glue to each joint. Assemble each set and clamp it up. Check and adjust for both square and flatness. Put to one side and leave for the glue to set.

Start to prepare some of the smaller components. You will need four side pegs, four drawer knobs, and half a dozen buttons. Pegs

9 The centers and shoulders of the tenons can be cut out on a bandsaw.

10 The round mortise holes for the two pegs are cut on a pillar drill.

and knobs can be turned out of waste from the rack rails and legs. You will need access to a lathe. Roughly chop off to length, allowing for a section of waste. Find, mark, and shallowly drill out the centers at each end. Initially, mount in a lathe between the head and tail stock and turn down to a cylinder to match the finished diameter. Now, probably on the tail stock end, turn down and test a round tenon to fit the holes you have previously drilled in the top, side rails. The same size will be sufficient for the knobs.

The tenon needs to be longer than required so that when it is fitted in the chuck it has plenty to grip on. Fit a Jacobs chuck into the head stock and mount the peg or knob in it. You can recenter the tail stock for extra support at this stage if you wish. Turn the final shape. To finish off, withdraw the tailstock and turn off the final bit of waste. The peg or knob can now be sanded to a suitable finish in the lathe. If you don't have a chuck, just turn between centers and clean up the cut off point out of the lathe.

11 The positions of the front and back rails are marked out on the legs.

12 Deciding on the spacing of the rack rails.

13 A dry run with the rails in place to make sure it all fits and to establish the shoulder lengths of the rack rails.

14 The edge of the bottom rail is cleaned up with a spokeshave.

Prepare the buttons by planing a strip to size to start. Mark this out with trenches that, when cut off, will produce a button with a tongue. Cut out the trenches, drill the retaining screw holes, and cut off to length. Countersink the holes if you wish (15). Each needs to be cleaned up and checked for fit.

Rather than start the main assembly process at this stage, apply one coat of sealer while you can get at all the fiddly bits. Providing you don't get too much sealer in or on the joints, this will not affect their integrity. Apply the acrylic sealer to the three sets of racks, one drawer runner assembly, two side rails, pegs and knobs, the top, and the legs. The latter must be center-drilled at the bottom and a small cup hook inserted (16). Once coated, they can be hung up from the ceiling to dry.

Whilst this is going on, try to find some suitable castors. Fit them, with four screws, so they are good and strong and will not come off. Cut the dry legs as necessary to accommodate the height of the castors and mark and drill

the retaining screw holes. These holes must be deliberately bored at an angle to ensure the screws have some purchase across the grain.

The main sub-frame assembly can now finally begin. Use a powdered resin mixed with water to provide a rigid joint and set everything out before you get started (17, overleaf). Attach the two top side rails to the legs first. All the other rack and drawer runner assemblies can then be slotted in and the whole thing clamped up square. Once the glue has set thoroughly, any excess can be removed and all surfaces lightly sanded back, prior to a second coating with sealer. Apply a couple of extra coats to the top, to ensure that it provides a tough surface to work on.

15 The buttons are made, drilled, and countersunk ready for use.

16 At this stage, everything needs a coat of sealer applied.

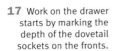

17 Work on the drawer starts by marking the depth of the dovetail sockets on the fronts.

18 A small, dovetail square is used to mark out the sockets and pins.

At this stage, the actual size of the drawer can be established. In this case, it was decided that access to the drawer would be from both sides, to make it more accessible—hence the four knobs. Each of the four components should now be cut and planed square to their finished sizes. The depth of the lap dovetails is marked out on the fronts with a gauge first. (**18**). It is handy to have a series of small dovetail squares to use for marking out. Once the spacing had been decided upon, making sure that the drawer bottom groove ran round where a tail was, the sockets and pins were marked out. The edges were cut with a dovetail saw across the angles and the bulk of the waste removed on the bench with a chisel (**19**).

A straight cutter mounted at the right depth in a router is another useful way to achieve this, if you have a lot of dovetails to cut. Each series of sockets and pins must then be cleaned up in the vise with a range of smaller chisels. With the corresponding tails marked on the drawer sides, cut out the bulk of this waste

on the bandsaw. Each side now needs to be trimmed to fit a front and tested (**20**). No more than a reasonable amount of pressure should be needed to knock the joint up together. Mark or number each corner as it is fitted. Finally, select your drawer bottom material. Some old, thin ply would suffice. Cut a groove around the inside of the drawer on the fronts and sides to take the bottom. This is not the traditional method of creating a drawer, but will suffice in this case if you use a sheet material rather than solid wood. Once you have cleaned up, apply plenty of glue to the joints and begin to assemble the drawer (**21**, opposite). When you have set it up in the clamps, check that it is square and flat and leave everything to one side to set (**22**, opposite).

Now you need to finalize the drawer to catch up with progress on the other parts of the project. Clean off the excess glue and sand the faces down. Check and adjust for fit in the unit recess. Cover the show wood faces with two consecutive coats of sealer, lightly sanding

19 The bulk of the waste is chiseled out on the bench.

20 Testing the tails for fit.

21 Plenty of glue is applied to the drawer dovetail joints.

22 The drawer is clamped and squared up.

down in between. While this is going on, fit the castors. Partly drive in two screws first (**23**). The adjusted base plates of the castors can then be fitted over these before the other two screws are driven in to hold it in place (**24**). Ideally, use two braked castors on opposite corners to make sure that the unit does not move around. Fit and glue the pegs into the top, side rails. Use some gash stock between them and the cramps to avoid any marks (**25**). Once the drawer has been sealed,

fit and glue the knobs on. Again, use something to protect them from damage or marking while being clamped in place.

With luck and a fair wind you should now be on the home run! Place the top, bottom side up, on a protective sheet to avoid marks. Up-end the sub-assembly unit onto it. Position the buttons, not too tight to the legs, and drive the retaining screws home (**26**). Turn the whole unit over, slide the drawer in, and the job is done.

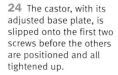

23 Here you can see the first two securing screws for the castors being partly driven in.

24 The castor, with its adjusted base plate, is slipped onto the first two screws before the others are positioned and all tightened up.

25 A bit of gash, soft stock protects the pegs while they are being glued in place.

26 Finally the pegs are used to fix the top to the sub-frame structure.

Pests and diseases

Wood comes under attack from both boring insects and fungi, sometimes working alone and occasionally together. The most invasive feed off the wood—sometimes while the tree is still growing—and, in the process, physically destroy it. Attack or infestation can also occur if logs are left in damp conditions. However, with the application of common sense, good housekeeping, and a few chemicals, you can normally prevent and eradicate wood attack.

Right An ambrosia beetle, the scourge of many timbers and freshly harvested lumber.

Wood borers

These include wasps, bees, ants, and marine borers. However, here we will concentrate on beetles, as your wood is most likely to be attacked by them.

Beetles

Beetles mate and lay eggs that hatch into grubs, turn into pupae, metamorphose into beetles—and then the cycle starts all over again. The lifecycle usually lasts three to four years.

Sometimes infestation is caused by the adult insect boring into the wood and laying its eggs in a breeding tunnel. Eggs can also be laid on the surface, in cracks and crevices, or under bark. Once hatched, the grub bores into the wood and the effects of its activity can be devastating if they are not dealt with in time. Your first clue as to their presence might be the appearance of exit, or flight, holes. If you see these, sadly it may already be too late to save the wood.

Above Beetle larvae, clustered together on the bark of a tree.

Types of beetle

There are many different types of beetle. Here we consider the three most common:

Ambrosia beetle

(Families: *Platypodidae*, *Scolytidae* and *Lymexylidae*)
The ambrosia beetle is found in forests worldwide, especially in the tropics. It attacks any type of timber—tropical hardwoods (in Africa and the Far East), Douglas fir and hemlock (North America), as well as softwoods and hardwoods throughout Europe and Scandinavia. The beetle also infests standing timber, felled logs, and cut lumber. It bores into the wood, creating a tunnel system in which the eggs are laid.

On lighter woods there is often an associated fungal staining in and around the tunnels that can be even more devastating than the beetle attack. The fungi is introduced by the larvae and grown as a food source. This survives as long as the wood has a moisture content of 30 percent or more. Otherwise, it dies, depriving the larvae of its food source, and the infestation ceases.

The best way to prevent an attack is via rapid conversion and drying of the lumber. You can also apply some chemical treatments to thicker material if it is to be predried before kilning.

Deathwatch beetle

(*Xestobium rufovillosum*)
Most prevalent in Europe, the deathwatch beetle causes significant damage to structural timbers in older buildings. The beetle concentrates on hardwoods and has a particular fondness for oak. It operates in damp conditions, feeding off woods that have been attacked by fungi.

After mating, up to two hundred eggs are laid and the hatched larvae bore into the host wood,

hundred eggs are laid onto unpolished surfaces and the grubs hatch and bore into the wood. After pupation, the beetle bores out of the wood producing typically round exit holes. Bore-dust or "frass" (beetle droppings) can often be found below the infestation.

Insecticidal treatments should be applied to all surfaces and directly into old flight holes. Nearby grubs quickly die off. Deeply buried ones will only do so when they ingest treated materials while attempting to exit as a beetle. Special conservation techniques can be used on expensive or heritage pieces of furniture. These may involve specialist heat treatments or freezing the object.

House longhorn beetle
(*Hylotrupes bajulus*)
Originally indigenous in Europe and the Mediterranean, this beetle has spread throughout North and South America, Australia, and southern Africa. It does not, however, breed in colder climates and when weather in warmer countries cools down, infestation ceases.

The house longhorn beetle poses a real threat to structural timbers, because it attacks seasoned woods. It goes for the sapwood of softwood in house timbers, rafters, joists, and other joinery products.

Untreated timbers in newer buildings, where moisture is still present from the construction process, also provide an ideal breeding ground. In wood with high levels of sapwood, the degradation can lead to total collapse of that section and eventually to structural failure.

After mating the female lays up to two hundred eggs. The hatched larvae can travel some way before burrowing for four years or more. The adult beetle is a strong flier and, on warm days, can fly to other locations, further spreading the infestation.

To avoid attack, all new-build timbers should be treated with an insecticidal preservative and the wood allowed to dry thoroughly before installation. In existing buildings, providing the infestation is not too advanced, insecticide that is sprayed or brushed on will contribute toward eradication over time. Where the damage is extensive, the affected timber should be removed and freshly installed.

causing serious damage. They can stay within the wood for at least five years, depending upon the conditions. The only evidence of attack may be from the emerging beetle's flight holes and piles of wood dust.

The key to avoiding attack is to keep the wood dry. As a precaution, all sapwood should be removed as early as possible or treated with an insecticide.

Common furniture beetle
(*Anobium punctatum*)
The furniture beetle (also known as woodworm) is indigenous to the temperate regions of Europe but has spread to other similar climates. It is usually found outdoors but, under the right conditions, it can travel indoors to infest furniture and other wooden items.

Its primary areas of attack are the sapwood of both hardwoods and softwoods. In older furniture, the grubs bore into the carcass from the back, cracks, or crevices. They also like wicker basketwork and similar light wood products. Depending upon the nutritional quality of the host wood, the lifecycle of the furniture beetle varies from three to five years. Up to one

Above The house longhorn beetle.

Fungi

Generally, there are two types of fungal attack. The first grows on the cell contents, possibly causing staining, but leaving the structure sound. The other—wood-rotting fungi—eats the cell tissue, causing decay and serious degradation of the timber's structure, eventually leading to the total collapse of affected timbers.

Structure of fungi

There are two parts. The first is the fruiting body, the mushroom or visible plate. The spores or seeds are dispersed from its underside. The second part, which does the damage, is the vegetative system or "mycelium." This is comprised of a mass of fine tubes called hyphae that invade and eat the cell or its contents.

In order to survive, fungi need four elements: adequate moisture; suitable temperature; a food source; and air. If these are all available, and spores are introduced, the fungi will thrive.

Above A serious infestation of dry rot at work in a wooden cupboard.

Wood-attacking fungi

Many types of fungi attack wood. Below are three of the most common.

Dry rot

(*Serpula lacrymans*, formerly *Merulius lactymans*)

Despite its name, dry rot needs moisture to survive. In the advanced stages of decay this brown rot breaks the wood down into cube-like sections. The fine, leading mycelium can cover extensive areas, penetrating mortar and crossing steel and concrete in its quest for fresh wood to attack.

As a result, dry rot is the most invasive of the wood-attacking rots. Where it can be seen, an absorbent cotton-type effect spreads across the surface of the timber. The fruiting body is a soft, fleshy plate often with white edges, which produces a microscopic, red dust-like spore. In areas where the attack is hidden, the first indications of the presence of the fungi are depressions and splits on the surface.

Removal of some or all of the four components (needed for fungi survival) will halt the attack. Eradication is achieved by the total removal of affected timbers, fungicidal preservative treatment of the surrounding areas, and replacement with treated components.

Wet rot

(*Coniophora puteana*, formerly *Coniophora cerebella*)

This grows in areas that are always moist. An advanced attack is characterized by longitudinal cracking with horizontal breaks, creating a cube-like appearance in infected areas. The affected wood eventually becomes brittle and powders to the touch. The mycelium grows as per dry rot, extending from the tip and invading fresh wood. When visible, it is usually a dark brown color and threadlike in substance. The fruiting body is a small, green platelike structure. Unfortunately, while it remains localized and cannot penetrate masonry and mortar, it cannot be seen on the surface until it is well advanced.

You can eradicate this fungi in the same way as dry rot, but you must also remove the source of the moisture.

Blue or sap-stain fungi

Several fungi cause this mold-like blue stain in the sapwood of softwoods and in the less durable, light hardwoods. Although the wood becomes discolored, there is no structural effect on the timber.

To avoid attack, timber should be dried as quickly as possible. Some tropical timbers are dipped or sprayed with a fungicidal solution.

Right Blue-colored, moldy rot like this afflicts many woods and can be a serious problem.

Glossary of wood terms

AD An abbreviation describing timber that is "air dried." Reducing the moisture content further has to be done artificially.

Adze A paring tool that is most commonly used for large shaping work, such as chair seats.

Angiosperms These are hardwoods or "dicotyledons"—generally, deciduous trees with characteristically broad leaves and seeds enclosed in a seed case.

Annual rings Sometimes referred to as "Growth Rings." These are the concentric rings of wood that are added annually to the growing tree in temperate and certain tropical countries. In most tropical countries growth is continuous, so these rings do not appear.

Auger A long twist bit for boring large holes by hand. Most twist bits used in powered tools are called augers.

Awl A pointed tool used for boring small lead holes. It should also be sharp enough to use as a marking tool.

Back saw A tenon, dovetail, or similar thin-bladed saw that has been stiffened along the top edge for added strength, helping to produce a straight cut.

Balk A square lump of timber, sawn or hewn, which is at least nine inches (225 millimeters) square.

Bandings Decorative narrow inlays used in cabinet work. They can be plain or checkered.

Bandrack saw A large bandsaw for converting logs into lumber.

Bare When timber is measured undersize or a measurement is taken to fit and needs to be underside by a fraction that is not measurable.

Blue stain A bluish staining of sapwood created by a fungi attack.

Book-matched A term used when two pieces of veneer cut from the same stock are opened out like a book and fixed to the base material.

Burrs Odd-shaped growths that occur on the sides of some trees. Twig burr is sought after and valued for the production of fancy veneers.

Cabinet maker This is the skill that is used to make fine furniture.

Carpenter The art of "carpentry" is related to the structural use of wood in buildings. A carpenter is a practitioner of carpentry.

Case hardening A drying defect that can be rectified. The outer skin of timber has been placed in tension by drying it more than the middle.

Caul This is the flat or slightly shaped tool used in veneering to hold the veneer in place.

Caulk A joint that has been filled to make it watertight is "caulked." A boatbuilding practice that fills the deck joints with tar or a similar substance.

Center matched A term used to describe a method of veneering in which a number of pieces have a central meeting point.

Check A small split in the surface of a board that does not go right through.

Clear lumber Or "clears." This is a phrase mainly used in the softwood sector that refers to defect-free material—that is, material that does not feature knots and so on.

Cleft This term refers to when a block of wood is split rather than sawn.

Cock bead Normally refers to a small bead that stands proud of the adjacent face; for example, around a drawer.

Collapse A defect created by excessive shrinkage during drying. The core of the wood collapses in on itself in extreme examples.

Common furniture beetle Otherwise known as "woodworm." It is an infestation by *Anobium punctatum*, a wood-boring beetle.

Coniferous Refers to a conifer tree; softwoods, which are generally, but not always, evergreen.

Converting A sawmill phrase that describes an action of converting one size into several others.

Cross-cut Cutting across the width of a plank or board, across the grain.

Cupping A distortion in the width of a board when the edges curl up to create a cup effect.

Curl This refers to a veneer that has been cut from the fork of a tree. Also known as fan, crotch, or crutch veneers.

Cut nails These are flat nails that are cut or stamped out of a sheet of metal.

Deciduous This term applies to trees that shed their leaves annually.

Deep cut This is the long cut through the width and down the length of a board as opposed to through the thickness (see Rip cut).

Density Timber density is arrived at by comparing the weight of a constant volume with specific moisture content.

Dote A type of wood rot caused by fungal decay. Timber affected will smell of mold and become discolored on the surface. Also referred to as doty, dosy, and dozy.

Dressed This term is used to describe timber that has been planed on one or more sides.

Durability The factors affecting durability are things like density, hardness, oil, or mineral content and so on.

Earlywood This is the layers of growth that trees in temperate climates put on rapidly at the start of the growing season in spring; also known as springwood.

End check Or "split." The small splits in the end of a board that naturally occur during drying.

End matched Usually refers to flooring. The matching occurs when the end is square-cut, so that there is no gap in the joint.

Equilibrium Moisture Content Wood is hygroscopic—it has the ability to take up and give off moisture. When the wood's moisture content has become equal to that of its environment, it is said to have reached its EMC.

Evergreen Those trees that bear leaves throughout the year. Mainly softwoods but not all. European Larch sheds it needles. Some hardwoods, Evergreen Oak, and some eucalyptus retain their leaves.

Flight hole The exit hole created when a wood-boring beetle bores its way to the surface.

Frass Wood-boring beetle droppings. Each type of beetle produces a different textured dropping. Examination under a microscope will help determine which it is.

Fuming The darkening of oak, and some other timbers, by the use of ammonia.

Gash A piece or pieces of waste or spare wood that can be used in a secondary position and not as the primary show wood.

Girdling This is the technique of cutting right through the bark of a standing, live tree, to the wood underneath. It effectively kills the tree, stopping the flow of sap and allowing the tree to dry before felling.

Girth This is the outside measurement around a log or tree—the circumference.

Green Often used to describe freshly felled timber that has high moisture content.

Hammering The use of a veneer hammer to press down on a veneer and squeeze the excess glue out.

Hand Left- or right-handed. Can refer to a variety of subjects, including doors and door furniture.

Hardwood A conventional term used to denote timber of broad-leaved trees with porous wood belonging to the botanical group known as Angiosperms.

Honeycombing Another drying defect in wood. Similar to collapse, it is difficult to spot until the wood is cut.

Hoppus measure A volume measure for round wood logs.

Hygroscopic All wood has the ability to take on and give off moisture like a sponge; this is known as "hygroscopic."

Incipient decay The initial stages of fungal decay. Associated signs are a discoloration of the wood.

Indigenous Native wood of a particular country.

Joinery This is the art of making and fixing wooden items in buildings, such as windows and doors.

Joint This is the generic term relating to the junction between timbers; the act of jointing wood together.

KD The abbreviation for "kiln dried." KD does not always mean that the timber is dry enough for the purpose that you intend.

Kerf The width of a saw cut. Also used

to describe the width at which the teeth of a saw are set to cut.

Late wood The growth layer of wood laid down later in the annual cycle.

Linear measure The length measure of timber, either as an individual piece or as a cumulative total.

Lumber A phrase that refers to converted wood.

MDF This is the abbreviation of "medium density fiber board."

m^2/m^3 The surface area and volume abbreviations of "square meter" and "cubic meter."

Moisture content The weight of moisture contained in wood expressed as a percentage. In some cases it is possible for the moisture content of timber to exceed 100 percent.

Moisture gradient Because timber is hygroscopic, it tends to dry quicker on the outside than it does in the middle.

Nominal size This refers to timber sizes before they have been dressed to a "finished size."

Nonporous wood Timbers that contain no pores in their structure; usually softwoods.

PAR The abbreviation that refers to "planed all round."

Patina The deep gloss or luster finish that a piece of furniture acquires over years of polishing and handling.

Plain-sawn Any timber that is not "quarter-sawn."

Pores The pores, or "vessels," are the principal water/food conduction elements in the structure of hardwoods. Their size, shape, and distribution, along with other factors, helps with the identification of specific timbers.

Prime The best possible grade available for that particular timber species; the highest quality.

Quarter-sawn The best cut to produce planks from a log, but not always the most economical.

Rays Correctly called "medullary" rays, in hardwoods. These are the cells that when cut on the quarter produce the figure seen in quarter-sawn material.

Redwood A trade term that refers to the pine group of timbers.

Regularized Pieces of wood of a given size that have been sawn or partly planed to a consistent size.

Resaw This is a bandsaw, or larger circular saw, used to cut and produce a number of pieces from larger stock.

Rip cut Also known as flatting, cutting down the length of the wood. The cuts are made through the thickness rather than through the width.

Rough timber Rough timber is lumber that is sawn only—not planed, dressed, or even molded.

Round timber These are logs ready for conversion into lumber. They may be referred to as "in the round."

Sapwood The layer of growing wood just underneath the bark of a tree.

Saw doctor Someone who "doctors" saws. This is the person who has the knowledge to sharpen, tension, and set saws of all sizes so that they cut efficiently.

Sawyer A person who is trained to operate one or more saws.

Scant When a plank or board is under the specified size, it is referred to as scant.

Shake Any split, cleavage, or partial separation between adjacent layers of wood fibers.

Show wood Literally the wood that is showing as opposed to hidden. Any polished wooden surface showing on upholstered furniture is called show wood.

Shrinkage As wood dries it shrinks, because the cellular structure reduces in size as moisture is lost.

Skiver This is the name given to a piece of leather set into a desk top.

Softwood Gymnosperms, coniferous, or needle-leaved trees that have a nonporous wood structure.

Species In the classification of plants, thus trees, a species is a sub-division of a "genus."

Specification A listing of requirements.

Square-edged This is effectively lumber, planks, or boards with both edges sawn square and straight.

Stickers These are the regular-sized strips

of wood used to separate layers of boards or planks when in the air and kiln drying process; sometimes called "strips."

Sticker stain Or "shadow." This is when there has been some sort of chemical reaction between the sticker and the stock being dried.

Surfaced When one or both wider faces of a board have been planed or dressed.

T & G The abbreviation of tongued and grooved; a machined profile usually used as floor boarding.

Tally The record of timber sizes picked and prepared against an order.

Thicknesser A powered planing machine that can plane wood to a regular thickness.

Through and through The most commonly used method of cutting logs to produce lumber.

To cut Timber, machined or sawn, supplied so that the customer is able to cut his or her specific requirements from it.

Tyloses Found in porous hardwoods, this is a thin, bubble-like obstruction within the vessel cell structure, in the pore cavity.

Veneers Thin slices of decorative wood used to face up a cheaper, plainer wood.

Wane The outer, uneven edge or edges of timber planks that have been cut "through and through."

Warp This term refers to any distortion in a board when it is not flat and straight.

Whitewood The general classification that covers softwood species such as spruces and firs.

Worm holes This is the common name for the flight hole of a mature wood-boring beetle.

Yield The amount of timber products of value that is cut or produced from logs.

Index

Acknowledgments

Many of the photographs in this book were commissioned exclusively for use therein. Please see details below. In addition, the author and publishers should like to thank a number of individuals and organizations for supplying the balance of images, as listed below.

All the step-by-step photographs for the woodworking projects (pages 198–291) were taken by the author, Peter Bishop, as well as the following images:
114–15, 117 (top), 130 (top), 134 (main picture), 135 (main picture), 142 (top), 143 (top), 144, 145 (bottom), 146 (top,), 147 (top), 150 (top and bottom left), 151 (bottom), 152–3, 154 (top), 160–1, 164 (bottom), 166 (top), 168 (bottom left and right), 169 (top), 170, 172–5, 183, 186 (top), 197 (bottom).

All the completed project pictures for the projects (pages 198–291) were taken by Tim Sandall, as well as the following:
116 (bottom), 118 (top and bottom right), 120 (bottom middle and right), 121 (top), 122, 126 (bottom right), 127 (top left), 131 (top left), 132, 136 (top), 138, 149 (bottom), 157 (top right and left, bottom left), 162–3, 164 (top), 166 (bottom), 167, 168 (top), 169 (bottom left and right), 177–9, 182, 184–5, 187–9, 190 (top left and right, bottom right), 191 (top), 192, 193 (top), 196 (right), 197 (top left, middle and right).

The following pictures are provided courtesy of Toolbank Ltd:
118 (bottom left), 120 (bottom left), 121 (bottom left, middle and right), 128, 130 (bottom), 131 (top right), 134 saws pictures (1, 2 and 4), 135 (top), 140 (top left, bottom left), 141 (top left, bottom left), 142 (bottom left, bottom right), 143 (bottom right), 145 (top left, top right), 146 (bottom left, top, and bottom left, bottom), 147 (middle right), 148 (bottom), 149 (top row; bottom row: top right, middle), 150 (top left, middle left), 151 (top right, middle), 154 (middle, bottom), 155–6, 157 (side pictures: top, middle, bottom right), 159 (bottom), 186 (bottom).

The following images are provided courtesy of Focus Publishing:
120 (saws group), 126 (bottom left), 127 (top right), 133, 134 top left (number 3 saws), 137 (bottom), 140 (top right, bottom right), 141 (top right, bottom right), 147 (bottom), 148 (middle), 176 (bottom left, bottom right).

Other pictures are provided courtesy of the following organizations:
Kahrs: 190 (bottom left), 272–3
Oxford Forestry Institute: The Directory of Wood chapter (pages 32–113)
www.active-Services.org.Uk: 294
www.carboneutraldesign.com: 193 (bottom)
www.sxc.hu: 1–4, 6–22, 24–8, 30–1, 101, 116 (top), 117 (bottom), 120 (top), 126 (top), 137 (top right), 148 (top), 158, 159 (top), 176 (top), 191 (bottom), 196 (left).
www.zionet.com: 293

The author and the packager, Focus Publishing, would also like to thank James Latham and Timbmet for kindly providing the wood for the projects (pages 198–291).